PENGUIN BOOKS

THE FINANCIAL TIMES

THE BIRTH OF THE EURO

Dan Bilefsky has recently joined the fellow at the Centre for European Reform, a London-based think-tank. He has written on European issues for the *New Statesman* and *World Link* and was a reporter for *SmartMoney* (the *Wall Street Journal* magazine).

Ben Hall is research director at the Centre for European Reform. He helped set up the Centre in 1996 and now manages its research and publications programme. He worked on EU affairs in Robin Cook's office prior to the general election.

Lionel Barber is the UK news editor of the *Financial Times*. He was the *FT*'s Brussels correspondent from 1992 to 1998. He has also worked as the *FT*'s Washington correspondent. He has lectured widely in the US and Europe on the EU, transatlantic relations and US foreign policy.

The Birth of the Euro: the *Financial Times*'s Guide to Emu

Edited by
DAN BILEFSKY & BEN HALL
With LIONEL BARBER

PENGUIN BOOKS
in association with the
Financial Times

PENGUIN BOOKS

Published by the Penguin Group
Penguin Books Ltd, 27 Wrights Lane, London W8 5TZ, England
Penguin Putnam Inc., 375 Hudson Street, New York, New York 10014, USA
Penguin Books Australia Ltd, Ringwood, Victoria, Australia
Penguin Books Canada Ltd, 10 Alcorn Avenue, Toronto, Ontario, Canada M4V 3B2
Penguin Books (NZ) Ltd, Private Bag 102902, NSMC, Auckland, New Zealand

Penguin Books Ltd, Registered Offices: Harmondsworth, Middlesex, England

Published in Penguin Books 1998
10 9 8 7 6 5 4 3 2 1

Set in 9.5/12 PostScript Adobe Minion
Typeset by Rowland Phototypesetting Ltd, Bury St Edmunds, Suffolk
Printed in England by Clays Ltd, St Ives plc

Contents

Foreword

In the pantheon of journalistic clichés, the word 'historic' must rank among the most over-used. Yet the experiment on which Europe is about to embark – the launch of its new single currency, the euro – is one of the rare events to merit this description.

For the eleven initial member countries of the euro and their partners, economic and monetary union changes everything: the nature of competition and cooperation within the European Union; the ability of individual member states to shape their economic destiny; the debate about political integration and accountability. It means countries finding new ways of working together, with altogether unpredictable results. It is, quite literally, a leap into the unknown.

For European business, it is a transformation of the battleground – the final step towards creating Europe as a genuine single market, and the likely catalyst for a wave of financial and industrial restructuring. And for the world at large, the arrival of the euro spells the biggest shake-up in the international monetary system since the second world war: a new currency to rival the dollar, and a major new factor in banking, trade and political relationships.

For all these reasons the *Financial Times* is keenly interested in the euro and how it works. As the world's leading business newspaper, with Europe as its home market, we have been charting the single currency for many years, from failed attempts at monetary cooperation in the 1970s and 1980s through negotiation and implementation of the Maastricht treaty.

Through the work of specialist writers and an unparalleled network of European correspondents, we have closely followed the political battles, exhaustively explained the economic and business background, and in the process we have built up a considerable body of expert writing.

This book offers a carefully edited selection as a guide for those who need to know about Emu. It is intended to be helpful, whether your need to know derives from your business or from general interest, and whether you already know a little or a lot. I hope you enjoy and profit from it, and that you will be encouraged to follow this great but uncertain project in the pages of the *Financial Times*.

ANDREW GOWERS
Acting Editor

Contributors

GERARD BAKER *FT* Washington Bureau Chief
VICKI BAKHSHI *FT* Leader Writer
LIONEL BARBER *FT* News Editor
RICCARDO BARBIERI Analyst – Morgan Stanley Dean Witter, London
JAMES BLITZ *FT* Rome Correspondent
SIR SAMUEL BRITTAN *FT* Economics Commentator
DAVID BUCHAN *FT* Diplomatic Correspondent
ROBERT CHOTE *FT* Economics Editor
TRACY CORRIGAN *FT* New York Correspondent
REGINALD DALE *International Herald Tribune* – Washington
SCHEHERAZADE DANESHKHU *FT* Leisure Industries Correspondent
IAN DAVIDSON Former *FT* Foreign Affairs Columnist
SIMON DAVIES Former Head of *FT* Capital Markets Team
IVO DAWNAY Managing Director – GJW (Brussels office)
PAUL DE GRAUWE Professor of Economics – Catholic University of Louvain (Belgium)
GUY DE JONQUIÈRES *FT* World Trade Editor
NICK DENTON Former *FT* West Coast Technology Writer
HUGO DIXON *FT* Head of Lex
RUDI DORNBUSCH Professor of Economics – Massachusetts Institute of Technology
JOACHIM FELS Analyst – Morgan Stanley Dean Witter, London
STEPHEN FIDLER *FT* US Diplomatic Editor
ANDREW FISHER *FT* Frankfurt Correspondent
MICHAEL GARDINER Partner, Ernst & Young
ANDREW GOWERS *FT* Acting Editor
GEORGE GRAHAM *FT* Banking Editor
CLAY HARRIS *FT* Banking Correspondent
PEGGY HOLLINGER *FT* Retailing Correspondent
GIORGIO LA MALFA Leader of Italy's Republican Party and a member of the European Parliament
EDWARD LUCE *FT* Capital Markets Writer

PETER MARSH *FT* Industry Correspondent
PETER MARTIN *FT* Editor, International Edition
JANE MARTINSON *FT* Investment Correspondent
FRANCO MODIGLIANI Institute Professor Emeritus – Massachusetts Institute of Technology
WOLFGANG MÜNCHAU *FT* Economics Correspondent, Frankfurt
WILHELM ÑOLLING Former member of the Bundesbank council
PETER NORMAN *FT* Bonn Bureau Chief
DAVID OWEN *FT* Paris Correspondent
QUENTIN PEEL *FT* International Affairs Editor
ROBERT PESTON *FT* Political Editor
RICHARD PORTES Director – Centre for Economic Policy Research
MICHAEL PREST Partner – Chancery Communications
STEVEN RATTNER Deputy Chief Executive of Lazard Freres (New York)
BARRY RILEY *FT* Associate Editor
HÉLÈNE REY Lecturer in International Economics, London School of Economics
WOLFGANG SCHÄUBLE Leader of CDU/CSU MPs – in the German Bundestag
PHILIP STEPHENS *FT* Associate Editor & Political Commentator
DOMINIQUE STRAUSS-KAHN French Finance Minister
LAWRENCE SUMMERS Deputy US Treasury Secretary
JENS TARTLER *FT* Contributor
ROBERT TAYLOR *FT* Employment Editor
YVES THIBAULT DE SILGUY EU monetary affairs commissioner
EMMA TUCKER *FT* Brussels Correspondent
ADAIR TURNER Director General, Confederation of British Industry
MAGGIE URRY *FT* Agriculture Correspondent
STEFAN WAGSTYL *FT* East European Editor
JOHN WILLMAN *FT* Consumer Industries Editor
MARTIN WOLF *FT* Associate Editor & Chief Economic Commentator

Introduction
Let the great experiment begin

LIONEL BARBER

The launch of the euro is the most far-reaching development in Europe since the fall of the Berlin Wall. It marks a decisive step forward in the integration of the economies of western Europe, the climax of a project more than thirty years in the making.

Eleven members of the European Union will form the new euro zone: Austria, Belgium, Finland, France, Germany, Ireland, Italy, Luxembourg, the Netherlands, Portugal and Spain. The United Kingdom, Denmark, Sweden and Greece will remain outside initially. The euro zone will encompass almost 300 million consumers. It will make up the second largest economy in the world behind the US, accounting for more than one-fifth of global trade. The euro is widely viewed as a rival to the dollar, at least in the medium term. But statistics tell only half the story.

The launch of the euro on 1 January 1999 supplies a vital missing link in Europe's single market. The elimination of transaction costs should mean greater competition, more efficiency and better deals for the consumer. Price transparency will send a juddering shock through business, commerce and the capital markets, accelerating the widespread restructuring under way.

Emu marks a cultural revolution, institutionalizing monetary orthodoxy and exporting German-style anti-inflationary rigour Europe-wide through a new institution, the Frankfurt-based European Central Bank. If Emu advocates are correct, the birth of the euro heralds a second economic renaissance for Europe built on stable prices, enduring fiscal discipline, and lower interest rates.

But Emu is a gamble, too. Contrary to initial expectations, the new monetary union in Europe will extend beyond the natural D-Mark zone to include inflation-prone economies in the south such as Italy and Spain. It remains a project conceived by Europe's political elite, without deep-rooted support among the European public. It is a great experiment without precedent.

Whatever the prospects for success or failure, Emu enjoys an impressive pedigree. Its origins go back to the late 1960s, when the Europeans were searching for a response to the upheaval in the Bretton Woods international monetary system, in which the US dollar was the dominant currency. In 1970, Pierre Werner, Luxembourg prime minister, produced a three-stage plan for achieving monetary union within a decade. The first oil crisis intervened, but Europe's search for currency stability took on fresh momentum in 1979 with the creation of the European Monetary System built on the concept of stable but adjustable exchange rates. A combination of factors – the launch of a single European market freeing the circulation of capital, goods, and services, the fall of the Berlin Wall and German unification – gave the decisive impetus to Emu as a political project. The result was the 1992 Maastricht treaty, in which the EU adopted a blueprint remarkably similar to the Werner plan.

Between 1992 and 1993, a wave of speculation almost forced the Emu show off the road. But the member states, by now fifteen, gritted their teeth, squeezed inflation, and cut budget deficits to within striking distance of the Maastricht target of 3 per cent of gross domestic product.

The birth of the euro is a testimony to the power of political will. For former Chancellor Helmut Kohl of Germany, Emu is a means of anchoring a united Germany into a united Europe. For the late President François Mitterrand, Emu offered a strategic opening to break the monetary hegemony of the German Bundesbank through the creation of a supranational central bank. For better or worse, the launch of the euro has become a pre-condition for the EU's second historic task after the end of the Cold War: enlargement to the former communist countries of central and eastern Europe. Without the quantum leap towards deeper economic integration in western Europe, many governments have argued that an enlargement to up to twenty-five countries would eventually reduce the Union to little more than a free trade zone.

More positively, Emu has also inspired traditionally weak governments to take courageous steps to slash profligate spending to meet the entry criteria for monetary union. Political leaders such as Romano Prodi of Italy and José Maria Aznar in Spain can reasonably argue that the need to qualify for Europe's elite single-currency club offered the essential spur to economic reform and the restoration of public finances.

Emu points to a second powerful alliance, this time between the financial markets and the technocrats in Brussels and Frankfurt who have laboured over the blueprint to launch the single currency like medieval monks working on the great religious texts, seemingly oblivious to famine, pestilence and war in the outside world. The combination of political will and first-class technical preparation – first through the European Commission's Green Paper on the transition to monetary union published in spring 1995, and later through successive papers published by the

European Monetary Institute in Frankfurt – has turned once-sceptical financial markets into true believers in the single currency. Once market sentiment changed – some time after the December 1995 summit naming the euro and agreeing on a three-year transition to the introduction of euro notes and coins in early 2002 – there was too much money riding on a successful launch for currency traders and hedge funds to back off their original bet.

Now that these political and technical issues are settled, Emu is ready to move from the drawing board to reality. What are the practical consequences for business, industry and finance? For manufacturers, the elimination of exchange-rate risk offers immediate benefits. Smaller companies will gain because they have previously lacked resources for foreign exchange-rate management. But as Niall FitzGerald, chairman of Unilever, the Anglo-Dutch consumer products giant, points out: Emu will also deliver a competitive shock to the European economy. Price transparency will allow consumers to purchase more easily across borders. Technological innovation – such as the growth of the Internet and home-based shopping – will probably accelerate the process. Fleet-footed companies will be able to tap instantaneously into a large customer base; but the less agile risk being swamped by the competition.

For the financial sector, the effects of the single currency are likely to be even more dramatic. From 1 January 1999, when exchange rates for euro currencies are locked irrevocably, foreign exchange trading, a big money-spinner in the City of London, will disappear. To an extent, the forex market has anticipated this shift by betting heavily on Emu going ahead on schedule. One big question after 1999 is whether traders will target peripheral currencies such as sterling or the Swiss franc or whether they will focus on euro-dollar and euro-yen trades.

The competitive impact will be even more severe in banking. As Professor David Currie says in his report, 'The Pros and Cons of the Emu' (London: The Economist Intelligence Unit, 1997), the single currency will deliver a much-needed fillip to the various EU banking directives associated with the single market. Previously, the circulation of national currencies has stifled competition because banks have set up systems allowing them to operate in another national currency, leading to the perpetuation of 'balkanized' national banking systems. In Europe, a wave of cross-border banking mergers and associated consolidation indicates that the *ancien régime* is about to be swept away. In Belgium, the national banking system has been transformed in the past 12–18 months. Only the biggest banks will survive, says one senior corporate financier involved in the restructuring.

In terms of its impact on the financial markets, the advent of the euro will be even more impressive. Emu will create a new market for government debt denominated in euros and a new pool of euro-denominated equity. National stock markets, numbering more than thirty, will be forced to rationalize. Many predict that in the single-market-driven Europe of the future, there will be one Euro-wide group of blue-chip stocks to trade and one Euro-wide blue-chip stock market to trade them on. How soon this dream can turn into reality is an open question; but the most powerful players in Europe are bidding to corner the market. In the summer of 1998, the Frankfurt and London stock exchanges announced a 'strategic alliance'. Their plans involved harmonizing their listing rules and market conventions, to offer reciprocal access to each other's members, and, eventually, to build a single electronic trading platform for the 300 largest European companies which would be required in every fund-manager's portfolio.

The creation of a more liquid pan-European equity market is likely to encourage smaller, private companies to come forward. In Italy, where private companies have traditionally preferred to deal with cosy local banking relationships, there are already signs of a shift in mentality. Since small companies – rather than large conglomerates – offer the best chance of creating jobs and reversing chronic unemployment in Europe, this development could be highly significant.

One market, one money has a seductive ring. But its success will ultimately depend on the stability of the macroeconomic framework operating in the euro zone. Four factors are likely to be decisive. First, the sustainability of economic convergence inside the euro zone. On balance, the circumstances for launching the euro are favourable. Despite the Asian financial crisis, growth is picking up, perhaps reaching an average of nearly 3 per cent across the Emu zone. In terms of consumer price inflation and long-term interest rates, progress has been spectacular. The reduction of public deficits has also been impressive, even if some countries resorted to one-off measures and gimmicks to qualify for Emu. The next step is to use the recovery to further reduce 'structural' rather than cyclical deficits. Debt is another matter. Belgium and Italy are running debt levels which are twice the Maastricht target of 60 per cent.

The optimistic view is that the euro will serve as a catalyst for structural reform, the big gap in the performance of member states in the 1980s and 1990s. Emu should deliver a painful prod to governments to tackle labour market flexibility. Yet there are risks. Monetary union will be subject to immense strains if the necessary structural adjustments are not made. And if countries shirk reform, the traditional safety valves for adjustment – exchange rate flexibility and provisions for large fiscal transfers from the EU budget – are absent.

The second test turns on the strength of political commitments to Emu-led discipline. The German-inspired Stability and Growth pact envisages balanced budgets over the economic cycle, buttressed by sanctions against transgressors running excessive deficits above 3 per cent of GDP. But many believe that these fines will prove unworkable. At issue is whether euro-bloc countries will continue the combination of peer pressure and economic policy co-ordination which worked so successfully under Maastricht or whether selfish national interests will prevail in time of crisis. Much will depend on the Franco-German relationship. So far the political elite in both countries have demonstrated an impressive strategic commitment to the project, despite several wobbles on the way and evidence of divisions between Bonn and Paris about the operation of Emu and the obligations it entails.

First, President Chirac and latterly the Socialist government have sought to resist German pressure for iron-clad guarantees on fiscal discipline in the future euro zone and to introduce a more flexible approach in which growth and employment are given greater priority. On the other side, German ministers and the Bundesbank have balked at what they view as political interference in the future European Central Bank, notably Mr Chirac's insistence on nominating Jean-Claude Trichet, governor of France, as a rival to Dutchman Wim Duisenberg as head of the ECB. The *de facto* split term between Duisenberg and Trichet agreed after a spectacular row at the May 1998 summit marks an uneasy compromise.

The differences between the French and the Germans are deep because they go to the heart of their respective political cultures. Germany's post-war economic success is built on anti-inflationary rigour, the so-called Stability Culture. The guarantor of this culture is the Bundesbank, whose independence is guaranteed in the constitution. Stability *über alles* and confidence in the national currency – each guaranteed by independent professionals acting above the political fray – still exercise a powerful hold on the German popular imagination.

The French tradition is very different. The French state may have been compromised in World War II but it was not destroyed, as it was in Germany. The tradition of state interference or state management of the economy is ingrained, going back three centuries to the days of Colbert. Thus, the notion of an independent central bank is new. Legislation guaranteeing the independence of the Banque de France only completed passage in the summer of 1998 *after* EU leaders had decided on the eleven founder members of Emu. In France, it is still inconceivable that all power should rest with unelected central bankers. As the French have stressed time and again, there must be a political counterweight to the future European Central Bank.

The third area of potential conflict seems bound to turn on the role of the European Central Bank. The ECB's independence is enshrined in the Maastricht treaty; so is the commitment to price stability. But this is a new, untested institution which is certain to face heavy political pressure if Europe continues to shamble along a path of slow growth and high unemployment. The ECB lacks the legitimacy which the Federal Reserve enjoys in the US; nor is it accountable in the way the Federal Reserve is to the US Congress. The European Parliament – which is trying to establish itself as the natural democratic counterweight in this area – remains a fledgeling institution of mixed reputation. National parliaments – not the European Parliament – still command the loyalty of Europe's citizens.

In practice, the role of political counterweight is likely to fall to the Ecofin council of EU finance ministers, the main decision-making body on macro-economic policy in the Union. What is still unclear is how far Ecofin could be undermined or superseded by the new French-inspired Euro-eleven informal council of members of the euro zone. At the very least, the existence of the Euro-eleven club puts more pressure on outsiders such as Britain to join – or risk being sidelined.

Finally, the pessimists argue that monetary union cannot exist without a broader political union which enjoys legitimacy, as in the US. But political union implies further acts of Euro-integration such as tax harmonization to complement the harmonization of currency and monetary policy. On the other hand, the Europe of the euro is still a collection of nation states with widely varying unemployment rates, different labour markets and welfare systems. Emu is likely to expose the risks of running a unified monetary policy without a common fiscal authority. But it would be wrong to be too pessimistic. Emu represents a formidable act of political will. Only the bravest – or the most foolhardy – would have predicted that eleven countries, including Italy, would be ready to launch the single currency on schedule in 1999. Having embarked on this historic venture, Europe's leaders have no intention of abandoning it at the first sign of trouble.

The lesson of European integration over the past forty years is that political leaders have moved forward incrementally, occasionally suffering setbacks such as the demise of the European Defence Community in 1954 or the virtual collapse of the European Monetary System in 1993. But they have always recovered, either by taking a big step forward such as the Treaty of Rome in 1957, which laid the basis for the Common Market; or through such agile leaps as the reinvention of the Exchange Rate Mechanism in 1993 which saved the single market and the Emu project. We can expect similar improvisation in future. Let the Great Experiment begin.

1 Emu – a leap into the unknown

Economic and monetary union is a once-in-a-century experiment which will transform the political and economic governance of Europe. But it is also a journey into the unknown. Those in favour argue it will act as a shot-in-the-arm for Europe's slow-growth economies by offering stable prices and enduring fiscal discipline. Those against argue it is an act of folly which will divide Europe, reinforcing the post-Maastricht deflationary spiral, robbing nation states of their sovereignty, and alienating a European public already worried about the political legitimacy of European institutions and decision-making.

This chapter offers a full flavour of the controversy surrounding the single currency. Wolfgang Schäuble, the CDU's Chancellor-in-waiting in Germany, sums up the case for Emu in 'Hard sell for a hard euro'. Yves-Thibault de Silguy, the EU commissioner for monetary affairs, suggests that Emu's success can only be guaranteed by political will. As Lionel Barber, the *FT*'s Brussels correspondent, shows in his article 'The point of no return', political will was decisive in 1997 when EU governments scraped for every pfennig, franc and peseta to meet the entry criteria for monetary union. Emu became the make-or-break project for governments in northern and southern Europe, occasionally triggering huge controversy, as in the story of the revaluation of the Bundesbank's gold reserves.

On the other side of the debate, Wilhelm Nölling, a member of the Bundesbank council, calls for a delay in Europe's 'test-tube currency'. Robert Chote, the *FT*'s economics editor, likens Emu to 'Cliffhanging imprudence'.

Many of their reservations stem from one question: is there genuine economic convergence between the future members of the euro zone or are there underlying tensions which, in the event of a crisis, could lead to the collapse of Emu with devastating economic and political repercussions for the rest of the continent?

Beyond the polemics, the collection of *FT* articles offers a closer look at life in euroland. Peter Martin offers a sweeping analysis of the impact and influence of a single currency on business, the financial markets and the consumer in his commentary 'Where Europe boldly goes'. Hugo Dixon analyses the revolutionary consequences of the euro for Europe's capital markets. Lionel Barber notes how the launch of the euro will affect the candidates for EU membership from central and eastern Europe.

The chapter also offers an attempt to answer the billion-euro question: will monetary union lead inexorably to political union? Lionel Barber cautions that the evolution of European political union will be slow and tortuous – not least because of the sensitivities surrounding control of national taxation policy. Other authors examine in more detail the perils of operating a single currency area with a centralized monetary policy and a decentralized fiscal policy.

The chapter concludes with a layman's guide to Emu, offering questions and answers to everything you ever wanted to know about the single currency.

LIONEL BARBER

A The Euro and ever closer union

The point of no return: *Emu has gone through many twists and turns, but the project is now more solid than ever*

LIONEL BARBER

The world woke up to economic and monetary union in 1997, when the single currency moved from a distant dream to a virtual certainty. There were plenty of heart-stopping moments along the way. A few more lie ahead, but Europe's leaders have passed the point of no return.

So has big business. European banks, insurance companies and industrial groups have been preparing actively for the euro. They hired expensive computer staff, modified billing and payroll systems, and launched a wave of pan-European bids and mergers on a scale not seen since the launch of the single market a decade ago.

The corporate restructuring anticipated the competitive pressures that will arise from price transparency and capital mobility across the euro zone. It helped to make the single currency a reality. Not in the sense of euro coins jangling in the pockets of Mr and Mrs Euro-citizen, but by creating momentum towards monetary union that no one – not even the hawks in the Bundesbank – could stop.

Other forces have transformed Emu's fortunes. By far the most important was economic recovery in the European Union. Renewed growth spelt higher tax revenues. Hard-pressed governments suddenly had a breathing space in which to meet the Maastricht budget deficit target of 3 per cent of gross domestic product needed to qualify for Emu membership.

In late February 1998, it became official what financial markets had been expecting for a long time: 14 out of 15 EU countries – all except Greece – met the key condition of the Maastricht treaty: a ratio of budget deficits to gross domestic product of 3 per cent or less. Only four countries – Luxembourg, Finland, France and the UK – complied strictly with the debt-to-GDP ceiling of 60 per cent. But this condition has been interpreted more flexibly than the others. Italy and Belgium, for example, have made it into the first division of Emu members, despite debt-to-GDP ratios running at twice the reference level.

The second favourable development has been a prolonged spell of record low interest rates in Germany, magnified by the weakness of the D-Mark against the dollar. Washington took a relaxed view, seeing the currency alignment as one of the few stimuli to growth in Europe. 'If Emu goes ahead,' says David Hale, chief economist of Zurich Kemper Investment, 'they should put [US treasury secretary] Bob Rubin's head on the euro notes.'

Third, Europe's leaders and central bankers learned the lessons of the 'currency wars' of 1992–3 when they fought in vain to defend exchange-rate parities. The decisive move came in September 1997 in the spa town of Mondorf-les-Bains. EU finance ministers declared they would announce in May 1998 the rates at which individual currencies would enter Emu. Currency traders were put on notice not to second-guess the conversion rates between the selection of Emu founder members in May and the launch of the euro on 1 January 1999.

Mondorf was confirmation that the politicians and the central bankers would hold their nerve. Whatever the public's own doubts about Emu or the calls for a postponement, particularly in Britain and Germany, the Emu timetable remained intact. This was a tribute to the French and German governments, which were determined to keep to the commitments under the 1992 Maastricht treaty. It was also a testament to the skill of a handful of independent professionals in Brussels and Frankfurt who stuck to the script even when the chief actors occasionally forgot their lines.

Baron Alexandre Lamfalussy, who stepped down in mid-1997 as president of the European Monetary Institute, the forerunner of the ECB, played a central role. Known as the Holy Spirit hovering over the project, he earned the trust of politicians and central bank governors alike. Another unsung hero was Sir Nigel Wicks, the British chairman of the EU's secretive monetary committee, which prepared all the key meetings of EU finance ministers. At times, the Emu show threatened to come off the road. The decision by Jacques Chirac, the French president, to call for early parliamentary elections in France still looks like the action of a desperate man out of touch with the mood of the public. For two fraught weeks, the unexpected victory of the Left threatened to provoke a crisis with the Germans over the Socialist-led government's commitment to fiscal discipline.

The stand-off ended at the Amsterdam summit in June 1997. It was there that Lionel Jospin, France's prime minister, signed up to the stability pact enforcing budgetary discipline in return for vague assurances about growth and employment. This allowed the government to introduce extra measures to trim the 1997 deficit, which had threatened to spiral to more than 3.5 per cent.

The Franco-German confrontation pointed to underlying tensions within the Emu project, but it also showed that French policy towards monetary union had stayed consistent since François Mitterrand abandoned socialism in 1983. Occasional wavering aside, France's strategic objective of creating a European Central Bank to dismantle the Bundesbank's *de facto* power to set interest rates across the EU has always prevailed.

Germany's government, too, stuck to its long-term Emu goal. Helmut Kohl, the chancellor, declared solemnly that the alternative to the single currency was a collapse of the EU and the risk of renewed conflict in Europe. By early 1998, German unemployment had risen above 4.8m, the highest since 1933. A slower-than-expected recovery was hurting tax revenues. Germany, once the model economy in Europe, had to admit that an extra effort was needed to meet the self-ordained target of 3 per cent.

In May 1997 Theo Waigel, Germany's finance minister, flew by helicopter to Frankfurt with a plan to revalue the Bundesbank's gold and foreign exchange reserves. It was a defining moment. Operation Rheingold, as it was dubbed by critics, left Bonn open to charges that it was engaged in accounting gimmickry. It weakened Germany's case for keeping other countries, notably Italy, out of the first wave of Emu. Yet the debacle over the gold reserves had a perversely positive result. Mr Waigel's manoeuvres – which surely had Mr Kohl's blessing – showed how desperate Bonn was to meet the Emu-deficit target. The gold revaluation was postponed for twelve months, keeping the Bundesbank's honour intact. Mr Waigel kept his job, and German public opinion on Emu began to shift from sceptical opposition to passive resignation that the single currency was coming. The Hamburg state elections in late September 1997 marked a final turning point. Henning Voscherau, the city mayor, ran an anti-Emu campaign that backfired. The Social Democrats suffered their worst defeat since the second world war. The result sapped the confidence of those in the SPD and the governing CDU–CSU coalition who were pressing for a delay.

The other battlefield was in Italy, where the centre-left Olive Tree coalition, led by Romano Prodi, was mounting a strong effort to meet the Maastricht deficit. In early February 1997, the *Financial Times* revealed a plan to delay Italy's participation in the first wave of single-currency countries. Uproar ensued. Traders sold off the lira, but by the end of the day the market had staged a strong recovery. The message was clear. As long as Mr Prodi could stay the course, he could expect the markets to give Italy the benefit of the doubt. The crisis in autumn 1997 over pension reform met with astonishing calm. Although the government fell, Mr Prodi was back in power within a week.

The rest of the world has also begun to catch up with events in Europe. Larry Summers, deputy US Treasury secretary, gave a qualified blessing to Emu in testimony to Congress. Americans remain generally sceptical about whether Europe can stand the rigours of a single currency. But Mr Summers has given a clear sign that Washington believes Emu is coming. As with German unification, it has no intention of standing in the way.

The new Labour government in Britain has taken the same view. After much internal agonizing, Labour has declared its intent to join the single currency – though not until after the next general election, due by 2002. Some have dismissed the qualified commitment as unnecessarily timid. But Tony Blair, the prime minister, insists he needs more time to turn round sceptical British public opinion.

As Mr Blair discovered at the EU summit in Luxembourg in December 1997, the rest of the Union will not wait for Britain. On tax, employment, and budgetary policy, the trend is towards more intensive co-operation, especially among euro-zone countries. The Emu group will even form its own club. Outsiders can apply, but have no guaranteed seat at the table.

The post-Emu world is taking shape. No one can pretend they know exactly how it will work or what forces it will unleash. One peak is within sight, though others remain to be scaled.

First appeared 30 December 1997

Europe boldly goes: *eleven countries are embarking upon an exhilarating, yet frightening, experiment*

PETER MARTIN

When you walk into the glossy Continent hypermarket at Mondeville, just outside Caen in northern France, the first thing you notice are posters of the latest special offers in food or clothing – with prices marked in euros as well as French francs. The euro figures are no more than guesses. But those posters symbolize perfectly the event that took place on 25 March 1998, when two official reports confirmed that eleven countries are eligible for membership of European economic and monetary union. Emu will now go ahead from 1 January 1999. The posters, with their guessed-at prices, reflect both the essentially prosaic nature of the process (surely the exact denomination in which you pay for your cheese cannot be that important?) and the blind stab at the future that Europe is undertaking.

The reports from the European Commission and the European Monetary Institute – forerunner of the planned European Central Bank – concentrated on the prosaic bit. They assessed the sustainability of the convergence process between the likely Emu members in extremely narrow terms. But how far will governments be able to continue to meet the Maastricht criteria for entry once the immediate pressure to qualify is past? And how successful will the German-inspired stability pact be, with its even tighter limits on government borrowing? These are not trivial issues. But they are dwarfed by the broader, still unimaginable, consequences of Emu.

Now that Emu is a certainty, two powerful and immediate consequences flow: a shift to a new Europe-wide monetary policy and the creation of a single, integrated capital market. And from the moment euro prices become the norm – officially in 2002, but possibly sooner if the Caen hypermarket is a guide – the third immediate consequence ensues: the completion of the European single market, with effects on business that most companies and investors have yet to grasp.

Because they will be set on the basis of economic conditions in many countries, not just one, interest rates will oscillate less than before. But because the preponderant weight in decision-making will be given to the countries of the slow-growing Franco-German core, it will be laxer in peripheral countries such as Italy, Ireland and Spain than would otherwise have been the case. There will be a sustained boom in these regions – at least until their costs render them uncompetitive.

Until now, German companies or French institutional investors have had at the back of their minds the notion that attractive opportunities in the peripheral countries might be offset by a subsequent adjustment of foreign-exchange rates, which might render them less appealing. That fear will now be banished. There is little to be lost – and much to be gained – from switching investment from the core to the periphery.

The common monetary policy will also contribute to the creation of a single, closely integrated capital market. A common currency, and a newly harmonized set of market conventions – thanks to many months of painstaking work by bankers and bureaucrats – will create a single pool of capital. The greater liquidity this provides will make it easier for private-sector borrowers to issue debt – including junk bonds from companies that until now have had little access to cross-border capital.

Similar changes will take place in the equity markets, as the euro confirms the emergence of a superleague of about 300 European companies. Even if stock exchanges continue, for the time being at least, to operate on national lines, that will have little impact on these companies. Their share prices and accounts denominated in euros, their tax treatment increasingly common, their corporate governance prodded towards the Anglo-Saxon model by US shareholders, these companies will look much more like each other than like their smaller national siblings. Unfamiliar pan-European indices such as Eurotop or Stoxx will replace the familiar Dax, CAC and FTSE 100 indices. For financial institutions, especially, the competitive pressures are likely to produce a wave of mergers, first among banks (which will lose revenue from foreign-exchange trading and underwriting local-currency equity and bond issues), then among insurance companies and other retail financial services groups.

Financial markets will be quickly integrated. Consumer goods markets will take longer – because the final moment for retail prices to shift to the euro is not until 2002. But once prices are all set in the new currency, consumers will be able to see more clearly – and punish more effectively – those companies that are attempting to keep prices at different levels in different markets. This process would normally be a slow one. But the shift to euros will have a galvanizing effect on consumer attitudes, especially because of the need to adjust price points.

Manufacturers' prices usually differ from market to market – FFr9.99, for example, or DM299. Translated into euros, those prices will lose their appeal. There will be big rewards for companies that quickly adjust all their products to new, Europe-wide price points. That may mean changing, and harmonizing, product specifications and packages. This will create dire pressures on companies to push prices downwards. They will be helped in their hunt for lower costs by the absence of currency barriers, making it psychologically and practically easier to purchase from the far reaches of the euro zone. Companies failing to seize these opportunities will find themselves victims of the takeover wave that will spread from banks to manufacturing companies.

These are all the immediate effects of Emu. They will be clearly visible in the early years of the next century. But the second-order effects will be even more powerful, if a little delayed. They can be summed up in a single phrase: the growing irrelevance of national boundaries. Cultural boundaries, regional boundaries, ethnic boundaries may well be strengthened in reaction to the growing homogenization of the European Union. But national boundaries, the boundaries of statehood, will be progressively less important. As national economies become integrated with the euro zone, it will be less and less relevant to use them as a frame of reference. Some companies in Spain will do well, others do badly. So what? That tells us something about individual managers, industries, styles of business. But it tells us little else of value.

National statistics will capture ever-less-important facts. Government spending, constrained by the stability pact and the ease of business migration across national boundaries, will differ less between countries. Tax policies will be brought into line by European peer pressure. France will still be very different from Finland – but Louisiana is very different from Vermont.

The process of integration will not be smooth. Growing tensions – between companies, between governments, between organized interest groups – will threaten to blow the union apart. Such fissures will be greatest if France and Germany prove unable to cope with competition from the periphery, and unemployment continues to rise in the core of the euro zone. But if Emu does not collapse – and there is an outside chance of that – the processes required to find a solution will enormously strengthen the European entity.

That is the future to which the March 1998 convergence reports committed Europe. It is hardly surprising that those nations least anxious to submerge themselves in the emerging European polity – the UK, Denmark, Sweden – are hanging back from Emu. But for those countries committed to the process, Europe's future is already under way. You have only to go to Mondeville to discover that.

First appeared 28 March 1998

Harmony a sensitive issue *– now that Emu is within reach, a familiar question arises: will the single currency lead to a harmonization of fiscal policy?*

LIONEL BARBER

Almost ten years ago, a committee of central bank governors under the chairmanship of Jacques Delors, European Commission president, left the matter open. They preferred to agree on a blueprint to launch the euro rather than disagree over its likely consequences. The politics of fiscal harmonization or fiscal co-ordination are delicate. Tax policy is one of the last bastions of national sovereignty. All decisions must pass the unanimity rule in the EU, which is why progress in areas such as value-added tax has been halting at best. But once Emu becomes a reality, the link between the single currency and the single market will become more explicit. The competitive forces unleashed by Emu – notably price transparency across borders – will make all governments more sensitive to accusations that others are using unfair methods or policies to gain advantage. Tax regimes present inviting targets.

One of the more remarkable developments of the past twelve months is the way in which tax policy has crept to the top of the EU agenda. Governments and the European Commission have begun to anticipate the impact of the single currency, starting with a joint approach towards 'tax poaching' or harmful tax competition.

The breakthrough came in December 1997 in the run-up to the EU summit in Luxembourg. EU finance ministers agreed a voluntary code of conduct on business taxation; a commitment to consider a minimum withholding tax on non-residents' savings income; and an agreement to discuss a directive making it easier for companies to transfer interest and royalties across borders without the risk of double taxation.

The impact of the deal was softened by several unilateral declarations by member states. Ireland insisted on a five-year deadline for phasing out its 10 per cent tax rate for manufacturers which France and other countries insist is siphoning off investment. Luxembourg declared it would not accept the introduction of any EU-wide withholding tax unless it is balanced by legislation to enforce a minimum corporate tax regime – an argument rejected by Ireland and most likely by other countries, including the UK.

Despite these escape clauses, work on tax co-ordination is edging forward under the guidance of Mario Monti, the methodical and cerebral Italian commissioner responsible for the single market. In March 1998, he unveiled proposals for a directive eliminating withholding taxes on payment of interest and royalties between associated companies. Mr Monti is also contemplating the content of the coming directive on withholding tax on foreign savings. The latter is based on a French initiative which seeks to deal with the conflicting demands of banking secrecy and the need to exchange information among EU tax authorities. The approach would allow, say, a French saver to pay withholding tax in Luxembourg, most likely set at a stiff level to compensate for the privilege of remaining anonymous. Alternatively, the French saver could pay tax direct to the French authorities, thus removing all doubts about tax avoidance. It looks like a neat solution, but important practical questions remain on who gets what share of the revenue.

Mr Monti believes that momentum on this issue should pick up over the next eighteen months because the three governments in the EU chair – Austria, Germany and Finland – are nominally committed to advancing tax co-ordination. More important, all are certain to participate in monetary union.

But Mr Monti is not putting all his eggs in the legislative basket. The code of conduct remains a useful means of applying collective pressure to limit predatory tax competition. Hence the creation of a new EU-wide peer review group meeting not less than twice a year. With luck it could be as effective as the peer pressure which member states have used to great effect in the drive to reduce public deficits and debt ahead of Emu. The dilemma is how far to go. The single currency means the end of differentials in national interest rates and national exchange rates. Tax policy will be the last discriminating element between countries. Why should countries such as Ireland be penalized for seeking comparative advantage through tax havens such as Dublin Docks?

On the other hand, influential politicians such as Jean-Claude Juncker, prime minister of Luxembourg, argue that Emu will force greater harmonization of economic policies across the board. The logic points to some agreements or understandings on minimum standards on tax and social security just as they apply to EU social policy. After all, Emu does not just stand for monetary union: it means economic and monetary union.

Finally, EU-wide directives seeking to limit predatory tax competition will be ineffective unless they are extended to other OECD countries, notably Switzerland. Without a common tax regime, money would simply flow out of the member states into safer havens such as Geneva or Zurich. In this sense, the announcement by the British government that it was reviewing the status of the Channel Islands could be a straw in the wind.

In a world of global markets, instant communications, and volatile money, European governments are discovering that greater fiscal co-ordination – if not actual harmonization – is one step towards recapturing sovereignty. We can expect further progress, however halting.

First appeared 23 March 1998

Emu's capital consequences: *Emu will put the heat on Europe's industrialists. But they will end up the better for it.*

HUGO DIXON

Replacing European-style capitalism with the Anglo-Saxon variety can hardly have been the aim of the politicians who concocted economic and monetary union in Europe. But that, paradoxically, is just what is likely to happen. One way it will do so is through labour markets. Emu's one-size-fits-all monetary policy will be such a straitjacket that flexibility will be needed elsewhere. That could help freer (Anglo-Saxon) labour practices spread more widely. But a less explored and potentially even more rapid way in which Anglo-Saxon capitalism will catch on is via the capital markets. The single currency will give birth to a large single capital market. This is likely to smell less like continental Europe's stakeholder capitalism and more like the shareholder capitalism predominant in the US and UK.

As companies in all sectors start competing for funds on a Europe-wide basis, they will have to change their behaviour and embrace the philosophy of shareholder value. A chain reaction beginning with the political decision to launch Emu will unintentionally alter the way investment is channelled and hence end up affecting the entire corporate sector.

European capitalism is transforming itself anyway. Companies are paying increasing attention to shareholders' needs. Evidence for this ranges from the growth of employee share-option schemes to the number of share buy-backs. The reasons why companies are doing these things – intensifying global competition and the growth of funded pension schemes – would exist even without the single currency. But Emu will accelerate the changes. There are many channels through which the euro will affect European capitalism. The clearest will be through investors' portfolio allocations.

At present, European capital is largely trapped at home. Of the big countries, only the UK invested more than 15 per cent of its financial assets abroad in 1996, according to figures compiled by Intersec, the fund management research organization (*see* chart, p. 13). The figures in Germany, France and Italy all hovered around 5 per cent. One reason for this home country bias is that individual savers do not want to run the risk of a fall in the foreign currency they invest in. Another is that in most countries insurance companies and, to a lesser extent, pension funds are prevented by regulations from investing more than a small portion of their assets in foreign currencies.

Once the euro is launched in January 1999, currency risk for investments within euroland will vanish. French investors have no need to stay in France to escape currency risk – Germany or Italy will do just as well. Institutional investors are increasingly focusing on this already. Of course, this will not happen overnight. Investors' clients realize this is going ahead and are looking at stocks on a pan-European basis, says Ben Funnell, European equity strategist at Morgan Stanley Dean Witter. There is no question that capital will flow within this zone to a broader extent. But how far will the process go? The Europeanization of portfolios could eventually be fairly dramatic as investors realize foreign investment actually cuts risk through diversification rather than increasing it.

Standard portfolio theory says investors should own a bit of everything pretty much in proportion to its weight in the total market, says David Miles, professor of finance at London's Imperial College. If that happened in euroland, investors would end up with the vast majority of their assets abroad instead of the current tiny proportion.

Of course, this will not happen overnight. Investors' greater familiarity with local opportunities, residual regulations favouring domestic investment and just plain inertia will slow the change. But those expecting a long-drawn-out process are in for a shock if recent flows into Italian mutual funds are a herald of things to come. Not only is a torrent of money pouring into these funds but, in most months, more is going into foreign than Italian equities – and that is even before the euro is launched.

The single currency will also spur Europe's incipient love affair with equities. At present, shares play a surprisingly small role in most European portfolios: cash and government bonds dominate. The UK, where over half private-sector financial assets were in equities in 1996 according to Intersec, is the glaring exception among the big countries. The figures in Germany, France and Italy were all around 20 per cent.

The main factor causing the growth of equities as an asset class is the trend towards private pensions. When it comes to saving for retirement, shares are a particularly appropriate asset. This is because returns tend to be higher than with bonds or cash and, although their value swings around from year to year, over the long term the peaks and troughs are normally smoothed out. The growth of private pensions is happening anyway. Governments are trimming generous state pension schemes because they fear that ageing populations could bankrupt them. But the Emu process will make this happen faster. Under the stability pact

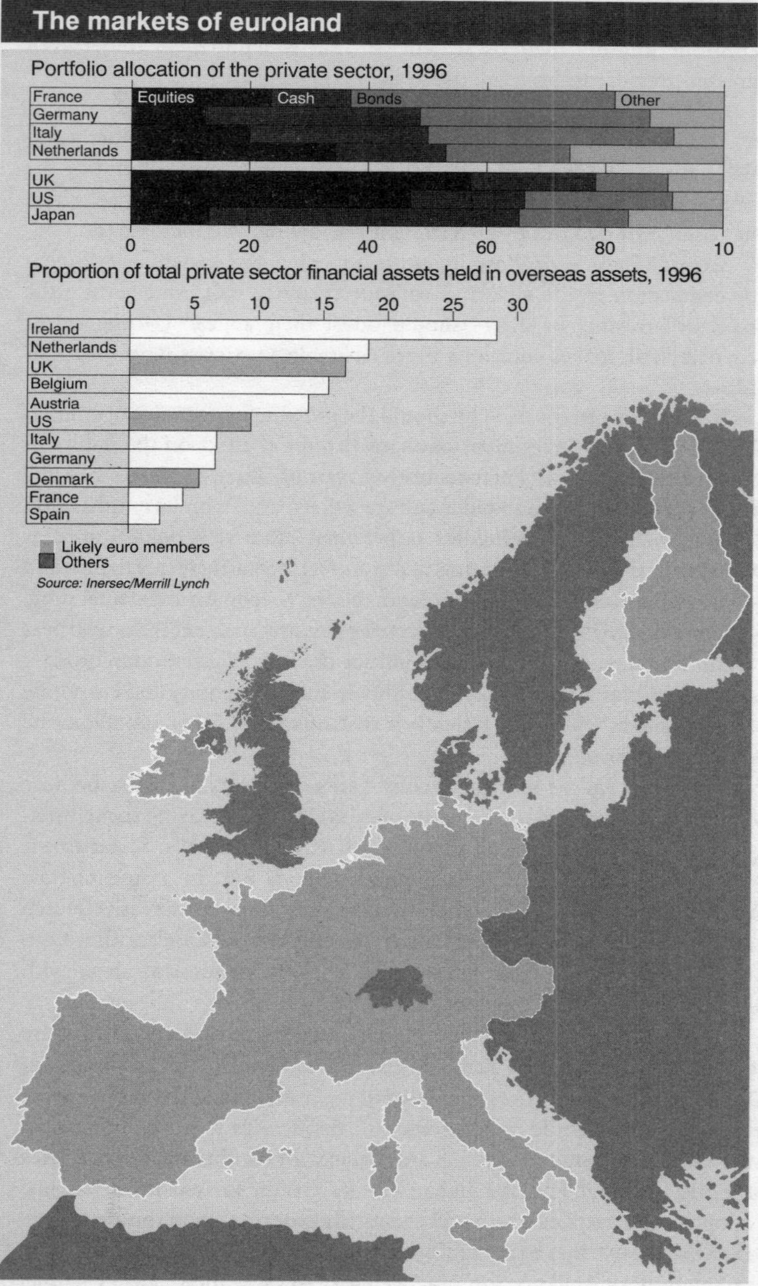
The markets of euroland
Portfolio allocation of the private sector, 1996
France
Germany
Italy
Netherlands
UK
US
Japan
Equities
Cash
Bonds
Other
0
20
40
60
80
10
Proportion of total private sector financial assets held in overseas assets, 1996
0
5
10
15
20
25
30
Ireland
Netherlands
UK
Belgium
Austria
US
Italy
Germany
Denmark
France
Spain
Likely euro members
Others
Source: Inersec/Merrill Lynch

accompanying monetary union, countries have committed themselves to continue limiting their fiscal deficits. That will put them under even greater pressure to privatize pensions.

In two other ways, Emu will fuel Europe's affection for equities. First, at a time when the supply of government bonds is shrinking, other assets will naturally fill the hole in investors' portfolios. Shares will not be the only asset class to benefit from this trend: corporate bond issuance, which has been crowded out by government borrowing, will increase too.

Second, Emu will allow investors to enjoy the benefits of foreign diversification inside euroland without currency risk. And cutting the risks of investing in shares should boost their appeal. Getting rid of currency risk makes equities a more desirable asset class, says Professor Miles.

So what? one may ask. Why should the growing importance of equities and cross-border investment have any profound effect on the nature of European capitalism? For two related reasons. First, as shares become more prevalent, so shareholder culture will expand, with its emphasis on creating value for shareholders rather than other stakeholders such as workers or managers. Second, as investors feel increasingly free to pick and choose opportunities across euroland, they will become more demanding.

Sub-standard companies will perceive this as a stick being used to beat them. Dynamic organizations should see the opportunity to tap broader capital pools as a carrot. More liquidity in Europe's equity and corporate bond markets will lower industry's cost of capital. This will allow the strong to grow stronger.

One trend will be more share buy-backs. Investors like these because they typically cut companies' costs of capital while removing the temptation to waste spare cash on investments with low returns. So far this is still largely an Anglo-American phenomenon. But, in a sign of how attitudes are changing, Royal Dutch, the previously conservative Dutch arm of the Shell Oil giant, last week has said it would seek authority to buy its shares. Meanwhile, France and Germany are pressing ahead with legislation to facilitate buy-backs.

Another embryonic trend is linking executive remuneration to share price performance. The fact that executives stand to make significant money if their share prices rise is one of the most powerful tools to ensure they pursue shareholders' interests with vigour. Again, stock options and the like are common in the US and Britain. In continental Europe, they are just starting. Eni, the Italian energy group, for example, has just adopted a share plan which will eventually cover its 2,000 top managers. Elsewhere, laws that make options unattractive are being reformed.

Yet another Anglo-Saxon practice likely to cross the English Channel is the hostile takeover. So far, these are still extremely rare on the Continent. And even when they do occur, as in last year's bid by Generali, the Italian insurance company, for France's AGF, they do not always succeed. That, in part, is due to shareholding structures that protect incumbent managements. In France and Italy, webs of cross-shareholdings and *noyaux durs*, or shareholder pacts, fulfil this function. In Germany, the house bank system – under which banks own big stakes in industrial companies – plays a similar role. But these links are being dissolved, while independent shareholders are becoming increasingly demanding. At the same time, countries like Italy are reforming their takeover rules to remove some of the barriers to making a successful hostile bid.

Do not expect a tidal wave of hostile takeovers. But there may not need to be many to keep top management on their toes. After all, as Voltaire said, you only need to execute the occasional admiral to encourage the others. Or, as Dr Pangloss might have said from the same book, Emu is for the best in the best of all possible worlds. For shareholders, at least.

First appeared 30 April 1998

Strains of a monetary marriage: *Emu defies modern taboos*

MARTIN WOLF

In the very long run, almost anything that can go wrong will do so. Within European economic and monetary union, this raises a simple question: will it cope with the political strains that sharing a common money is bound, occasionally, to create?

In an age too impatient for long courtships and too cautious for life-long marriage, Emu violates both taboos. The 'Werner plan' for monetary union saw the light of day back in 1970. Yet, however long and hard the preliminaries, their end marks but the closing of a chapter. The next one will be at least as difficult: the management of a supposedly indissoluble marriage among – initially – eleven sovereign member states of the European Union.

The view that the member states remain sovereign is controversial. Many argue that they are surrendering or 'pooling' their sovereignty within Emu. This is an error. The members are delegating powers. Their peoples could, if they wished, elect governments committed to withdrawal from Emu – or the EU – and then withdraw. This is true for all members, but particularly for the larger European powers. The gossamer threads of monetary union cannot 'bind' Germany against its will; they merely symbolize and reinforce its willingness to be bound. Unhappy history suggests that monetary unions, unaccompanied by a credible merger of sovereignty, do not last, examples being the Latin, German–Austrian and Scandinavian monetary unions. Long-lasting monetary zones are defined not by whether they are what economists call 'optional currency areas', but by the boundaries of a state.

Money is political, particularly in the modern world. Yet Emu is an attempt to separate it from politics. This is true in two respects. First, decisions at the EU level are made by guardian bureaucracies and intergovernmental committees, subject to the oversight of a remote and feeble parliament. Meanwhile, democratic politics is almost entirely confined to member states.

Second, the EU has established an unprecedentedly independent central bank, one entitled by treaty to determine both its goals and the instruments it uses to achieve them. The EU's Maastricht treaty also imposed constraints on the fiscal policies of member states, subsequently reinforced in the 'pact for stability and growth' agreed in Amsterdam in June 1997.

Politics may seem to be kennelled, like an obstreperous dog. But it has a nasty habit of escaping. If the question is whether the depoliticized European monetary system can survive, the answer depends, first and foremost, on how well it works. Suppose Emu proved consistent with steadily rising prosperity, not just in the EU as a whole, but in all member states. Suppose the decisions of the European Central Bank (ECB) were uncontentious and each member state abided by the obligations it has assumed. Under these circumstances, the conflict between European money and national politics would remain purely theoretical.

A single monetary area stretching from the Arctic to the Mediterranean and from the Atlantic to the Oder will not work like this all of the time. It may well be better for every member, in the long term, than any alternative. But things are still going to go wrong somewhere, sometimes. One source of pressure might be regionally differentiated shocks to supply or demand. An industry that is especially important for a particular country might become globally uncompetitive, or demand might be relatively sluggish within one or more countries.

US experience suggests that both are possible within a long-standing and successful monetary union. Attempts by member states to offset the impact might then run into the constraints imposed by the stability pact. Another difficulty could be divergent initial conditions. In 1997, for example, the rate of unemployment varied from 5.6 per cent of the labour force in the Netherlands to 20.8 per cent in Spain. This has little, or nothing, to do with monetary policy, but it would hardly be surprising if those responsible for unemployment blamed the ECB instead. In future, the obstacles to adjustment inherent in Europe's inflexible labour markets might create still more serious difficulties for member states. Again, the temptation to blame the ECB is likely to prove overwhelming.

No less potentially important are differences in economic philosophy. The essentially Germanic ideas underpinning the Maastricht treaty are not universally accepted. France, for example, is far from comfortable with the model of extreme central bank independence embodied in Emu. Nothing is more likely than condemnation of the Frankfurt-based institution for alleged deflationary bias.

Moreover, the constraints accepted by member states, particularly over fiscal policy, are likely to conflict with domestic commitments and pressures. Most member states have big public pension liabilities; some start with high ratios of public debt to gross domestic product; Italy has both. The 1998 report on convergence from the European Commission noted that Italy would need to run a primary fiscal surplus – balance before interest payments – of 4.5 per cent of GDP for almost twenty years if it is to lower its debt ratio to the Maastricht standard of 60 per cent. The strain could easily prove too much.

In all, the number of ways in which unhappiness with Emu might emerge is depressingly large. Worse, when this takes political form it is bound to do so where politics works – at the national level. Awareness in financial markets of what is going on is then likely to be priced into assets, accelerating the onset of crisis.

The underlying reality is that power will lie with one group of people operating at a supranational level, while legitimacy will remain with another group operating at the national level. The risk that conflict will then emerge between democratic national politics and Europe's intergovernmental order is the greatest threat to the survival of Emu.

First appeared 30 April 1998

Eastern Europe: *candidates move into a closer orbit*

LIONEL BARBER

The decision to create the euro has aroused much controversy, but so has the relationship between the single currency and enlargement of the European Union.

Opponents of European economic and monetary union argue that Emu is a distraction from the challenge of uniting Europe after the cold war. Instead of the old Iron Curtain, they fear that a new 'velvet curtain' will divide a rich core of 'ins' from a poorer periphery of 'outs'. But Emu advocates insist that euro-driven 'deepening' in western Europe remains a precondition for 'widening' the EU in the east. The launch of the euro will help rather than hinder enlargement, they believe.

What these partisan arguments overlook is that the introduction of the euro will have an impact on the ten central and eastern European candidate countries (and Cyprus) whether or not they join the EU as planned early next century. The impact will be felt not only among the five countries on a fast track to membership – the Czech Republic, Estonia, Hungary, Poland and Slovenia – as well as Cyprus. It will also reverberate among those countries which have yet to open formal accession negotiations with the EU: Bulgaria, Latvia, Lithuania, Romania and Slovakia.

The first area to watch is foreign exchange-rate policy, particularly in those candidate countries which tie their exchange rates to a single currency – such as the D-Mark – or to a basket in which European currencies enjoy a strong weighting. The Czech government, for example, operates a managed float against the D-Mark, while Hungary operates against a basket weighted around 70 per cent D-Mark and 30 per cent US dollar. In Poland, the currency basket is about 45 per cent US dollar, 35 per cent D-Mark, 10 per cent British pound, 5 per cent Swiss franc and 5 per cent French franc. In each case, the euro will benefit from the shift out of Emu-participant currencies.

More broadly, once the accession process accelerates with the lifting of tariff and non-tariff barriers and capital controls, the applicant countries will be drawn increasingly into the EU's economic and monetary orbit, says Gabor Bognar, an economist at Goldman Sachs. The effect will be pronounced in front-rank candidates for membership such as the Czech Republic, Hungary and Poland, which have about 60 per cent of their merchandise trade with the EU. But it will affect those countries such as Bulgaria and Estonia which have currency boards based on the D-Mark. These will in future be linked one-to-one to the euro.

Central banks in central and eastern Europe are also likely to shift a portion of their reserves to the euro. Professor Hannah Scobie, director of the London-based Economic and Financial Centre, who has closely studied the link between eastern enlargement and the euro, is convinced that the emergence of a strong single currency will encourage the trend. In the real economy, Goldman Sachs predicts that the euro will circulate as a secondary means of payment. Office rents, often denominated in D-Mark or US dollars, will switch over to euros. Car prices will shift. Would-be purchasers of a BMW in, say, Slovenia will have to watch how the local currency is faring against the euro rather than the D-Mark.

Border regions between, say, the Czech Republic and Germany, are also likely to adopt the euro. But few are predicting a return to Communist-era black markets, where the dollar or D-Mark shoved aside the local currencies. Today, most currencies in the region are convertible, at least on the current account. If there is a threat of a shadow economy, it stems from tax avoidance rather than currency substitution, says Goldman Sachs.

The more intractable question is whether the eastern applicants have a realistic prospect of adopting the euro. Optimists such as Professor Scobie argue that, with the important exception of inflation, several candidate countries are performing well according to the EU's Maastricht criteria for joining Emu. On public deficits, the Czech Republic is close to balance. Hungary, with a deficit equivalent to 3.3 per cent of gross domestic product, and Poland, at 3.7 per cent, are within striking distance of the EU's 3 per cent target. On government debt, the Czechs (16 per cent), Hungary (64 per cent) and Poland (54 per cent) are performing better than their western counterparts.

But candidate countries face big hurdles. They must balance their high growth rates with the need to reduce inflation while sticking to a fixed or semi-fixed exchange rate – assuming they choose to shadow the euro or join the Exchange Rate Mechanism Mark II, once they have joined the EU.

How will their process of 'convergence' work in practice? In the first instance, all applicant countries are obliged to submit their macroeconomic programmes for review in Brussels. All candidates must also embrace the goal of Emu as part of their general effort to meet the *acquis communautaire* – the rules and obligations for members which have developed since the 1957 Treaty of Rome. At the forefront is the need to meet the standards of the single market and to comply with rules on state aid and competition policy. This means enforcing as well as passing EU laws – a big test for inexperienced, overstretched public administrations.

It is these tasks, rather than Emu itself, which may constitute the biggest barrier to future EU membership for the young democracies of the east.

First appeared 30 April 1998

Will Emu lead to political union? *The architects of the euro have never left any doubt that the single currency is more than a matter of money*

LIONEL BARBER

Jacques Delors, Helmut Kohl, and the late François Mitterrand have all paid lip service to the economic benefits of monetary union. But each has suggested that the political consequences would be momentous.

Chancellor Kohl sees the euro as a means of laying to rest the demons of nationalism and binding a united Germany of 80 million people irreversibly into a united Europe. In Brussels the expectation is that Emu will deliver a psychological boost to Europe's aspirations to play a greater role on the world stage. 'Whenever people talk about the dollar, they will also talk about the euro,' says Erkki Liikanen, the Finnish commissioner. 'Europe and the US will be spoken about in the same breath.'

Yet behind these aspirations the current reality is much less clear-cut. The EU is pushing ahead with a supranational independent central bank without a broader political union. But the imbalance between the carefully crafted blueprint for the operation of the ECB and the fuzzy division of power between national parliaments and remote institutions such as the European Commission and the European Parliament is striking. So is the fact that responsibility for core economic policy questions such as taxation remains in the hands of national governments.

Two questions arise. Is the muddled status quo sustainable? Or are critics – both euro-enthusiast and euro-sceptical – right when they argue that a political union is the logical development needed to establish the democratic legitimacy of the single currency? In other words, will Emu prove to be a catalyst for deeper political integration in Europe, complementing the acceleration of economic integration most predict will occur after the launch of the euro on 1 January 1999?

One way of looking at European integration is to imagine a medieval cathedral-in-the-making. The 1957 Treaty of Rome established the foundations. The 1986 Single European Act, the 1992 Maastricht treaty and the 1997 Amsterdam treaty supplied the altar and buttresses. Now that the single currency has provided the four walls, all that is lacking is a vault. In the past, France and Germany have acted as lead architects. Maastricht marked a watershed: for the first time, Europe's leaders entered areas such as money, defence and foreign policy where others had feared to tread. They even dared to give the European Community a new name: the European Union. A backlash followed, prompting Europe's leaders to become more wary of offending public opinion. Mr Kohl has stopped talking about 'the United States of Europe'. Inside the Commission, no one dares utter the term 'federalism' or 'political union'.

The April 1998 parliamentary debate in France underlined how sections of the left and right cling to their hostility to greater European integration. Jacques Chirac, the French president, could not persuade his own Gaullist party to vote for Emu. Much to the disgust of pro-Europeans such as Alain Juppé, former prime minister, the Gaullists argued that a yes vote would register a vote of confidence in the Socialist-led government. The rise of the far-right National Front – which is virulently anti-European and picking up support among France's disaffected, unemployed youth – has stirred up nationalist embers among the Gaullists.

In Germany, Mr Kohl won a resounding parliamentary vote of confidence in the euro. But the German public is nervous about surrendering the D-Mark. And the Bundesbank remains sceptical about an Emu project that includes high-debt economies such as Italy and Belgium without binding political commitments to fiscal discipline. If Mr Kohl fails to win an unprecedented fifth term in the September 1997 general election – a real possibility – Europe will lose the driving force behind deeper political integration. So an early test will be whether euro-building can continue independent of personalities.

The first area to watch will be economic policy. The eleven members of the single currency zone are planning to intensify co-operation inside the new euro-X forum for finance ministers which, in time, could evolve into a political counterweight to the European Central Bank. Ministers will not only apply the provisions of the German-designed Stability Pact to enforce fiscal discipline among euro-zone members. The French government is pressing hard for much closer co-ordination of macroeconomic policy. The aim is to align policies so that countries' economic cycles are more in tune. This would apply to individual countries, but could also apply to Europe as a whole.

The EU is also extending the Maastricht process of 'peer review' which helped countries reduce their public deficits. Employment policy is one area. Even Britain, which is staying out of Emu, is going along with this, if only because its record on unemployment is a strong card to play in Europe. In all these ways, the co-ordination of fiscal policies could add to pressures for more political co-ordination.

So, possibly, might pressure to 'complete the single market' by increasing the collective approach in certain areas. Taxation is one. EU governments agreed in December 1997 to a voluntary code of conduct restricting 'unfair' tax competition. The Commission is also bringing forward draft legislation. But whether Emu will actually stoke pressures for tax harmonization remains unclear. Yves-Thibault de Silguy, EU monetary affairs commissioner, argues that border regions in the euro-zone will be comfortable with high differentials in, say, value-added tax. Dutch and Irish officials argue that a dose of tax competition is vital to maintaining flexibility in a single currency zone, especially with a tight monetary and fiscal policy and without the safety valve of the exchange rate.

So, Economic and Monetary Europe does not by definition add up to Political Europe. Member states still regard certain areas as off-limits for the Union or the European Commission – particularly when it comes to defending entrenched privileges in international forums such as the Group of Seven industrialized countries. Thus, the UK and Germany are resisting the Commission's efforts to insert itself formally into the G7. Officials say it is vital to maximize Europe's united economic weight in the world. And the euro will, in some sense, make the G7 into the G3. But the pressure for greater political union that will come from international diplomacy is likely to be gradual. 'Member states will have to adjust their behaviour,' says one official, shaking his head in resignation, 'but it will take time.'

In the area of foreign policy, the picture of fifteen member states marching in lock-step would be the exception to the rule. Britain and France often behave like nineteenth-century colonial powers. The four 'neutral' member states – Austria, Finland, Ireland, Sweden – are by definition second-tier players. The institutional apparatus is creaking, too. The General Affairs council – the once-dominant decision-making forum in Brussels attended by foreign ministers – is in terminal decline compared with the up-and-coming Ecofin council of finance ministers. 'The whole process is a shambles,' says a senior EU diplomat.

One theory in Brussels is that EU leaders will become so dissatisfied with the preponderant power of the finance ministers that they will dispatch their own vice-premiers to Brussels to take charge of foreign policy. President Mitterrand floated the idea of a permanent high-level presence in a joint Franco-German initiative in late 1993, but the idea foundered on opposition from Mr Delors, former EU president, who worried that the Commission would be the big loser. Other member states feared the creation of a new French-dominated power centre in Brussels or, even worse, a quasi-federal government.

In Brussels the view is that the institutional status quo will hold – but not for long. And here, the single currency is not the only force for change. At least as important is the Union's longer-term plan to enlarge membership to the former communist countries of central and eastern Europe. The target date for the first new members is 2002–2003. This may be ambitious, because front-rank candidates such as Poland face massive adjustments to comply with the demands of the single market. The fifteen EU member states must also first reform the Common Agricultural Policy and produce a new budget deal to cope with the costs of expansion.

In the past, enlargement has forced the Union to adapt its institutions and decision-making through lengthy constitutional conventions known as intergovernmental conferences or IGCs. Thus, the accession of Britain, Ireland and Denmark in the early 1970s was followed by an extension of majority voting and a dilution of the national veto in the mid-1980s. Maastricht extended the process, but Amsterdam marked a holding operation – with the exception of closer co-operation on internal justice and immigration issues. Most insiders do not expect another all-embracing IGC ahead of the first wave of eastern enlargement. This implies a short, sharp conference, most likely in 1999, which would marginally extend majority voting, reduce the size of the European Commission and change the balance of voting between small and large countries.

In short, the process of euro-building will continue after the launch of the single currency, but perhaps in a more improvised and flexible manner than in the past. The euro will have political consequences, but they will take time to work through and they will entail a sharper division of responsibilities between nation states and Brussels. None of this amounts to the creation of a federal super-state.

First appeared 1 May 1998

B The case for and against Emu

Only politics can destroy Emu

WOLFGANG MÜNCHAU

Conspiracy theorists all over Europe love to speculate on the possibility that Emu will eventually collapse. Now that Emu is certain to start on schedule in January 1999, the forecast of a pending disaster has replaced the previously favoured prediction that Emu would never get off the ground. EU central bankers and monetary officials, who spent the past few years making sure that Emu will work, seem relatively unperturbed by the suggestion that it might eventually collapse. By contrast, euro-sceptic economists in the UK and the US are excited by the prospect of disaster. Can Emu collapse? The short answer is of course it can. But do not hold your breath.

When Emu begins in January 1999, there will be two phases. During the first phase, ranging from 1999 until the end of 2001, national banknotes will continue to circulate alongside a virtual euro, which will only exist as a non-cash transaction currency.

From July 2002, the euro will be the only legal tender in Emu for cash and non-cash transactions. During the first six months of 2002, the two phases will overlap. After July 2002, national banknotes will no longer exist.

Discussion of a breakdown must distinguish between the two different phases. A breakdown in the final phase of Emu would be similar to a breakdown of the dollar or of sterling. That would not happen unless national governments – probably backed by referendums or two-thirds parliamentary majorities – decided to pull out of Emu and reintroduce national currencies. Since these currencies would no longer exist, governments would be faced with an enormous problem. Because it took several years for central banks to prepare for the transition from national currencies to Emu, a reversion to national currencies could not be achieved overnight. It would take almost as long to get out of Emu as it took to get into Emu.

A government would have to muster political support for an orderly withdrawal followed by a relatively lengthy preparation process. There are other, more disturbing, but less likely scenarios. For example, Emu could break up as economic tension becomes unbearable. But those who believe in this scenario should try to put themselves into the position of future EU leaders who would have to take such a decision. An overnight break-up of a currency zone, without preparation, would entail massive risks. There would be no banknotes ready for distribution the next day. It could entail enormous systematic risk for the financial sector. Banks would find themselves with liabilities in expensive dollars, and assets of worthless euros. Once established, the life-or-death choices become highly asymmetric. The risk of continuing Emu will always be more calculable and more palatable than the risk of abolishing it after 2002.

In the 1999–2001 phase, the situation is not fundamentally different, despite the uninterrupted circulation of national banknotes. Since national currencies would remain in circulation, and since euro banknotes and coins would not yet have been distributed, a break-up of Emu would, during this phase, leave national governments free to re-issue national banknotes and coins under a domestic monetary regime. These national currencies would then presumably free-float against the others.

Walter Eltis, a UK economist, has argued that such a possibility could induce holders of, for example, lira banknotes and coins to pile into D-Mark banknotes after 1999. This could be a profitable tactic, if Emu were subsequently to break up. The assumption is that, under such circumstances, the D-Mark would be reintroduced as a bona fide currency and would appreciate sharply. But this theory ignores some realities. First, while piling into D-Marks is possible, it would by itself not jeopardize Emu. Unlike the exchange-rate mechanism, Emu cannot be driven apart by speculative attack. During the transition period, lira and D-Mark banknotes would be denominations of the same currency, the euro. If everybody piled into D-Marks, the money supply of the euro would not change. Only its composition would change. This scenario would be profitable if Emu were to break up for other reasons. It is, however, highly unlikely that governments would pull out of Emu so soon.

Furthermore, the scenario also misjudges the mechanism by which national currencies would be reintroduced. A break-up would be no orderly process. There would be no ERM to glue them together. There is nothing that would prevent a reincarnated Bundesbank treating these speculative D-Mark accounts held outside Germany as non-existent. It can be argued that these so-called D-Mark accounts would be merely denominations of a defunct euro. A newly introduced D-Mark would be a legally different currency from the old D-Mark.

The point is that Emu can only be destroyed by a political event. Such a political event would in all likelihood only occur in times of massive economic pressure and distortions. The sceptics are right in their assumption, but wrong in their conclusion. The chances of strong economic distortions at one point in the next ten or fifteen years must be very high. But this does not make a breakdown of Emu any more likely. On the contrary. If faced with the prospect of a break-up of Emu, with all the risks that this would involve, EU politicians would probably choose the soft option: joint action on taxes and mutual assistance, or whatever else it takes to reduce the disturbances.

This means that, under conditions of distress, EU leaders would be far more likely to opt for what the French call 'economic government' – a system of tax co-ordination, perhaps even an Emu-wide finance ministry, and a system of fund transfers to smooth the cyclical swings between booming and depressed economies.

The irony is that the conditions for the break-up of Emu are exactly the same as those that could lead to even more political and economic integration and centralization.

First appeared 23 March 1998

Cliffhanging imprudence: *the European single currency is a bad idea whose time has come*

ROBERT CHOTE

History and politics explain why Europe is adopting a single currency. Economics explains why it should not. In judging any economic reform, one should compare benefits and costs. The benefits of monetary union are predictable and will at best be modest; the costs are unpredictable but could easily be spectacular.

The abolition of currency fluctuations within Europe should reduce transaction costs, make national price differences more transparent, promote industrial specialization and encourage trade and investment flows. But Germany, France, Austria and the Benelux nations have in effect shared a single monetary policy for a decade, with exchange rates as good as fixed. They have not enjoyed an economic renaissance as a result: so why should the more disparate group that is now to adopt the euro?

Embracing the single currency also means losing both monetary autonomy and the ability to use nominal exchange-rate movements as a shock absorber. This need not matter if the currency area possessed three attributes that would allow it to cope with asymmetric shocks or a deterioration in competitiveness within a member country:

- Residents owning internationally diversified assets;
- Fiscal transfers between countries or the flexibility to use fiscal policy nationally;
- Flexible nominal wages or physical labour mobility.

Relative to the US – a successful single currency area of similar size – Europe performs poorly on all three.

Many US residents own significant financial assets in states other than their own, especially equities held in pension funds. So, when the economy in Massachusetts is doing badly, many residents will be cushioned by income from investments in Texas or California. In contrast, most residents of the putative euro-area do not own significant equity assets outside their own country.

Language, cultural and housing market differences also mean that people are less mobile in Europe than in the US. Some economists reply that US workers move only in response to long-term structural changes, not short-term fluctuations. But as monetary union should encourage national industrial specialization, Europe's lack of long-term labour mobility will still matter. Wages are also more rigid in Europe than in the US. High redundancy costs mean that movements in pay rates are less likely to absorb asymmetric shocks in Europe. Joining the single currency means accepting a single interest rate set by the European Central Bank. For some peripheral euro-area members this will mean adopting low interest rates suited to the sluggish economies of France and Germany when their domestic conditions argue for tighter policy to stem inflationary pressures.

By joining monetary union at this stage in their economic cycles, Ireland and Spain are behaving like the eponymous characters in the film *Thelma and Louise*: driving straight for the cliff, pushing the accelerator. Inappropriate monetary policies need not matter if national fiscal policies compensate. Euro-members will retain the ability to compensate for loose monetary policy with tight fiscal policy, but the mind boggles to think how much more tightening Ireland needs to avoid its looming boom and bust. But what if the ECB's monetary policy is too tight for a country's domestic needs? Its ability to loosen fiscal policy will be constrained by the absurd 'growth and stability pact', which is specially designed to punish a country for running too big a budget deficit by making it even bigger.

But the growth and stability pact may be overtaken by events. The largely unaccountable ECB is likely to run a tight monetary policy in its early years, to establish the 'credibility' to which every central bank aspires. Eventually, as unemployment rises and political extremism foments, fiscal prudence will crack. Unless, of course, the disciplines of the single currency have by then inspired the liberalizing structural reforms that years of excessive tight monetary policy in France have so conspicuously failed to deliver. Floating exchange rates are no more a panacea than fixed ones or a single currency. But Europe would be better served by a regime in which monetary union was confined to those economies that are in effect subsets of Germany's. The remainder should retain their own currencies and pursue monetary policies aimed at low and stable domestic inflation. Unfortunately, it is too late for this. The broadly based single currency is a bad idea whose time has come.

First appeared 23 March 1998

The test-tube currency: *the Maastricht treaty plan for the euro should be delayed to avoid a financial fiasco*

WILHELM NÖLLING

During his election campaign, Mr Tony Blair, the new UK prime minister, successfully built his quest for credibility around two words: 'Trust me.' With the best will in the world, I do not believe that the future president of the European Central Bank, on present plans, could pull off a similar achievement. Applied to the euro, these words would ring profoundly hollow.

The Maastricht plan for the euro is an experiment full of unprecedented risks. It tampers with a fundamental pillar of economic management, namely people's trust in the value and the proper functioning of their own money. According to the timetable, the euro will be with us in January 1999. Yet it is not too late to avert what could be a financial and political fiasco. The best solution would be to postpone the project. We must take a fresh look at how the European Union could move towards a single currency without the dangers and dissonances that have dogged the Maastricht project.

If the plan for European monetary union were really as simple, as risk-free and as advantageous as its protagonists claim, I would be in the vanguard of those fighting to introduce it on time. Unfortunately, this project has more 'ifs' than Rudyard Kipling's celebrated poem. Under the Maastricht plan, a number of internationally traded and held currencies that have a high degree of stability and confidence are to be replaced by a new artificial unit, the euro – the ultimate test-tube currency.

Many people believe most EU members will start Emu, as planned, in January 1999. Such predictions may turn out to be wholly misplaced. It is worth enumerating the many reasons for doubt.

First, the unpopularity of Emu in Germany, which would have most to lose if Emu failed, cannot be ignored. Popular scepticism about the German government's Emu policy has increased since Maastricht was agreed in 1991. This has political consequences that could cast a shadow over Chancellor Helmut Kohl's bid for re-election in 1998.

Second, European politicians made a grave mistake by pushing forward a fundamental change in monetary arrangements without any new political institutions. Monetary union needs to come after political union, not the other way around. In fact, there have been only desultory steps towards political union, and anything more concrete in coming years is most unlikely.

Third, in the absence of political union, politicians are preparing to set up a fully independent European Central Bank without any constraints and countervailing political force. Possessing the power to set uniform interest rates and determine inflation rates throughout the euro area, and tied to no other obligation than the maintenance of price stability, the central bank will be uncontrolled and uncontrollable – a monetary version of George Orwell's Big Brother.

Pressed by the Germans, EU governments have agreed a stability pact designed to rein in budget deficits after monetary union, but this is a wholly unsatisfactory approach. The stability pact will not produce the 'automatic' sanctions on deficit-running governments that German devotees of monetary stability desire. It will force governments and parliaments to take into account the strictures of the European Central Bank in running their budgetary policies. Yet there is no mechanism for redistributing fiscal resources between the richer members of the single currency area to the poorer ones.

Fourth, people throughout Europe are likely to focus attention on the need for monetary union to be accompanied by much more mobility and flexibility on labour markets. This is necessary, but not popular. If it becomes evident that Emu is being used as an instrument to push through painful free-market reforms, this could lead to an electoral backlash and the eventual unravelling of monetary union.

A fifth source of problems stems from the colossal technical and organizational challenge and huge costs of preparing for Emu. In many important areas preparations are falling behind what is required. Businesses are uncertain whether monetary union will take place and in which countries. In Germany, public sector bodies responsible for huge volumes of transactions are wholly unready for the euro. Many larger banks are making well-publicized preparations, but smaller ones are lagging behind.

The question remains whether EU countries will be able to continue to meet the celebrated convergence criteria once Emu has begun. Europe has had some success in bringing down inflation and stabilizing exchange rates. But there has been a sensational degree of upward harmonization in unemployment and public sector debt. Germany's public finances, meanwhile, are stretched to the utmost. We face a disturbing fall in revenues and a continued need for large transfers to east Germany, plus steep increases in payments for social welfare and unemployment. All this increases public debt.

Bonn is making increasingly desperate attempts to find a way round the problem, for instance by revaluing the Bundesbank's gold reserves, thereby printing money, or by selling further shares in Deutsche Telekom. Regardless of these measures, over the next decade Germany will find it most difficult to meet the key Maastricht requirement of sustainable fiscal stability.

There are two possible outcomes to the dilemma. Neither would help the euro. If governments step even harder on the fiscal brakes to achieve the budgetary criteria, that will cause pain in many countries, confirming fears that Maastricht's main effects are highly deflationary. Yet if governments try to bend the criteria through manipulating statistics, that will endanger the stability of the new currency. Politicians throughout Europe may derive help from the 1997 general elections in France and in Britain. In France, the tensions brought to the surface during the campaign, and the eventual outcome of the election, may prove helpful in steering the right choice for the euro.

In Britain, the new government's decisions to grant the right degree of independence to the Bank of England may prove constructive in re-establishing much-needed British influence on European affairs. UK-style operational central banking independence leaves overall anti-inflation policy in the hands of the government. This is clearly superior to the Maastricht model for a European Central Bank.

Britain, Germany and France might this year have a joint interest in postponing Emu. That would provide breathing space for Europe to improve its underlying economic performance and restart the journey towards a single currency. Emu is supposed to last for decades, if not for centuries. Spending a few more years to ensure it proceeds on a sound basis would be an eminently sensible use of governments' time.

The author, a professor at Hamburg University, was president of the Hamburg Land central bank and a member of the Bundesbank council between 1982 and 1992.

First appeared 19 May 1997

Intellectual gulf: *outsiders are obsessed with the perils of Europe's single currency; insiders are working out how it will change things*

PHILIP STEPHENS

The euro is upon us. The Anglo-Saxon reflex is to foresee catastrophe. This is an enterprise that Britain never wanted and the US never troubled to understand. It would be curious if either now gave it their blessing. From policymakers in Whitehall and the Bank of England we are offered an interminable list of the snares and pitfalls. Warnings from luminaries on the other side of the Atlantic have been positively funereal. Europe's economies are already sclerotic. Emu invites famine, pestilence and war.

The assumption, shot through with Anglo-Saxon arrogance, is that among those committed to this project there is no debate on its consequences. They are blinded by dogma. Governments in Bonn, Paris, Rome, Madrid and the rest will not confront the issues because to do so would be to admit the horrors that lie ahead.

The truth is otherwise. There is a debate among its authors about the single currency. But it is one that simply does not connect with the dialogue in the Anglo-Saxon world. While the cleverest minds in London and Washington focus obsessively on the dangers, those on the other side of the English Channel concern themselves with how it will remould the contours of their continent.

To the outsiders, the enterprise is a perilous excursion into the unknown. The door to Emu opens on to the edge of a cliff. To its prospective parents, the single currency represents another stage, albeit imprecisely mapped, of a long-established journey. It is hardly a surprise, then, that the two sides talk past each other.

I make these observations not as a persuader for Emu. You do not have to have hang-ups about national sovereignty to think the European Union's energies could have been better directed in the aftermath of the fall of the Berlin wall. And I, too, glance at the high levels of unemployment, the deflation wrought by efforts to meet the Maastricht criteria, and the prospect of a one-size-fits-all monetary policy and wonder whether it can work. That, though, is no longer the point.

The gulf between the prospective insiders and the outsiders was brought home to me at a gathering of the Franco-British Colloque in January 1998. The Colloque was the idea of David Simon long before he left the helm of British Petroleum to join Tony Blair's government. Sir Christopher Mallaby, a former ambassador in both Paris and Bonn, now holds the British reins. On the French side it is run by Jean-Louis Beffa, president of Saint-Gobain. Over the years, the Colloque has developed as a vital forum for the two countries' political and business elites.

It would be misleading to say that the French representatives at this latest meeting were entirely immune to Anglo-Saxon scepticism. There was much straight talking about the risks to the euro zone economies of asymmetric shocks. French industrialists and policymakers were candid also about the link between excessive social costs and regulation and the country's high unemployment – even if they gently reminded their British hosts that France's tradeable goods sector has never been more competitive.

Their conclusion, though, is that these are supply-side problems to be tackled inside Emu. In macro-economic management, the single currency represents continuity rather than dislocation. As one of France's most influential policymakers remarked, seven of the prospective members have been running a single monetary policy for the past eleven years. For Germany, France, the Benelux and Austria, the euro represents the exchange of wedding rings between partners that have long been cohabiting. As for high unemployment, it is a problem demanding micro- rather than macro-economic solutions. Greater transparency in labour and product markets will hasten the process of structural reform.

In this analysis, the traditional British concern that the single currency is the precursor to a United States of Europe is also wide of the mark. Britain tends to see political union in terms of the construction of new federal institutions. For its continental partners, it is much more about process than architecture. If one looks at the complex of mutual obligations to which the prospective participants have signed up, political union is integral to Emu. Here, I think, many have underestimated the role of the prospective club of single currency finance ministers. Mr Blair has extracted reassurances that Britain's voice will still be heard. Bonn has said the club cannot challenge the independence of the European Central Bank.

These supposed constraints will not stop euro-11 from developing into one of Europe's most powerful institutions. Formally or informally, it will intensify and extend the process of policy co-ordination. Taxes and social costs may not be harmonized, but new frameworks will be established. The central bank needs this political counterpoint. The future of Emu will depend as much on decisions taken by governments as on the euro interest rate.

In the U S, Alan Greenspan, chairman of the Federal Reserve, sits down to breakfast every week with Robert Rubin, U S Treasury secretary. Before long euro-11 will elect a chairman to sit down likewise with the head of Europe's Central Bank. There will be a similar political role to be played within international institutions like the Group of Eight and the International Monetary Fund. And here, euro-11 will challenge U S hegemony. Europe's four largest nations have collectively contributed as much as the U S to the international rescue operation for South Korea. But the terms have been written entirely in Washington. That will change when the euro bloc speaks with a single voice.

In all this there are still great uncertainties. Euro-11 offers only a partial answer to the serious questions of political legitimacy raised by the single currency. For Anglo-Saxons, though, the moment is fast approaching to stop explaining why Emu cannot work and to start thinking about how it will change things.

First appeared 19 January 1998

Now for the real test: *making a success of the euro depends on the political will of the member states*

YVES-THIBAULT DE SILGUY

After the launch of Europe's single currency, the big test for participating countries is how to collectively manage their economies. Are they ready for a bigger European dimension in national economic policies? This is key to the success of the euro in terms of growth and job creation. The necessary institutions and procedures are now in place. Making them work is a question of political will.

Monetary policy will be clear. From 1 January 1999, the independent European Central Bank will set interest rates for all participating countries with the primary aim of price stability. Joint decision-making among the governors of national central banks and the newly appointed members of the ECB executive board will allow countries to regain influence over their short-term interest rates, which today are largely driven by external factors. Even if the monetary policy needs of all participating countries are not identical, the ECB will be well placed to strike an appropriate balance. Look at the US, where big structural and wealth differentials between states such as California and Mississippi do not prevent the success of a single monetary policy for the dollar.

Other aspects of economic policy management are more complicated. The natural reaction of member states is jealously to guard their own autonomy while seeking maximum influence over the policies of other countries. To take a concrete example, we hear ministers in the council talking about the need to eliminate unfair tax competition (or even piracy) while fighting to defend the right to veto European Union taxation measures they do not like. How member states resolve this contradiction is crucial for the success of the euro.

There are three immediate challenges. First, to ensure lasting sound public finances. Irresponsible budgetary policies in one country can fuel inflation and push up interest rates throughout the euro zone. Recent progress has been impressive; the average deficit in the EU was 2.4 per cent of gross domestic product in 1997, down from 6.1 per cent in 1993. The goal of a balanced budget is not out of reach: without new measures, the average deficit in Europe should fall to 1.6 per cent by 1999. But countries must take advantage of the present period of healthy growth to make further progress on cutting spending rather than tax increases. In this way, they can create a cushion against any future economic downturn, and reduce the debt burden for future generations. This explains the limits on borrowing set by the treaty and the stability and growth pact. At the May 1998 EU summit in Brussels, Europe's leaders renewed their political commitment to the principle of sound budgetary discipline, providing further encouraging evidence of an emerging stability culture in Europe.

Second, the euro zone faces the challenge of a massive boost to competition in the single market, fuelled by greater price transparency and the end of exchange rate uncertainty. Governments will have a greater incentive to foster an enterprise culture to maintain the competitiveness of their economies. Participating countries will need some flexibility to adjust national policy instruments in response to local or regional conditions. But there will also be strong incentives to work together. Co-ordination will be needed to resist market pressures in areas such as taxation and the labour market. For example, member states are today unable to shift the burden of taxation from static labour and fixed investment, although this could contribute to reducing unemployment.

Instead they face pressure to cut taxes on more mobile things such as capital and business. This perverse situation explains why member states have become more willing to discuss increasing minimum EU tax rates in these areas.

The third challenge is to ensure the maximum benefits from the emergence of the euro on the international monetary scene. A euro zone of eleven countries accounting for one-fifth of world output and one-fifth of world trade will have similar economic weight to the US. It has the potential to play a greater role in international economic and monetary discussions than the sum of its component countries. But the necessary pre-condition is to ensure the euro zone is capable of defining a single position and of speaking with a single voice in international forums such as the International Monetary Fund or G7. The ECB will be able to present a single EU view. And euro-zone governments will have an incentive to do likewise.

The necessary framework exists for finance ministers to work together on their economic policies in the council, without undermining legitimate national economic sovereignty. We are not talking about line-by-line approval of national budgets or other policies before they are presented to parliaments. Governments will continue to set their own public expenditure priorities and tax systems in line with national needs and circumstances. But the overall thrust of economic policies will be subject to more frequent and intense examination at European level.

The commission will have a central role, providing analyses and recommendations on countries' policies. The informal meetings of the euro-11 finance ministers will allow frank discussion of sensitive issues. In public finances, the ultimate possibility of financial sanctions will be a deterrent for countries under pressure to relax fiscal discipline.

The consequences of the euro for the collective management of economic policies are becoming clearer. We have seen the determination of governments to prepare for Emu. The fruits of the resulting sound policies are emerging in the form of stronger growth and job creation. There is every reason for optimism about the ability of EU leaders to maintain momentum, ensuring the benefits of the euro for the future prosperity of Europe.

The author is European commissioner for economic, monetary and financial affairs

First appeared 4 May 1998

One money – but many nations: *the argument that the euro will lead to a superstate is unfounded*

JOACHIM FELS

Fears that the introduction of the single European currency will pave the way for a federalist superstate are grossly exaggerated. Experience shows that the integration of markets for capital and goods, which will be helped by introducing the euro, goes hand-in-hand with political decentralization, not centralization. If anything, political power will devolve from the nation state to the regional level. This would increase the scope for institutional competition in Europe and should, for instance, result in labour market deregulation and lower taxes on mobile factors such as capital. As a consequence, investment would improve and structural unemployment would be reduced.

When the Maastricht treaty was signed in 1991, European economic and monetary union was widely seen as a precursor to European political union. Federalists across Europe hoped that merging European currencies would force governments and parliaments to transfer the bulk of their legislative and executive powers to Brussels. Therefore they supported Emu. The euro-sceptics, including many free-market economists such as myself, opposed Emu because they dreaded (and still dread) the idea of a federal superstate interfering with social and economic policies. These, they believe, would be better conducted on a national or regional level.

The crucial assumption by the proponents and opponents of Emu was – and, in many cases, still is – that monetary union would lead to political union. Yet that assumption is no longer valid: while the introduction of the euro in 1999 is now a *fait accompli*, the chances for a federal political Europe are increasingly remote.

The drive towards political union has stalled. One reason is that politicians with a perceived taste for the federalist approach, such as Helmut Kohl, the German chancellor, find it hard to relinquish to a higher authority the final word on various policy issues. Take, for instance, the German insistence on a veto right for nation states in asylum matters at the European summit in Amsterdam in June 1997. Most other European Union governments are equally reluctant to move from the unanimity requirement in important matters to a majority voting system.

Much of this reflects the European electorate's disenchantment with the idea of transferring political decisions to yet another, higher level of government that is even further detached from local conditions than national governments. This distrust is not just a British or Danish peculiarity. It is widespread, also present in Germany and France, the two countries thought to be the motors of European political integration. The drive towards political union has stalled just when the effort towards monetary union has intensified.

Research on the link between economic integration and political separatism helps explain why politics become more local as markets become more global. In a world of trade restrictions and capital immobility, small states are economically unviable since the size of the market is determined by the size of the country. Nation-building or even empire-building makes sense in such a world, as it is the only way to reap the economic benefits of market size. Conversely, in a world of free trade and capital flows, the size of the market is global. Political separatism becomes less costly in a globalized economy. There will thus be a trend towards smaller political units based on cultural or ethnic identities, embedded in an open world economy.

There has been a strong positive correlation, from 1870 onwards, between the degree of economic openness and the number of countries in the world. The relationship also holds for the post-war period. Trade volume as a share of world gross domestic product rose by 40 per cent between 1946 and 1995; over the same period, the number of countries increased from 74 to 192. Today more than half of the countries are smaller in population than the state of Massachusetts, suggesting that globalization encourages political disintegration.

So what are the lessons for Emu? Consider that the single currency secures the internal market, and thus the free flow of goods and services, and enhances the mobility of productive capital – foreign direct investment. Closer economic integration should militate against a move towards political union. If anything, the trend towards devolution – under way in many EU countries – can be expected to accelerate. With the common market for goods, services and capital secured by Emu, regions will seek to gain a greater say in economic and social policies.

If devolution of power to the regions is the answer, it becomes unlikely that a European federalist agenda of harmonizing social security standards, taxes, and labour market regulations can be put into practice. Nor should it. The various nation states, regions and cities would rather compete for mobile jobs and investment by offering higher after-tax returns on capital. As a consequence, taxes on capital and skilled labour will fall and labour markets will become more flexible. This is what Europe needs to fight structural unemployment. And this is why I have developed from a euro-sceptic dreading a federalist political Europe into a euro-optimist. One money for Europe – yes; one government for Europe – no.

The author is senior economist at Morgan Stanley Dean Witter.

First appeared 22 December 1997

Hard sell for a hard euro: *Germans must accept monetary union as part of their future*

WOLFGANG SCHÄUBLE

The debate about monetary union in Germany has intensified. It will continue to do so since the connection between monetary union and the government's austerity reforms is not really understood. That is why 80 per cent of the population feel they have been inadequately informed. The foremost concern must now be to make clear the fundamental significance of Emu.

Going beyond the completion of the single market, monetary union is directed towards a radical rehabilitation and modernization of Europe's economies. This is intended to stabilize the economic and social systems of the participating countries and could have positive effects on the political order. A single currency will underpin and complete the single market, save costs and facilitate investment.

Germany has a direct interest in, and a special responsibility for, the completion of monetary union. This is due not only to economic factors, but also to the fact that monetary union takes up the idea of the 'social market economy'. It is clear that the strongest economy with the strongest currency will exert the strongest influence on the convergence process. Hence Germany must signal security and confidence to encourage its partners and reassure the markets.

But it was the success of the 'social market economy' that impressed our EU partners, combining as it did a liberal and productive economic system with a social order based on justice and solidarity. The model includes competition and an independent Bundesbank committed to maintaining price stability as well as the consensus principle and social partnership. Success in reforming the model will be crucial if the idea behind the Maastricht treaty is to gain lasting acceptance.

Germans must be told what this new Europe means. France, for instance, has kept its inflation rate below that of Germany for almost five years; in the last three years France's debt interest payments have fallen below those of Germany; the French franc has for many years held its own against the D-Mark and now figures among the most stable currencies in the world. Italy too has made remarkable progress in consolidating its public finances since 1992. Spain has not only undertaken massive efforts to bring down its deficit, but has also got to grips with the chief structural problem of its highly regulated labour market. There are many other examples of such achievements, few of which are known inside Germany.

The fear of a weak euro is without foundation. All EU member states are aware of the need for stability. The rate of price rises in most countries is below 2 per cent. The independence of the future European Central Bank goes beyond the statutes of the Bundesbank and is unmatched worldwide. Wages in EU countries have been developing moderately for years and have risen less than prices. Interest rates on the European capital markets are at an all-time low.

The financial markets do not demand any interest rate premiums since they apparently do not expect inflation rates to rise after the introduction of the euro. Neither money supply (central bank), nor money demand (wages, price rises) nor market expectations about the development of both parameters (interest rates) indicate a 'soft euro' in terms of its domestic purchasing power.

Wim Duisenberg, president of the ECB, has rightly observed that the external value of the euro need not concern participants any more than the external value of the dollar concerns the US. The significance of foreign trade for the gross national product of Emu countries would be just as small as for the US.

Participants in the single currency must continue to implement structural reforms even after the start of monetary union. This will be decisive in making Europe more attractive as a business location and enhance the appeal of a European currency to international investors and creditors. In view of the past successes of European stability policy and the efforts of individual EU member states to attain stability, there is no reason to doubt that Emu will remain on firm macroeconomic ground. A stability- and reform-orientated course must continue. This is especially important for Germany.

Emu is vital for the continuation of the process of European unification. It plays a crucial role in enabling Europe and its nations to meet the challenges of the future. The internal consolidation of the EU is, along with institutional reform, an essential requirement for mastering the enormous external challenges now confronting the union.

Germany faces its most daunting test. Resolving its internal problems by means of radical reforms is a prerequisite for attaining its principal foreign policy goal: a strong Europe, which is itself a requirement for safeguarding Germany's future.

This is an edited version of a statement written by Wolfgang Schäuble, leader of the CDU and CSU MPs in the Bundestag

First appeared 18 September 1997

Strange love: *or how I have not stopped worrying but learned to love the euro*

MARTIN WOLF

At least since the French revolution, Europe has been the cradle of visionary politics. European intellectuals and politicians have repeatedly tried to infuse the mundane business of government with some higher aspiration. Today, just one dream remains: Europe itself. The continent's leaders seek a Europe not only of peace and prosperity, but also of renewed power and prestige. That is why they have decided to start economic and monetary union in January 1999. Given the continent's often terrible history, it is natural to ask whether Europe is pursuing the right goal in the right way. Peace and prosperity across the continent is a noble goal. But will the huge step now being taken promote it, or produce precisely the opposite result?

My own views have evolved in the past ten years. When I first learned of the intention of the 1988 Hanover summit to set European monetary union in motion, I thought it insanely risky. I still think it risky. But it no longer looks insane. Whether Emu will lay the foundation of a harmonious and potent Europe remains an open question. But I am now convinced it offers at least two substantial advantages.

First, the currency union will largely eliminate exchange-rate uncertainty from the minds of those responsible for long-term economic decisions. The consequences ought to include enhanced competition, greater specialization, a more integrated European capital market and therefore higher incomes. Second, and perhaps more important, the alternatives to a currency union have come to look ever less attractive.

Floating exchange rates have proved disappointing. At one time it seemed possible to hope that inexplicable currency gyrations would disappear once inflation had been eliminated and fiscal policy been placed under secure control. Experience of the 1990s, including sterling's recent giddy climb, has demolished such optimism. For highly integrated European economies, currency instability must impose a high price.

An adjustable-peg regime has also proved far from ideal. This is not just because of the instability to which such regimes are prone but, within Europe, it also makes limited sense for the central bank that forms the monetary policy of the fixed-rate area to take the performance of only one economy, Germany, into account. But even Germany generates less than 30 per cent of European Union gross domestic product.

Have I learned to stop worrying and love Emu after all? Only up to a point. When I ask myself why I remain doubtful, the answer remains the enormity of the gamble. The upside is an improvement in EU prosperity and, for some, an enhanced ability to look the Americans in the face. The downside is constant friction over economic policy and, conceivably, a breakdown in the EU itself.

At present, these downside risks seem remote. One of the most important reasons for looking on Emu with a more welcoming eye than a decade ago is the effort made by the eleven participants. Germany's stability culture is far more deeply embedded across Europe than almost anybody had imagined. Who then foresaw a time when every EU member state, except Greece, would have inflation below 2 per cent? Similarly, Emu may even force countries to embark on long-needed structural reforms, particularly of labour markets. Here we see a powerful determination to embark on a project with intrinsic economic merits. Surely those that have managed the painful journey to the promised land will not let the difficulties involved in staying there disturb them. In any case, since the price of withdrawal would be enormous, member states are doomed to make the project succeed.

All this is plausible. But it is not enough to calm every one of my fears. One explanation for my worry is that, in spite of a mountain of books and articles on the subject, the economic and political implications of Emu remain inevitably unknown. This conclusion leaps from the pages of a fascinating special issue on Emu in the journal, *Economic Policy* (David Begg *et al.* (eds), 'Emu: Prospects and Challenges for the euro', Oxford, Basil Blackwell for Centre for Economic Policy Research, 1998). Does the stability and growth pact agreed in Amsterdam in June 1997 make sense? Or will it impose a damaging constraint on the ability of member states to smooth country-specific temporary shocks? The authors of one paper argue that the pact is unjustified, but should prove only a minor nuisance. Up pipes someone else insisting the costs will be large and another that the pact is justified.

Can Emu survive without large-scale internal fiscal transfers? One pair of authors argues that the absence of labour mobility and regional wage flexibility within member states has generated irresistible pressure for internal transfers. Since the problem will be still greater across national frontiers, the EU will be under pressure to become a sort of fiscal federation. Yes, responds one discussant, but Europe's political divisions make this unlikely; unnecessary, in any case, says another, because intra-country transfers have not done much to offset asymmetric shocks.

If we do not – and cannot – know how Emu will work, some things we do know:

- Emu is an experiment in running a unified monetary policy, without a common fiscal authority, among a group of sovereign countries – as French demands over the central bank presidency have just reminded everybody.

- The incentives for a country to show good behaviour before Emu are different from those to behave well after it starts.
- Europe's labour markets are catastrophically inflexible.
- Individual Emu countries are likely to go through long periods of recession or overheating, with few instruments to influence the outcome.

Emu is for ever. The course of Emu and the European economy may run smoothly, decade after decade. But both initial conditions and history suggest this is most unlikely. Emu is also a grand vision. The visionaries are Europe's elites, with their desire to transcend the dangers and limits of national politics. Emu will separate central areas of economic policy from national politics. Yet political legitimacy and identity will remain largely national. The risk then is that conflicts will emerge between the states that remain the focus of political life, on the one hand, and other member states or unaccountable European institutions, on the other. Many argue, for this reason, that there will either emerge a widely spread European consciousness embedded in a Europe-wide political process, or Emu will fail. Both historical precedent and common sense suggest this argument is correct.

I now appreciate the economic case for Emu and admire the bravery of those who are starting it. No one who wants the best for Europe can hope for anything but a triumphant success. Yet I still quail before the risks of this historic gamble.

First appeared 5 May 1998

Everything you ever wanted to know about Emu: *questions and answers*

WOLFGANG MÜNCHAU AND LIONEL BARBER

1. What is the point of it all?

Proponents say that Emu completes the European Union's barrier-free internal market. It is true that free-market areas do not need a single currency to operate successfully. But Europe's internal market is not just a free trade area. In theory, the single market was supposed to end barriers to intra-EU trade. In practice, most companies did not treat the EU as a domestic market. Emu will also do away with the remaining currency risk within Europe's exchange-rate mechanism.

2. Will Emu start on time?
Yes, on 1 January 1999.

3. When and how was this decided?
Formally, EU leaders announced the participants of the first wave of Emu at a special summit in Brussels on 2 May 1998. They chose eleven countries – all EU members except Greece, which has not qualified under the economic criteria, and the UK, Sweden and Denmark, which have opted out for political reasons. Financial markets have long expected a start-up group of eleven. This became a near-certainty when EU governments published their economic data for 1997, showing that all fulfilled the deficit condition.

4. Will Emu make the European economy more competitive?
That's the idea. Emu enthusiasts say a single currency will bring large-scale efficiency gains. Reduced exchange rate risk is an obvious gain, but a relatively insignificant one economically. Economic efficiency could be improved by stronger competition in product and labour markets. Companies may find it harder to charge different prices in different countries. Several economists are forecasting that prices will, on average, be lower under Emu than today.

5. What are the greatest short-term risks?
Emu imposes a one-size-fits-all monetary policy on its members, which means that interest rates will be the same in the entire Emu zone. Governments also have relatively little leeway in their fiscal policy, since the stability and growth pact – a fiscal pact agreed at the Amsterdam summit of EU leaders in June 1997 – imposes a ceiling on members' budget deficits of 3 per cent of gross domestic product. Given Europe's relatively inflexible labour markets and high degree of regulation, the risks are significant. Lack of flexibility will make it difficult for the Emu zone to react to asymmetric economic shocks. These are shocks that affect some countries or regions but not others – the impact of German unification was one recent example. Under Emu, if shocks trigger recession in some regions, national governments will have no effective counteracting policy instruments at their disposal.

Without sufficient labour mobility and a political union that allows fiscal transfers from wealthy to poorer regions – as in the US or within Germany – the constraints of Emu could lead to extreme economic and political tensions in times of crisis. Emu would be particularly vulnerable during an economic downturn.

6. What are the greatest long-term risks?

The long-term risks largely stem from uncertainty about the EU's political future. Emu is not the first monetary union in history, but it is by far the most ambitious. The economic consequences of Emu are unpredictable. Emu's success might depend on the ability of EU countries to move towards harmonized taxes, or towards a system of fiscal transfers, a common immigration policy or even a common foreign and defence policy.

One lesson from history is that monetary unions without eventual political union tend to collapse. Given the lack of momentum towards political union in the EU, Emu's long-term survival is far from guaranteed.

7. Who are the winners, who are the losers?

Multinationals and Europe's largest banks are likely winners. It is possible that Emu will increase competitive pressure in various sectors, especially banking. Some experts forecast a strong consolidation in the European banking sector. Also among the relative losers are companies which will have to pay the costs of the change over without benefiting from the trading effects, for example companies that trade only locally, such as shops and restaurants. A simple example: slot machine operators will be relative losers because they will have to adapt the machine for the new euro coins. Slot machine producers will be net gainers.

8. How should you prepare if your country joins Emu?

Emu will have massive effects on the way companies and banks operate. It will involve substantial changes to accountancy, financial and computer systems, and will also have strategic implications on areas such as pricing policy, wage levels, banking relations, perhaps even factory location.

9. How should you prepare if your country does not join Emu?

That is far more difficult. Obviously no preparation is needed if you operate purely locally, or even nationally. In other cases, however, Emu could affect your competitive position in the EU. UK banks, for example, are adopting a dual-track approach: they are fully preparing their wholesale operations for Emu, while paying less attention to the retail side. They should, however, be aware that they will probably have much less time for preparation than their German or French competitors, if their governments decide to join at a later stage.

10. Will the euro be a strong currency?

Probably yes (although economists disagree on this); the euro will be backed by one of the most independent central banks in the world, more independent than the German Bundesbank or the Federal Reserve in the US. The central bank's main function – enshrined in the Maastricht treaty and thus practically irrevocable – will be to safeguard the stability of the currency. Furthermore, the European Central Bank is more likely to err on the side of caution, at least in its first years of operation, in order to establish what central bankers refer to as 'credibility' with the financial markets. There are many observers who fear that there will be a substantially greater risk that the euro will be 'too hard' than 'too soft'.

11. How does the European Central Bank work?
The ECB is based in Frankfurt. It became operational at the beginning of June 1998. It will have responsibility for Emu-wide monetary policy from 1 January 1999. The ECB will be headed by a president, whose term will run for eight years under the Maastricht treaty. But after a controversial compromise, the ECB's first president, Dutchman Wim Duisenberg, has agreed to step down after four years in order to make room for a French candidate. The ECB's executive board will also consist of a vice-president and four further executives drawn from participating member states. Interest rates will be set by the governing council: this consists of the members of the executive board and the heads of the participating national central banks.

12. What will happen to the national central banks?
The ECB and the national central banks will form the European System of Central Banks (ESCB). Broadly, the ECB will take the policy decisions, while the national central banks will conduct most of the operating functions, for example certain open market interventions. There is a dispute inside the ECB – specifically between France and Germany – about the precise division of responsibilities. France prefers a more decentralized system. Germany fears that this would undermine the effectiveness of the ECB.

13. How will conversion rates between the national currencies be fixed?
At a summit in May 1998, EU leaders announced the bilateral conversion rates among the participating Emu members. These are the current central rates in the exchange-rate mechanism.

14. So does this mean we now know how many euros we can get for DM1 or FFr1?
Again, no. All we will know is how many D-Marks we can exchange for French francs, for example. What we will not know are the exchange

rates between national currencies and the euro. The Maastricht treaty says that these rates will be determined on 1 January 1999.

15. Does this have to be so complicated?
Unfortunately yes, because of the Ecu, the basket of twelve EU currencies. EU leaders decided some time ago that the Ecu must convert to the euro at a rate of one-for-one. The problem is that not all Ecu members will also join the Emu in 1999 – for example, the UK. What this means is that the euro exchange rate of each participating currency will depend on their Ecu rates on 31 December 1998, the day before monetary union. But the Ecu rate also depends on non-participating currencies. In other words, there will be a risk that the euro rates could be contaminated by a fluctuating currency such as sterling.

16. Why do we have to have a two-stage approach?
The priority is to remove uncertainty, which could tempt speculators to mount an attack against the euro group. If they waited until 1999, there could be frenzied speculation in the final countdown to 1 January 1999. The idea is to create a self-fulfilling prophecy, so that exchange rates will gradually float towards the announced conversion rates. The closer we get to euro, the closer exchange rates should get to their conversion rates. A speculator who is told that the D-Mark/franc conversion rate will be FFr3.4 in seven months has little incentive to trade a fundamentally different exchange rate today.

17. Could speculators find a way to attack the system?
They might, but it will not be straightforward. They could attack the rates if they do not find the selection of Emu members credible, in which case they might attack the exchange rate of the most vulnerable country. But it will not be as easy as it was in 1992, when massive speculation forced the pound out of the exchange-rate mechanism. The old ERM had narrow fluctuation margins, which gave speculators fixed targets to attack at relatively little risk. This time EU leaders seem certain to continue the present wide-band arrangement – or get rid of bands altogether – leaving speculators guessing.

18. Where does this leave the ERM?
The ERM with its current fluctuation margin of 15 per cent either side of the central parity will continue until the end of 1998. There is some pressure, however, for a new ERM – also known as ERM 2. This grid is to regulate the relationship between euro and non-participating currencies. Membership of the ERM 2 will be voluntary.

19. Will the UK join the ERM2?
The British government said no. Continental central bankers insist that membership of ERM is a precondition for entry into Emu. This issue is bound to give rise to a dispute ahead of the UK's eventual entry into Emu.

20. Can it still go wrong?
Having spent the last six years preparing for Emu at all levels of government, industry and finance, EU countries will not give it up lightly.

Central bankers have pointed out that once Emu starts up in 1999, the economic consequences of a collapse would be massive. A sudden collapse could put strain on the financial system, by triggering bank failures, for instance. EU politicians will probably seek alternative ways of relieving any pressure before pulling the plug on Emu.

Adapted from three articles which first appeared on 28 May 1997, 15 September 1997 and 5 January 1998

2 Events so far

The road to economic and monetary union looks like an obstacle course. There were plenty of stumbles on the way, many occasions when the outcome of the race to launch the euro looked in doubt.

This chapter begins with the intellectual godfather of monetary union, a man who remains relatively unknown outside his native Luxembourg. His name is Pierre Werner, the long-serving prime minister of the Grand Duchy. In 1969, Werner was asked to chair a high-level group on how Emu could be achieved by 1980. His report in October 1970 proposed a three-stage process for achieving a complete monetary union within a decade. The Werner plan was eventually derailed by currency turbulence linked to the first oil crisis, but it served as the blueprint for launching a single currency in the Maastricht treaty.

The next step in Europe's search for currency stability came in 1978 with the creation of the European Monetary System, the personal initiative of two men – Helmut Schmidt, chancellor of Germany and Valéry Giscard d'Estaing, president of France, aided by a third, Roy Jenkins, then president of the European Commission. The EMS restored a measure of exchange rate stability, but it took two separate phenomena – the arrival of Jacques Delors as Commission president and his plan to launch a single European market by 1992 – to give decisive impetus to Emu.

Delors had already presided over the strategic shift in French economic policy in 1983 when President François Mitterrand abandoned 'socialism in one country' and opted for a hard franc to achieve parity with the D-Mark. As Commission president in Brussels, Delors was the essential link between President Mitterrand in Paris and Chancellor Kohl in Bonn, each seeking to contain German power in European institutions.

Several themes emerge in the *FT*'s coverage. First, the formidable political will in France and Germany which kept Emu on track in the early 1990s. Emu survived the crisis over Maastricht ratification and the economic shocks unleashed by German unification. But it was a near-run thing.

Second, the failure of successive British government to grasp the depth of Europe's commitment to Emu. We see how Margaret Thatcher was outmanoeuvred by the French and Italians at the Madrid summit in 1989. We read the sorry tale of British membership of the Exchange Rate Mechanism which ended in humiliation in September 1992 when sterling and the lira were forced to leave the ERM. But we also see a glimpse of change with the new Labour government's qualified embrace of the single currency in late 1997.

Finally, we observe how Emu remains a project conceived and executed by an elite. Europe's leaders have largely ignored public opinion on economic and monetary union. Chancellor Kohl brushed aside the protest of 300 German economics professors in early 1997. Not one was going to interrupt his rendezvous with history.

LIONEL BARBER

March 1970 Werner Plan – Blueprint For European monetary union

REGINALD DALE

A blueprint for economic and monetary union in the Common Market by 1980 was completed here late last night by a working group of Community experts. The so-called Werner plan now goes to the six governments for adoption by the end of this year.

The final plan fills some of the blanks left by the interim report produced by the Committee, chaired by Luxembourg's Prime Minister, Pierre Werner, earlier this year. But although the idea of an initial three-year stage starting on 1 January next year is confirmed in the report, several question marks remain over the exact timing of the different phases in the progressive move to economic and monetary union.

In the monetary field, the first moves will be left to the Community's central bank governors, who will next year start to narrow the fluctuation margins between Common Market currencies as a first step towards a common European currency. It has also been agreed by the Committee that a Community 'stabilization fund', the nucleus of a future European federal reserve system, could perhaps be introduced before the end of the first stage.

But progress in the monetary field will be linked to greater convergence of the six's economic policies – detailed proposals for closed budgetary co-ordination were finalized by the Committee last night. After the meeting ended in the early hours of this morning M. Werner said that the initially experimental reductions in fluctuation margins would only be formalized after it had been generally agreed that 'real progress' had been achieved in the economic field.

Nevertheless, it is now clearer than ever that national governments will have to hand over a large amount of their own decision-making authority to central Community organizations – whether they be the committees of central bank governments, the Commission or the Council of Ministers – once economic and monetary union has been achieved at the end of the decade.

To compensate for the loss of national control over economic policy, the powers of the European parliament in Strasbourg would have to be considerably reinforced, officials said last night. Before the end of the first three-year period, the six would have to decide on how the existing Community treaties should be adapted to cater for the new institutional arrangements and define the precise working of the system after 1980.

If, as is widely assumed, Britain were to enter the Community at the beginning of 1973, the UK would thus still have the chance to participate in the decisions on the ultimate nature of economic and monetary union. But the UK would still, of course, be required to accept all the elements that have already been agreed by the six alone before then.

The introduction of sterling into the narrower Community fluctuation margin and British participation in the stabilization fund could present considerable problems, it was said here. For this reason some Community experts would like to push ahead with setting up the fund before British entry in order to ensure that its establishment should not be delayed by protracted discussions with the UK.

The fund, M. Werner said, would be started with small quantities of reserves, and then progressively expanded.

First appeared 9 October 1970

April 1989 Delors report *– Mr Delors offers a leap in the dark: the proposed steps to European monetary union*

PETER NORMAN

Central bankers are normally a conservative lot. Thus last week's unanimous agreement by the central bank-dominated Delors committee to a three-stage route towards economic and monetary union in the European Community appears at first sight surprising.

The 38-page report of the Delors committee, published yesterday, is unambiguous: economic and monetary union is a goal at which the EC should aim, it says. In this respect, the report of the seventeen-strong group provides a clear platform for political action. And for political criticism: Mr Nigel Lawson, Britain's Chancellor of the Exchequer, wasted no time in describing it as totally unacceptable, because of the transfer of sovereignty implied. Comments from other countries were more welcoming – but the report's implications for national sovereignty are likely to cause qualms in many of the EC's twelve capitals.

None the less, the report is an impressive document on first reading, particularly that part of it which sets out the steps required to achieve economic and monetary union. It requires a conscious effort on the part of the reader to realize that it is not, and cannot be, a precise blueprint for change. It contains no timetable for action. Skilful drafting has obscured widely divergent attitudes. Difficult decisions, which mainly concern greater integration of non-monetary policies, will be left to a shifting population of politicians with very different views in twelve nation states over what could be a very long period of time. These qualifications, however, are unlikely to hinder political pressure for early action of the report. Mr Felipe González, the Spanish Prime Minister, says Spain will seek a 'fundamental political debate' on monetary union at the Madrid summit of EC leaders at the end of June 1989.

The report has had to reconcile two broad differences of opinion in the committee. One group of pragmatists, headed by the representatives of West Germany, Britain and Luxembourg, argued that economic and monetary union should be an evolutionary process, based on the existing achievements of the European Monetary System. For them, the creation of a common currency and what is now to be called a European System of Central Banks would come after a lengthy process of economic integration. The other more enthusiastic group, headed by France, Italy and Spain, wanted more rapid progress towards monetary union, with an early commitment to institutional change.

The three-stage process agreed in the Delors report marks a victory of sorts for the pragmatists. It would leave institutional developments out of the first phase of the move to union. This would be devoted to achieving a greater convergence of economic performance through stronger economic and monetary policy co-ordination within existing institutions. The first stage would see all members of the EC becoming full members of the EMS, for example.

The ESCB would start coming to life in the second stage, which would require changes to the EC treaties, and hence the unanimous support of EC member states. This would be a period of transition: decision making would gradually shift from the national to the community level. In stage two, macroeconomic policy guidelines, including precise but not yet binding rules relating to the size of annual budget deficits in the member states, would be adopted by a majority decision of the Council of Ministers. The ESCB would be independent of national governments and other community institutions. It would absorb the EC's existing co-operative monetary arrangements and start the transition from co-ordinated national monetary policies to a common monetary policy. During this phase, the margins of fluctuation in the EMS exchange-rate mechanism would be narrowed, in preparation for moving to zero in the final stage, economic and monetary union.

The final stage would start with an irrevocable move to lock exchange rates. Rules governing co-ordination in the macroeconomic and budgetary spheres of policy would become binding. The Council of Ministers, in co-operation with the European Parliament, would be empowered among other things to interfere with national budgets. The ESCB would take over responsibility for formulating and implementing monetary policy in the Community. It would decide intervention in third currencies and would manage the Community's pooled reserves.

However, a lot of problems have to be surmounted before this brave new world is reached. In a carefully nuanced way, to cover the divergent opinions among the members of the Delors group, the report makes clear that there is a pressing need for more economic integration in the EC before union can get very far. Even before contemplating union, the report points out that the creation of the single European market will entail 'profound structural changes in the economies of the member countries'. The single market will necessitate 'a more effective co-ordination of policy between separate national authorities'. Moreover, 'greater convergence of economic performance is needed', to avoid potential dangers inherent in the programme.

Looking further ahead, the committee is concerned that regional and sectoral imbalances in the EC could be aggravated unless there are common policies to create a more balanced economic structure in the EC. Unless such problems were addressed, the viability of economic and monetary union could be threatened. In the non-monetary sphere, the committee argues that the single-market programme would have to be supplemented by action in three areas: competition policy would have to be adapted to strengthen market mechanisms; enhanced regional and structural policies would be required; co-ordination of macroeconomic policy would be needed to limit economic divergences between member countries.

Without countervailing policies, says the report, historical experience suggests that economic and monetary union could have a negative impact on peripheral areas of the EC. Transport costs and economies of scale would favour a shift of economic activity to the highly developed areas at the centre of the Community.

The demand for successful macroeconomic co-ordination runs throughout the report. 'In particular, unco-ordinated and divergent national budgetary policies would undermine monetary stability and generate imbalances in the real and financial sectors of the community', the report says. The eventual locking of exchange rates would remove at a stroke the possibility of correcting economic imbalances in the EC through exchange-rate adjustment. The creation of a common currency, which would follow soon after the locking of exchange rates, would bring additional problems. The disappearance of exchange rates and national current account balance of payments statistics would deprive policy-makers of important indicators of what might be going wrong at national level.

There are likely to be few quarrels with the aims that the committee sets out for economic and monetary union. It should be geared to price stability, balanced growth, converging standards of living, high employment and external equilibrium. Achieving and maintaining this will be a problem. The committee recognizes that even after attaining economic and monetary union, the EC would continue to consist of individual nations with differing economic, social, cultural and political characteristics. This 'plurality' would require a degree of autonomy in decision making to remain with individual member countries and a balance to be struck between national and community competences. 'It would not be possible simply to follow the example of existing federal states; it would be necessary to develop an innovative and unique approach', the committee's report says.

The committee proposes that the Community would only exercise power where collective decision making is necessary. Policy functions which could be carried out at national or regional levels without hurting the functioning of the economic and monetary union would remain within the competence of member governments. That may sound fine in theory, but is more difficult in practice.

An even greater problem would be the transfers of sovereignty that member states would have to make to implement the Delors report. As Mr Lawson's comments indicate, this is an issue of contention for Mrs Margaret Thatcher's government. It remains to be seen how far the report jibes with the views of Europe's other heads of government. Close co-operation in running the European Monetary System has turned Europe's central bankers into a closely knit bunch who are often more accustomed to working together than with their respective national governments. This undoubtedly helped the Delors committee overcome differences and reach agreement on the text.

The growing integration of financial markets has taught central bankers, more than most officials, to recognize that national sovereignty has its limits, particularly in the realm of monetary policy. The avoidance of any detailed timetable for the moves towards economic and monetary union enabled the bankers to make progress in a technocratic manner. They were helped by the fact that – despite opposition from Mrs Thatcher – there was a political head of steam behind moves towards greater European integration when the Delors committee was established by the June 1988 Hanover summit to explore 'concrete steps' towards economic and monetary union.

The coming months will establish whether the political will to start the process towards economic and monetary union still exists. Much will depend on the attitude of Mr Helmut Kohl, the West German Chancellor, and of the French government which takes over the six-month presidency of the European Community at the end of June. Close reading of the Delors committee report makes clear that there are daunting problems before economic and monetary union can be achieved in Europe. But it also paints a tantalizing picture of how such a union could look.

Last week in Bonn, Mr Kohl restated his vision of a European Central Bank and a single currency at the end of the process towards unification of the twelve EC member countries. And France – one of the countries seeking rapid institutional moves towards union – celebrates the bicentenary of its revolution later this year. It could well use the occasion to launch an initiative that would start the process, mapped out by the Delors committee, towards economic and monetary union in the European Community.

First appeared 18 April 1989

June 1989 Madrid summit – *Thatcher runs charmingly into an ambush*

PHILIP STEPHENS

It could hardly have been a coincidence that Mrs Margaret Thatcher chose a black top for her summer outfit as the Madrid summit drew to a close yesterday. After all she had been tricked again by the perfidious Europeans. Worse still, the Foreign Office had done what it often seems best at – misjudged the mood of Britain's European partners.

So it was far from clear if the tensely gritted smile during the traditional 'family' photocall reflected as much her mood towards her own Foreign Secretary, Mr Geoffrey Howe, as towards some of her fellow heads of government. It was the Foreign Office, of course, which had persuaded her that it was time at last for Britain to climb aboard the Eurobus to monetary union in order to keep the temperature in Madrid's Palacio de Congresos a little below the 100 degrees outside.

Not a word was to be uttered about Marxist conspiracies or socialist superstates. Even Jacques Delors, the unwitting author of Mrs Thatcher's infamous Bruges speech, was to be offered the odd, admittedly strangled, compliment. But what the FO omitted to tell her was that the nasty François Mitterrand had persuaded the easily led Helmut Kohl that it was time the Community abandoned the bus in favour of a flight on Concorde.

Looking across the table at eyes he once described as those of a Caligula, Mr Mitterrand seemed to have forgotten that he had once likened Mrs Thatcher's mouth to that of Marilyn Monroe. The Iron Lady's charm offensive, as it was being dubbed by the British tabloid press, could never be enough to deflect a Frenchman in search of a place in the European history books. From Mr Delors, who now sees heads of national governments as mere mortals compared to European presidents, the reward for her new conciliatory tone could hardly have been more unkind – Mrs Thatcher was, he said, now engaged in a political 'striptease'.

Mr Kohl's ambitions were a little more modest. After breakfast yesterday morning with the French President, he was apparently prepared to sign up to virtually anything – as long as nothing was actually done until after the West German elections early next year. Long regarded as 'unsound' in Downing Street, he seemed content to let Hans-Dietrich Genscher, his Foreign Minister, swap his role as junior coalition partner for that of puppet-master. For Mr Genscher, a Euro-fanatic even by the standards of those eagerly snapping up the Ecu coins minted specially for the summit, it was the perfect opportunity to settle old scores. After all, last month Mrs Thatcher had simply refused to see him during his visit to London.

Sir Geoffrey, who only this week admitted that if Mrs Thatcher fell under the No. 12 bus to Brussels he would – ever so reluctantly – seek the key to her current Downing Street residence, was not much in evidence. After staying up late on Sunday to persuade the Prime Minister to say nice things about, of all things, the European Monetary System, he seemed content to spend his time dotting the 'i's' and crossing the 't's' on a series of typically anodyne statements on EC foreign policy. Getting 'words', 'language' and finally 'texts' rather than actually doing anything seemed the object.

Back in the real game, Mr Mitterrand did not have it entirely his own way. His manner, marked by a persistent habit of keeping everyone else waiting for him to arrive late, at times became too imperious even for his allies. Mrs Thatcher could even claim the satisfaction of an hour or so when he, rather than she, looked isolated. And her approach at least brought a plaudit from Felipe González, who emerged as one of the more gracious figures at the summit.

This week, though, was just the first round. In a year or two Mrs Thatcher will be sitting down at a conference she does not want to discuss a goal she does not want. On past evidence the charm may wear a bit thin.

First appeared 28 June 1989

December 1991 Maastricht summit *– A Heath Robinson design for Europe: the Maastricht treaty is a curious hybrid that will win no prizes for symmetry and will be hard to implement*

DAVID BUCHAN

They did it. In the small hours of a cold Maastricht morning, the twelve EC leaders agreed to turn their Community into a political and monetary union, now to be grandly called the European Union. The Maastricht treaty is indeed the biggest milestone in the Community's 34-year history. It contains, among the goals cited in its preamble, many of the attributes – common citizenship, defence and money – of a potential Euro-superstate. Yet it also makes clear that its intent is not to melt member countries into a United States of Europe, but rather to retain the present mosaic of ever more closely co-operating nation states.

The new treaty, which is part broad constitution, part detailed business plan, maps out the EC's course until the end of the century. The timetable is clearest on economic and monetary union (Emu), which is to be crowned with a single currency by 1 January 1999 at the latest.

In addition the treaty, or its annexes, charts the road ahead in developing a common EC defence policy through the Western European Union (WEU); its membership is to be expanded to match that of the EC and its future will be reviewed in 1998. Two years earlier, in 1996, there will be a more general constitutional review of the Maastricht treaty. The focus of the review – though Britain succeeded in preventing this being made explicit – will be to see whether the new inter-governmental co-operation in foreign/security and in immigration/criminal justice policies can be brought more under standard Community rules.

What Maastricht has brought forth is a strange, heterogeneous creature which, as a bleary-eyed official of the Dutch presidency of the EC admitted early yesterday morning, 'will win no beauty prizes' for clean symmetry. It has been made very clear that member states are now less inclined, or able, to keep together in pursuit of the Community's collective ambitions – ambitions which are being set ever higher. So member states are likely to start opting in or out. There is, for a start, now to be a giant opt-out for all of Britain's eleven EC partners, who have effectively decided to create a separate 'European Social Community' that will use EC institutions to make its laws.

Thus, the Brussels Commission, with British members, will propose social legislation, which the Strasbourg Parliament with its eighty-one British MEPs will then amend. In theory, Mr Michael Howard, the UK employment secretary, will absent himself from the Council of Ministers. But can he preside, yet not vote, during Britain's EC presidency in the second half of next year? Will the eleven have to find another president on this issue for that period of 1992? If so, how? Given these complexities, it was not surprising that many other EC delegations were yesterday hoping that Britain might have a Labour government next year, pledged to the Social Charter.

The opt-out on Emu for Britain and Denmark (which wants to hold a referendum) is also sure to lead to problems. One of these emerged late during the Maastricht summit. This is that Britain will be able to take part in the vote in 1996 – which it is agreed will be the first attempt to launch Emu – on whether there is a sufficient 'critical mass' of countries to form the currency union. This 'critical mass' is set at a majority (seven) of the twelve, or whatever number of countries then make up the Community. What happens if Britain is one of only seven countries deemed economically fit to pass to Emu, but London opts out? If only six were both ready and willing to go to Emu, the answer seems to be that Emu would remain stalled. A solution, but not a watertight one, to this problem lies in a protocol to the Maastricht treaty. This protocol on the 'irreversibility of movement towards Emu' states that no member should act so as to prevent a single currency coming into being.

It is the clear intention of the Maastricht treaty that countries should not be able to pick, à la carte, from the now-expanded menu of goals and policies prescribed for the European Union. But defence will pose a particular problem. At present the WEU has only nine of the EC states as its members. Greece passionately wants to join it, and now will be able to do so. So will Denmark and neutral Ireland, if they want.

However, enlargement of the Community may alter the geometry of its defence dimension again. Austria and Sweden, if they still feel strongly about their neutrality in the post-Cold War world, may shrink from joining WEU. On the other hand, Poland, Czechoslovakia and Hungary, which may join the Community around the turn of the century, would gladly jump into WEU. These are some of the complexities and inconsistencies – particularly in Emu and social policy – which will bring the Maastricht treaty under fire. It is true that there is much cleaning up of the text which has to be done before the treaty is ready, perhaps as late as next March, for formal signing by the twelve governments and presentation for ratification to their national parliaments. But this interval is for textual polishing, rather than substantive renegotiation.

And the first baptism of fire for the treaty will come as early as today when Mr Ruud Lubbers, the Dutch prime minister who presided over the Maastricht summit, and Mr Jacques Delors, the Commission president, go before the European Parliament to justify it.

The Strasbourg MEPs have no direct hold over the treaty in terms of being able to ratify it; they can only issue their opinion of it. But at least one national parliament – Italy's – has said it will be guided by Strasbourg's views when it comes to its own national ratification debate. And the European Parliament is sure to criticize Mr Lubbers and especially Mr Delors, as leader of a fellow supranational institution, on several counts. The Parliament has not got a bad deal for itself. It will now be able to negotiate amendments directly with the Council on all internal market legislation as well as measures covering infrastructure, education, health, culture, and some environment and research policies. If, too, the Parliament cannot get its amendments taken up by the Council, it will have a veto to kill the legislation. But MEPs wanted much more, which their champion, Chancellor Helmut Kohl, failed to win them at Maastricht.

Even the treaty's Emu provisions may come under fire. Emu is the only really solid achievement to come out of Maastricht. The Community does now genuinely seem to be on a course towards a single currency that is as irreversible as anything subject to the vagaries of economics can be. The stages have been clearly marked out, each with its own economic criteria and monetary institutions. The sites for the European Monetary Institute (in the second stage) and the European Central Bank (to manage the single currency in the final stage) have not been agreed, and probably will take a lot of unattractive horse-trading to settle. But at the moment this is not a key issue.

The Maastricht decision to set 1999 as effectively the final date for the single currency is perhaps not as hot-headed as it first seemed. The fact that no minimum quorum of countries has been set for the passage to Emu in 1999 means that EC leaders will be less tempted to bend politically the all-important economic convergence tests which countries must pass to qualify for Emu.

Mr Henning Christophersen, the EC commissioner for economic affairs, called it 'a very elegant solution, marrying clear dates with Germany's insistence on economic conditions'. And that seems to be why Mr Kohl this week overruled the doubts of his officials about accepting the formula. There is less involvement for both the Commission and Parliament in Emu than in standard EC business covered by the Treaty of Rome. Far greater, however, is the concern on the part of these institutions and some governments (Germany, Belgium and Italy to name three) that the Maastricht treaty makes decision-making on foreign and immigration/criminal justice policies almost purely an intergovernmental affair.

But that was the only way in which most governments were ready to take a first co-operative step in these sensitive fields, Mr Lubbers said yesterday morning. Outright involvement of the Commission and Parliament in foreign-policy decision-making would have made impossible agreement with the UK government, which as it was insisted that decisions to implement common EC foreign-policy measures by majority had themselves to be taken by unanimity among governments.

On immigration, the Dutch prime minister said that, when he was the first leader ever to raise the topic at an EC summit, at Hanover in 1988, 'I would have been amazed to think we could bring this matter within the scope of our Union only three years later.'

Once a few more years had elapsed, perhaps by the time of the 1996 constitutional review, immigration might be fully brought within the Community structure, Mr Lubbers added. However, that will not satisfy MEPs who are frustrated at being legally incompetent to discuss immigration, one of the hottest political issues on their Euro-constituents' minds. Clearly, it is distasteful for governments like Britain's to move sensitive policies from an intergovernmental forum to the Community proper. At Maastricht, all that Mr Major would do to please Mr Kohl on this score was to agree that the EC could settle policy on short-term visitors' visas by unanimity for the time being, and by qualified majority by 1996.

Far more problematic, however, would be movement in the opposite direction, from Community-level to intergovernmental decision-making. This is precisely what Mr Delors feared when Mr Lubbers, aided and abetted by Mr Kohl, decided on Tuesday to pursue their social policy ambitions outside the standard Community institutions of the twelve, to help the UK prime minister out of the political hole he had dug for himself. At one point, the Commission president believed that Britain's eleven partners were about to take future social policy right out of the Treaty of Rome. This is why Mr Delors came up with his 'least bad' alternative of legislating on social matters among the eleven.

As the man heading the EC executive which is going to have to make the Maastricht treaty work, Mr Delors now faces very considerable problems. Before Maastricht, the Commission president was railing against absurdities and 'organized schizophrenia' in the Community's political union treaty. But he could never have imagined that the twelve leaders would come up with such a Heath Robinson solution on social policy. While it may be the biggest step in Community integration in thirty-four years, the Maastricht treaty will take some selling, even to the most hardened of European enthusiasts.

First appeared 12 December 1991

June 1992 Danish referendum – *Mutiny rocks EC ship of state: Denmark's rejection of the Maastricht treaty poses a grave threat to hopes for European integration*

DAVID BUCHAN

Ratify or be damned. This was how Denmark's EC partners, and the European Commission, yesterday reacted to the thumbs down given by the Danish electorate on Tuesday to the Maastricht treaty on political and monetary union. Since they will not now ratify the treaty, Danes can expect damnation, or at least to be cast into Community limbo.

Some EC leaders were more diplomatic than others. Mr Jacques Delors, the Commission president, warned of 'consequences not only for the Community, but for Denmark and Danes'. Mr João de Deus Pinheiro, the Portuguese foreign minister who has the unenviable task of being in the EC presidency chair at this crisis moment, was very blunt. 'We can't have a member state which does not accept the fundamental goals of the Community (as contained in Maastricht) continuing to be a member state,' he said. 'It could have another status, another relationship with the EC.'

President François Mitterrand and Chancellor Helmut Kohl said they regretted the Danish decision, but pledged 'their determination to realize the European union unswervingly'. Mr Douglas Hurd, the UK foreign secretary, said the Danish vote was 'not a reason to stop others going ahead'. Do Denmark's partners mean business or just bluster? That will become clearer later today when EC foreign ministers hold an emergency meeting while they attend a Nato gathering in Oslo. But it is clear that the small number of Danish voters – some 46,000 – who tipped the referendum against Maastricht have precipitated the worst Community crisis since 1965. It was then that General Charles de Gaulle took France out of the Council of Ministers, insisting that his partners could not make decisions in his absence. They refused, stiffened by Dutch resistance, and six months later France came back into the Council.

There is a parallel to today's crisis. 'If Denmark's eleven partners stick together on Maastricht, this will not be a big crisis,' said a senior EC official yesterday. 'But if they start to have second thoughts, then this will indeed be a big crisis.' It is not a question of facing down a Danish government, which is wholly mortified by what its voters have done. Even if it were, small Denmark faces eleven, mostly larger, partners; big France dominated the original six.

It is the dark doubts that so many countries have, or have had, about aspects of the great integrationist leap of Maastricht that are the difference between now and the 1965–6 crisis. Darkest of these doubts is whether governments are not simply way ahead of their populaces in their acceptance or enthusiasm for tighter European integration. The only test of that would be to put Maastricht to an EC-wide plebiscite, which no one is proposing. But Mr Mitterrand yesterday grasped part of the nettle by announcing a French referendum on Maastricht; his gamble, high-risk for his own political domestic fortunes, is for a resounding French Yes to quash the impact of the marginal Danish No.

The initial, flat refusal yesterday of Denmark's partners to renegotiate Maastricht reflects their fear that the treaty was like a boat, carried safely to harbour by a high-tide of Europeanism that may now be ebbing away. Renegotiation could well sink it, in new cross-currents of fears about central control from Brussels; about immigrants flooding across newly opened borders within the EC; about Maastricht's new powers for the European Parliament robbing national parliaments of their legislative birthrights. Any renegotiation of Maastricht would also invite a double broadside against its key provisions for Emu and common foreign and eventually defence policies. Bonn would almost certainly not be able to renegotiate Emu, unless it secured the clear-cut opt-out that Britain and Denmark won; and if Germany were allowed a 'maybe' commitment to Emu, all momentum would be lost. The Maastricht commitment to a European foreign policy and defence would also be eroded by the Atlanticists – the UK, Portugal and the Netherlands – and by neutral Ireland and by Denmark, many of whose citizens showed this week that they want to keep the Community in civvies, not in military uniform.

But before Maastricht's opponents drain their champagne glasses, they should spare a thought about what might happen if the treaty dies. Its death will not necessarily mean the death of Emu or of European defence. Indeed, both could occur on terms vastly less pleasing to most EC states.

As Mr Karl Otto Pöhl used to say, only half-jokingly, when he was Bundesbank president, Germany is ready right now for Emu with some of its immediate neighbours – France, the Benelux (and he used to mention Denmark). But there would not be any democratic European structure to such a monetary union, outside the Community. Breathing a sigh of relief at not having to take in spendthrift southerners, or Britons, Germany could pick and choose its partners for a northern continental currency club. Emu on these terms might be very attractive to many of those Germans who currently rail against Maastricht. And the loud howls from excluded Italy would not make it any less so.

Likewise, the death of Maastricht might not make President Mitterrand and Chancellor Kohl any less keen to pursue their plan to create a European army corps by 1995. It might render them keener. At present, they only have a rather implausible joint brigade of 4,000 men. But in the absence of partners, they might try to put substantially more of their armies together. More important, Maastricht enshrined the Western European Union, the nine-nation defence organization with established links to Nato, as the body through which Europe would develop its defence interests. Any European force would come under a WEU umbrella. That umbrella could be blown away along with Maastricht, making the Americans even more irritated about Franco-German rivalry to Nato than they already are.

These, then, are some of the stakes involved in the current Maastricht mess. There are, basically, two ways of sorting it out. The first is for the eleven to stick to the line that most of them espoused yesterday. This involves them all plodding on with ratification, as if Tuesday's Danish rejection had never happened. Then, at the end of the year, they would tell Denmark to find some way of approving Maastricht, or take itself out of the Community, at least out of the European Union created by Maastricht.

The second option would involve listening carefully to what the Danish government suggests might mollify its voters, and trying to do something about it. A compromise might exploit the fact that European Union contains three 'pillars', in the Maastricht jargon – one covering standard EC business (enlarged to Emu), and two 'intergovernmental' pillars covering foreign, defence, police, immigration and home affairs. It was not ruled out in Brussels yesterday that Denmark could stay in the EC, but forgo participation in the new intergovernmental business. Myriad problems leap to mind; for instance, what about sanctions on Serbia which are decided intergovernmentally by all twelve, but implemented by EC machinery? 'But, legally, we can always arrange something,' said an EC expert.

The snag about letting countries dine à la carte off the European menu – as the complaints that followed Britain's Maastricht opt-out clause on social policy highlighted – is that it opens the way to ever-greater fragmentation of Community activity. In particular, if Denmark can pick and choose, why cannot the new members queuing to join the EC?

Ironically, it was enlargement, or rather its implications for EC integration and institutions, that may have just tipped the Danish vote against the treaty. At President Mitterrand's suggestion, last December's Maastricht summit decided to ask the Commission to prepare a report for this month's Lisbon summit on how the Community could cope with a more numerous membership. The Commission has taken the study seriously: perhaps, it belatedly realized, too seriously. Certain ideas for the report, which is still not finalized, started to leak out a month ago. These included reducing the required minimum votes for taking decisions by majority and transforming the Commission into a more powerful executive, particularly on the foreign policy side.

Alarmed at seeing all his work on Maastricht, particularly on Emu, slip away, the Commission president back-pedalled by rightly denying these ideas had any official status. But this was not before newspaper headlines such as 'Delors wants to rule Europe' had had their impact in Denmark. It is equally ironic that Danes were yesterday being sharply criticized by some of their fellow Nordics.

The one certain consequence of the Maastricht mess is that, unless it is very speedily sorted out, it will prevent accession negotiations with Sweden, Austria, Finland and Switzerland starting, as the forthcoming UK presidency planned, next January. Thus, Denmark may bring down on its heads the wrath of its fellow Nordics in Sweden and Finland, while perhaps indefinitely deferring an EC entry application from Norway.

Another item on the Community's agenda – that of its future financing over the next five years – now becomes even more pressing. Spain has warned that it will not ratify Maastricht until it gets satisfaction on more 'cohesion' cash, via the EC budget, from northern countries. But the latter may now reply: 'What's the point in paying the bill for Maastricht, with Maastricht itself in such doubt?' On such issues, the united front which Denmark's EC partners sought yesterday to present could well come apart.

First appeared 4 June 1992

September 1992 ERM collapse – *Behind the ERM crisis: the inside story of the events which led to Black Wednesday and made the Community's most important objective, monetary union, its least plausible goal*

PETER NORMAN AND LIONEL BARBER

The exact timing remains unclear. But, some time in the afternoon of Saturday 12 September, Mr Jean-Claude Trichet went through one of those chameleon-like changes which top international bureaucrats sometimes experience. As a senior French official, he had stood that morning alongside his boss, Mr Michel Sapin, the French finance minister, receiving high-level visitors from Germany in France's steel and glass finance ministry at the unfashionable end of Paris, near the Gare de Lyon.

Hans Tietmeyer, vice-president of the powerful Bundesbank, and Horst Kohler, state secretary at the Bonn finance ministry, were on their way to Rome. They had told the French government that Germany wanted to negotiate the first substantial realignment in the European exchange-rate mechanism in more than five years.

By late evening, Mr Trichet had switched roles. He had exchanged his French civil servant's hat for that of an EC functionary as he prepared to relay to Community member states two pieces of important news: Italy was planning to devalue the lira by 7 per cent in the European Monetary System; and Germany had promised a cut in interest rates in an attempt to calm turmoil in the ERM. What he did not tell them was the Germans wanted a broader realignment of currencies within the system, including sterling. The ERM, a system of fixed but adjustable exchange rates, was no longer capable of providing monetary stability for Europe. The planned realignment was a radical move to restore order to the system and keep alive hopes of progress to economic and monetary union.

Mr Trichet is director of the French treasury, the most coveted position in France's civil service hierarchy. He is also chairman of the European Community's monetary committee, the secretive group which helps manage European monetary affairs. His actions that weekend were to play a crucial role in determining how the ERM crisis unfolded. Some critics have accused him of putting French interests above those of the Community – by trying to place a protective 'ring-fence' around Italy's devaluation so that the French franc would be shielded from speculative attacks in the week ahead of France's closely contested 20 September referendum on the Maastricht treaty. Others charge that he failed to tell the UK that Germany wanted a broader realignment, including sterling. With hindsight, some officials have argued that, if Mr Trichet has pushed for an early weekend meeting of the monetary committee or of EC finance ministers, the EC might have organized a broader realignment that would have calmed the growing fever on financial markets and perhaps even have ensured Britain's continued ERM membership. He has been cast as the *éminence grise* who scuppered such an opportunity.

The truth, as a *Financial Times* investigation, which has included dozens of interviews with top officials across the EC, makes clear, is both more complex and Mr Trichet has told colleagues that, in his capacity as a French official, he could not use the highly sensitive information given to him by the Germans that morning to set in motion discussions leading to a broader realignment. When wearing his monetary committee hat later in the day, he accepted as a *fait accompli* the news of the Italian devaluation and took no steps to broaden the scope of the weekend's currency changes, arguing that he could not negotiate on behalf of individual member states. The crisis that has shaken the EC's system of fixed but adjustable exchange rates since September is a story of communications failures at all levels.

Mr Trichet's behaviour accorded with the letter of the Community's arcane rule-book, but it did nothing to avert turmoil. Yet Mr Trichet's split personality on that Saturday merely typified the bureaucratic contortions that drove the ERM into the biggest crisis in its thirteen-year history. Even though currencies will not feature on the formal agenda of the European Community's summit in Edinburgh today, the autumn crisis will haunt the twelve leaders of the EC member states. Ambitious plans for Emu by the end of the decade have been set back by Black Wednesday's traumatic suspension of sterling and the Italian lira from the ERM and by subsequent crises and disruptions. Time and again, this autumn's European crisis was bedevilled by human failure and institutional weakness. The crucial meeting of EC finance ministers in Bath on 4 and 5 September exemplified this; so, too, did the events which led to devaluation of the Italian lira and the turmoil which culminated in Black Wednesday.

The ERM looked ripe for change when the ministers met in Bath. Funds were haemorrhaging out of the lira into the D-Mark, threatening exchange rate relationships that had stood for 5 ¾ years. The UK government's policy of trying to hold sterling's ERM parity at DM2.95 against the D-Mark during a harsh recession was looking threadbare. The fact that opinion polls in France pointed to a possible government defeat in the September referendum increased the chances of a massive speculative attack against currencies in the EMS. The twice-yearly informal 'Ecofin council' is usually something of a treat for the ministers and governors, their close aides and their spouses. Bath was different. 'It was the worst I've ever attended,' said one veteran of nearly twenty such gatherings. 'A disaster,' concluded another. Nobody who attended has a good word to say about it, least of all senior British Treasury officials who were summoned late on Saturday 5 September to help break deadlock.

Mr Ruud Lubbers, the Dutch prime minister, was later to say that the failure to arrange a realignment at the meeting would go down as a 'black page in the book of 1992'. But a realignment was never properly discussed at Bath. Instead, the meeting set what was to become a familiar pattern of half-articulated expectations by some countries that were deliberately ignored by others. Neither Mr Lamont nor Mr Sapin, his close ally in the talks, would contemplate any devaluation of their currencies. Mr Sapin's position was that there could be no ERM realignment before the Maastricht referendum. The Italians, in office for only a few months, kept their heads down. Nobody uttered the 'R-word' in the meeting. Instead, Mr Lamont turned repeatedly on Mr Schlesinger, urging him to cut German interest rates. 'It was tense,' observed one continental official. 'Unilateral pressure was put on one partner in a repeated way.' Mr Schlesinger – as mere *primus inter pares* on the Bundesbank's decision-making council – was statutorily unable to deliver any such promise. He was also temperamentally disinclined to yield to political pressure. Faced with Mr Lamont's battering ram tactics, Mr Schlesinger nearly walked out. Some days later, he complained that he had been asked four times to cut rates and had to reply No four times 'when only once should have done'. Mr Lubbers later blamed Bath's failure on 'political motives'. Realignment, he said, 'was not possible – because England had its pride and France said that it couldn't be done because it was facing a difficult referendum and they couldn't discuss it; and the English said then that the Bundesbank should do something first, and so the discussion went.'

Certainly, realignment was in the air, despite Mr Lamont's and Mr Sapin's efforts to keep it off the agenda. Outside the Bath Assembly Rooms, Mr Waigel, the German finance minister, was asked by journalists whether a realignment was being discussed. He stonewalled, answering that such a move would need unanimous support from ERM states, which was not forthcoming. Inside the Assembly Rooms, Mr Schlesinger made comments that officials present were later to interpret as signals that the Bundesbank favoured a realignment. At the time, however, almost no one realized the significance of his words. The ministers finally knocked together a four-point statement which reaffirmed their opposition to a realignment and referred to a Bundesbank promise not to raise its interest rates. Mr Lamont was quick to imply that this had been a victory over the mighty Bundesbank, a suggestion that angered Mr Schlesinger. Any calming effect the statement might have had on financial markets was undermined the next day when Mr Schlesinger said the Bundesbank pledge represented no change in policy and distanced himself from the agreement not to realign ERM exchange rates.

In the days after Bath, the ERM suffered further blows. The Finnish markka, which had been pegged to the Ecu, the EC's embryonic currency, was allowed to float after suffering extended speculative attack. Sweden began a costly and ultimately futile bid to keep its krona pegged to the Ecu by intervening heavily on currency markets and pushing its interest rates to 500 per cent at one point. The Italian lira was sold heavily, finally falling below its ERM floor on Friday 11 September in spite of massive support from the Bundesbank and Bank of Italy. After having to buy an unprecedented DM24 billion worth of lire in less than a week, Mr Schlesinger sought the German government's support for a general realignment in the ERM.

It was at a special meeting in the Bundesbank, on Friday evening, when Mr Tietmeyer and Mr Kohler were asked to go to Rome by way of Paris, to negotiate a devaluation of the lira and seek a realignment involving other currencies.

In one respect, the monetary manoeuvrings of the September 12–13 weekend started under a more favourable star than in Bath. In discussions with Chancellor Kohl and his financial advisers, Mr Schlesinger made a potentially far-reaching concession that earned him criticism at home when it became known after the weekend. He made clear the Bundesbank would be prepared to bargain a cut in German interest rates in return for a realignment. The extent would depend on the number of countries taking part. On Saturday and Sunday, the Bundesbank president contacted members of the bank's council to discuss the scope of the interest rate cut. However, the Bundesbank made no effort to contact the Bank of England or British government. 'It was not our job to inform the British of our intentions,' Mr Schlesinger would say later.

The absence of timely communication with London was to diminish greatly prospects for the broad realignment the Bundesbank sought. Once a member state seeks a realignment, it is the job of the EC monetary committee, whose chairman is Mr Trichet, to find out the views of other member states. On that weekend, Mr Andreas Kees, the committee secretary who usually canvasses ERM members before convening a meeting of the committee, was away boating. Mr Trichet had to sound out members for a meeting. He decided against such a gathering. Mr Trichet's decision to handle the lira devaluation by phone is now recognized by all – including, it seems, Mr Trichet – as a mistake. It stifled a broader debate on currencies that weekend. There was no opportunity for bilateral meetings with the chairman in which room for compromise could be assessed. Instead, that weekend again illustrated how difficult it is for ERM member states to thrash out delicate policy issues. It is unclear whether Messrs Kohler and Tietmeyer realized Mr Trichet was acting as a French government official alone, and not as EC monetary committee chairman, when they met him and Mr Sapin in Paris en route to Rome. What is certain is that Mr Trichet interpreted their visit as a kind of courtesy call. He knew that the Germans wanted a broad realignment, but believed they had come to advise the French government of a potentially difficult situation just one week before the Maastricht referendum. The German visitors never made a precise request for London to devalue; nor did they propose new parities for the pound.

It was in the evening after he was told by telephone of the outcome of the German–Italian negotiations in Rome that Mr Trichet put on his monetary committee hat. It was his duty to see whether the other ERM members approved the planned 7 per cent lira devaluation, and he duly contacted them. But he did not consider it his job to sound out others about broader realignment. After all, he reasoned, the positions of the various countries were known. France had said it did not want to devalue. Both Mr Major and Lamont had publicly rejected devaluation, turning it into a prestige issue. Although it had been fairly clear since the Bath meeting that Germany wanted a broad realignment, it would have been a delicate matter to have suggested a devaluation to the British because the pound had not been under pressure in the previous week. Others have argued that he took a narrow view of his job. 'To do that realignment by phone was unacceptable,' complained one continental central banker. 'Not only was the issue too delicate to be handled by phone. The procedure meant that not everybody was in possession of the same information.' But any of the ERM countries could have insisted on a meeting of either the monetary committee or ministers if they wanted more than the 7 per cent lira devaluation of that weekend. They had an opportunity to act when Mr Trichet contacted them from Saturday evening onwards, or when the draft monetary committee communiqués announcing the realignment were circulated. But none did so.

Mr Trichet also felt confident a successful realignment could be handled by phone. On three previous occasions the lira parity had been changed in the EMS without a meeting. Moreover, by late Saturday, when he received the news from Rome, time was running short. This is acknowledged in Bonn. According to a senior German finance ministry official, Mr Trichet was 'under a very difficult time restraint, and operating in a very difficult environment'. 'We came together very late that weekend with the Italians, asking for a realignment,' the German official said. 'On

Friday evening, when invitations normally go out for monetary committee meetings, we were talking among ourselves. It was only on Saturday that we could really offer something in terms of interest rate moves, and we could really pull the Italians on board.' British officials say that the first they heard of a realignment was on Saturday evening when they were asked: 'Do you consent to the Italian devaluation against the D-Mark?' The weekend development was so unexpected that Whitehall had to mount a large-scale search operation to trace Sir Terry Burns, the permanent secretary to the Treasury. He was finally tracked down in Dulwich, a south London suburb, at a party celebrating a friend's 25th wedding anniversary.

He learned the news on a mobile phone from Sir Nigel Wicks, the second permanent secretary, who, conscious of recent security breaches on mobile phones, would only refer obliquely to a problem with 'our sick friend'. Mr Lamont, who was at the last night of the Proms, was also only told of developments at a late stage. Although there was some concern that the lira devaluation could mean further volatility in the ERM ahead of France's referendum, there was no sense of imminent doom early on Sunday when Mr Lamont met senior officials in the UK Treasury to discuss developments. By then, according to UK officials, it was known the Bundesbank would cut its Lombard rate by ¼ percentage point the next day and announce cuts of ½ point in its discount and money market rates. When Sir Terry asked, as a matter of form, whether sterling would join in the realignment with a devaluation, the answer from the chancellor was No.

Superficially, the 7 per cent lira devaluation appeared almost a textbook realignment. It had been carried out behind the scenes, apparently without fuss. But there were some worrying loose ends and signs that all might not be well. The Italian government was unhappy to be devaluing alone. On Sunday morning, Mr Guiliano Amato, the Italian prime minister, rang Mr Major, who was staying with the Queen at Balmoral, to tell him about the planned lira devaluation. He asked if the UK was joining the realignment. Mr Major said No. According to Downing Street, the Italian premier did not then press the UK to devalue.

Just before going to church with the Queen, Mr Major telephoned Mr Lamont at the Treasury meeting to confirm the no-devaluation line. But, by Sunday afternoon, some UK officials feared the lira devaluation would trigger further speculative pressure in the ERM ahead of the French referendum. They were to argue later that Germany should have 'nursed the lira through' until 20 September.

There was also concern in the Bundesbank that the changes would not satisfy the markets. The Italian government, it emerged later, thought the scale of the devaluation too small. Rome believed 15 per cent was necessary to restore competitiveness, although it recognized that such a large lira devaluation would almost certainly have been blocked by France because it would have given Italian exporters a big price advantage.

Whatever Mr Trichet's motives, the scene was set for the last act of the drama before Black Wednesday. The scale of inflows into Germany the week before showed that markets could wield awesome power in an age of almost unrestricted capital movements. The 7 per cent lira devaluation had been sufficiently large to reward speculators. There was enough dissonance among policy makers to encourage fund managers and corporate treasurers to take a further shot at the ERM.

By the afternoon of Tuesday 15 September, sterling was in trouble. It closed in London just a fifth of a pfennig above its ERM floor of DM2.778, at its lowest-ever level in the mechanism. The Treasury called a high-level crisis meeting in Chancellor Lamont's office with senior Bank of England officials to discuss tactics for the next day.

As the meeting was in progress sterling suffered its knock-out blow – as a result of yet another misunderstanding. News agency reports appeared on Tuesday evening of an interview by Mr Schlesinger with *Handelsblatt*, the German newspaper. He was quoted as favouring a more comprehensive realignment. The news pushed sterling through its ERM floor in after-hours dealings. Two frantic telephone calls between Mr Robin Leigh-Pemberton, the governor of the Bank of England, and Mr Schlesinger got the response that the remarks were 'not authorized'. While the governor was initially reassured, Mr Lamont, according to one participant, was angry and anticipated trouble. He abruptly silenced Mr Leigh-Pemberton.

Though denials were soon forthcoming, the scene had been set for a day of carnage on the foreign exchanges. Mr Schlesinger's purported remarks were too close to the known views of many top officials in the German central bank – including his own. Twenty-four hours later, Mr Lamont was outside the Treasury facing the television cameras. He announced Britain's withdrawal from the European exchange-rate mechanism. Massive intervention, possibly exceeding £15 billion, and two emergency interest rate increases, first to 12 per cent and later to 15 per cent, had failed to save the pound. The question facing the EC was whether the ERM and the strategic goal of economic and monetary union by the end of the millennium could be saved from the wreckage.

Additional reporting by Quentin Peel, David Marsh, Edward Mortimer, Ronald Van de Krol, Will Dawkins and Robert Graham

First appeared 11 December 1992

September 1992 Black Wednesday – The ERM and Maastricht: 'Sterling was being sold like water running out of a tap'

STEPHEN FIDLER, IVO DAWNAY, PETER MARSH, QUENTIN PEEL, JAMES BLITZ, EMMA TUCKER, DAVID MARSH AND TRACY CORRIGAN

If there was a moment when Norman Lamont knew that his economic policy was in ruins, it came a few seconds after 11 a.m. last Wednesday, 16 September. As sunshine streamed into Parliament Square, Britain's Chancellor of the Exchequer rose from his desk in the Treasury, and stepped into his richly panelled outer office. Half an hour earlier he had called John Major at the Old Admiralty building in Whitehall where the prime minister was temporarily housed while repairs were being undertaken to Number 10 Downing Street. Could he raise interest rates by 2 percentage points? Yes, said Major over the secure telephone line. Devaluation had to be avoided. The government's credibility was at stake.

The announcement was to be released to the news agencies on the stroke of 11 a.m. It would come as a hammer-blow to a nation battered by recession. A small group of advisers, the chancellor at their centre, gathered round the Reuters news-agency screen outside his inner sanctum. All morning the Bank of England had been fighting a desperate battle to save the pound from collapsing against the D-Mark and dropping through its agreed floor in the European Exchange Rate Mechanism. Billions of pounds were used to try to stem the tide. Sterling revived briefly, then dropped back. As Big Ben struck eleven, Lamont and his team remained transfixed by the numbers on the screen which monitored the currency markets. The chimes stopped and still the pound was sinking. A minute passed. The chancellor broke the silence. 'It is not moving,' he said. The government would fight a desperate, rearguard action, but the battle was already lost.

The extraordinary events which have engulfed the pound, shattered the British government's economic policy and shaken the ERM to its core began in earnest two weekends before in the elegant city of Bath. European finance officials, under Lamont's chairmanship, met to prepare, among other things, for the possibility of a No vote in the French referendum on the Maastricht treaty on European union. There would be turmoil on the markets. They would need to be united. But the cracks were beginning to appear. The Germans argued that the weaker currencies in the ERM, such as the pound and the lira, were out of line with the rest. Germany's partners responded that the Bundesbank was keeping interest rates too high and stifling growth.

Despite subsequent denials that this had ever been mooted, the German delegation, led by Theo Waigel, the finance minister, and Bundesbank president Helmut Schlesinger, offered to reduce their interest rates. The price: a wide-ranging realignment of the mechanism – one which, by definition, would involve the pound. 'In the event, the others weren't ready for it,' said one German official later. In his statement after the meeting Lamont presented the outcome as a victory for Britain. He had secured from the mighty Bundesbank a promise not to raise interest rates. The following morning German interest rates were cut by a grudging quarter of a percentage point and Britain's Tory tabloids took up the theme. The Bundesbank was portrayed as buckling to political pressure, its cherished independence compromised. The Bundesbank's president later confided that he was so angry at the conduct of the meeting that, at one point, he nearly walked out. When Schlesinger set the record straight the next day, the private disagreements became public. The markets began to smell blood. After that, the markets began seriously to test the ERM's resolve. Currency dealers sold Italian lire, the ERM's weakest link. In the week after the Bath meeting they had sold more than £8.5 billion-worth of lire for D-Marks.

That weekend increasingly worried finance officials across Europe hurriedly conferred and cobbled together a deal: Italy would devalue the lira by 7 per cent. In return the Italians would support a broader realignment. The British continued to resist. The Bank of England had plenty of ammunition to fight the speculators should they turn on the pound, or so it thought. Its $44.4 billion (£25 billion) in reserves at the end of August had been supplemented by a more recent £7.27 billion borrowing in foreign currencies.

Shortly before lunchtime on the Tuesday the lira began to sink. For sterling the die was cast. Traders were beginning to believe that one devaluation was not enough. 'As the lira fell, we started to notice that there was a big pick-up in trading in sterling against the D-Mark,' said Mark Austin of the Hongkong and Shanghai Bank. By Tuesday afternoon, the currency was again heading towards DM2.80. By late on Tuesday, traders reckoned the Bank of England had bought around £3 billion – but the pound was not responding. 'What are the British doing?' asked one French dealer. 'If the franc were in this situation, we would have overnight rates up at 40 per cent.' But Britain was in the grip of a deep recession. Raising interest rates was political anathema.

By Tuesday night the pound closed in London just a fifth of a pfennig above its ERM floor of DM2.778, its lowest ever in the mechanism. There was a growing feeling in Whitehall that the currency could be tipped over the edge unless something was done. The Treasury called a crisis meeting in Lamont's office with senior Bank of England officials. Beneath two glittering chandeliers, the details of the following day's tactics were plotted around a large oaken table. Besides the chancellor, the key actors who were to shape tactics on Black Wednesday were there: Sir Terry Burns, the Treasury's gritty permanent secretary ('keep smiling' is one of his aphorisms); his right-hand man, economist Alan Budd; Andrew Turnbull, in charge of monetary policy; Bill Robinson, the chancellor's special political adviser; and Sir Nigel Wicks, the Treasury's laconic second permanent secretary in charge of international affairs.

The Bank group included: Robin Leigh-Pemberton, the aristocratic governor; Eddie George, deputy governor and the man in overall charge of market operations; Ian Plenderleith, associate director in charge of markets; Tony Coleby, director of monetary affairs; and Andrew Crockett, international director. George, known in the City as Hard Eddie, outlined the strategy: take each part of the battle as it comes; escalate the defence in discrete stages. First there would be large and overt Bank intervention. A rise in interest rates would be held in reserve for later in the day. One official pondered as he left the room at about 8 p.m.: 'I wonder if it will be enough.'

Elsewhere, events were already conspiring to thwart their plans. Five hours earlier in Frankfurt, seat of the Bundesbank, two journalists, one from Germany's principal business newspaper, *Handelsblatt*, and one from the *Wall Street Journal*, were interviewing Schlesinger. They released a summary to the news agencies. Schlesinger was reported as saying that a more wide-ranging realignment of the ERM than the devaluation of the lira, agreed at the weekend, could have reduced turbulence in the currency markets. This was code for saying that the Germans believed a sterling devaluation was necessary.

The story was later denied. But what Schlesinger was quoted as saying was too close to the known views of many top officials in the central bank – including his own. It was dynamite. When the *FT* called the Bank of England and the Treasury to seek reaction, near panic ensued in Whitehall and Threadneedle Street. Lamont was with his wife Rosemary for dinner at the Regent's Park home of the US ambassador, Mr Ray Seitz. Treasury officials called him with the news as they fought desperately to lessen the impact of the story. Leigh-Pemberton twice called Schlesinger at his home near Frankfurt to try to clarify the report. The academic Mr Schlesinger – who years ago told a Bundesbank colleague: 'the markets do not interest me' – appeared bemused by the news that his quoted comments were creating havoc on the foreign-exchange markets. 'The interview has not been authorized,' he twice told the Bank of England governor, referring to the fact that both correspondents had promised to check their text with him before publication. He appeared 'puzzled' by the confusion, said a British official. Throughout the night, the Federal Reserve Bank of New York and the Bank of Japan supported sterling.

By 7.30 a.m. on Wednesday, a team of eight foreign-exchange dealers assembled in Eddie George's room in Threadneedle Street, hunched over their screens to buy pounds. Plenderleith ordered them to spend about £2 billion in three separate interventions. By 8 a.m. the pound was pinned to its floor. Dealers were baffled by the Bank of England's actions. Said David Cocker, Treasury adviser at Chemical Bank, at about 10 a.m., 'Why aren't interest rates going up? Can we really be sure that the government is that committed?' By 8.30, the Treasury crisis group re-assembled in the chancellor's room. The mood was sombre. Plenderleith called Lamont over a secure hot line. The chancellor, having spoken to the prime minister earlier, ordered more intervention from the Bank's foreign-currency reserves. Leigh-Pemberton and George were smuggled into the meeting through a side entrance to avoid photographers.

As the heavy artillery in the City began sterling's day-long pounding, Major took his armour-plated Jaguar the two-minute drive down Whitehall to the Admiralty for a long-scheduled 9 a.m. meeting with Michael Heseltine, Douglas Hurd, Kenneth Clarke, Richard Ryder, the chief whip, and Sir Norman Fowler, the Conservative party chairman. The subject was supposed to be Maastricht – but the meeting became a de facto war cabinet.

By 10.30 a.m., the call everyone was dreading from the chancellor came through. Major left the meeting to take it. Hearing that the pound was sinking, he calmly approved the two percentage point interest-rate hike to 12 per cent. The prime minister made certain that this core group of ministers would convene for the key decisions – an insurance policy that the law of 'collective responsibility' would be invoked in full.

At 11 a.m., the move was announced. The chancellor's group was aghast as the pound barely moved. One member of the group thought to himself: 'It's all over.' The currency market was coming to the same conclusion. Lamont made a statement to explain his move: 'As the current extraordinary pressures and uncertainties abate, I hope it will be possible to bring interest rates back down.'

The markets were less than impressed. According to one analyst at the time: 'This may be what the public wants to hear, but it isn't nearly enough.' By noon, Lamont ordered more intervention. He would say, later, that it was like trying to stop a whirlwind. There followed a short discussion about whether suspension from the ERM would be in the Treasury's best interests. At 1 p.m. sandwiches were called in to the war room. Many were left untouched. When US markets opened at around 1.30 in London, US fund managers dealt in huge sums. As one dealer put it: 'Sterling was being sold like water running out of a tap.'

At 2.15, the Bank fired its best shot, raising interest rates to 15 per cent, the first time in history it had raised rates twice in a day – both since rescinded. The stock market's reaction was telling: it rallied because traders believed even this would not stop the run on the pound. Sterling would have to be devalued. Total central bank intervention on Wednesday alone may have exceeded £15 billion. One senior minister commented afterwards: 'We were buying every single pound in the foreign-exchange markets. The reserves were haemorrhaging.'

Major began making plans for sterling's withdrawal from the ERM. He called Pierre Bérégovoy, the French prime minister, and Chancellor Kohl in Germany. Just before 4 p.m., the Bank of England organized a conference call with fellow central banks and told them sterling was being suspended from the ERM. Faced with the full scale of the defeat, Major once again summoned his cabinet colleagues at 5 p.m., this time with Lamont and Leigh-Pemberton. The prime minister and chancellor spelled out their drastic solution. One Whitehall insider says that while Treasury and Bank officials appeared close to panic, Major remained calm. Retreat from the ERM was formally agreed. Just over two hours later, with the twilight fading in the Treasury's neo-classical courtyard, Lamont adjusted his tie and began to speak to the forest of microphones and cameras. 'Today,' he began, 'has been an extremely difficult and turbulent day . . .' That night he worked till 3 a.m. Civil servants said the next morning he returned to his office with a smile on his face and a spring in his step. 'I have had an excellent night's sleep and I feel fine,' he told them. 'For the first time in a long while I haven't had to worry about the pound.'

First appeared 19 September 1992

September 1992 France's 'Petit Oui' – *The French vote: thin reprieve gives twelve the chance to take a deep breath – The Yes vote does not mean treaty can be implemented in its present form*

IAN DAVIDSON

The Yes vote in yesterday's French referendum is an almost unbelievably thin reprieve for the forty-year-old enterprise of European integration. For many years, public opinion polls in France have shown steady majority votes of 60 per cent or more in favour of Europe. On this occasion the French administration campaigned strongly in favour of Maastricht, eventually with the support of the national leaders of all the mainstream parties of government. If a 50.7 per cent majority was the best they could muster between them, the government (and the opposition, for that matter) are clearly under notice that the Maastricht treaty does not command the kind of popular support which would be required to implement it.

In reality, there was almost no chance, even before yesterday's vote, that the treaty could be implemented in its present form. The Danish people have rejected it, and they cannot vote again unless the government can claim that the situation has somehow changed. There has been loose talk of some kind of declaration or protocol which would reinforce the restraints on gratuitous meddling by Brussels in national affairs. But even if this is what would be required to bring the Danes back into the fold, it must mean a change in the treaty, which would open the door wide to a re-negotiation.

Secondly, the uncertain prospects of British ratification of the treaty must have been further reduced by last week's collapse in the government's strategy for sterling. Euro-sceptics in the Conservative party will be even less amenable to Maastricht rhetoric. Correspondingly, Mr Major's authority for imposing party discipline in favour of a monetary system, which even he does not wish to rejoin soon, would seem small. The Yes vote in France does not mean there is after all a chance for the Maastricht treaty to be implemented in its present form; but it does mean the twelve governments can take a deep breath and decide where they go from here.

First, they have to decide whether to try to rescue the specific objectives of the treaty by replacing it by another treaty or (more likely) several treaties; or whether to pause until circumstances are more auspicious. The most specific questions they have to consider are whether the cause of economic and monetary union is really being advanced by current conditions of recession, economic divergence, and monetary turbulence;

and whether a programme which requires the political leadership of Bonn to override the narrow monetarism of the Bundesbank is really plausible when the economic credibility of Bonn is so clearly at a discount.

But the most general question is more fundamental: are the twelve really committed to a programme of integration based on common interests; or was last week's fiasco in the currency markets a stark indication that we are seeing the re-emergence of conflicts of interests, between the internal German problems associated with unification, and those of the rest of the Community? It is too soon to give any general and durable answer to that question. Last week's temper tantrums by British ministers and officials showed that the UK government has no confidence that Germany is putting common interests first. But perhaps they should reflect that French ministers and officials, too, have repeatedly (if more temperately) revealed irritation with the high level of German interest rates. The difference is that the French economy is in much better shape to ride, at least for a time, the consequences of the egotism of German economic and monetary policy.

Here we have the bottom line. If the German government is still committed to the idea of economic and monetary union, eventually, the French are probably in a position to stay for the ride on the roller-coaster. But the British are not. If the French had voted No, we might have had a twelve-speed Europe, or even a No-speed Europe. What the Yes vote does is to preserve the option of a two-speed Europe. In that sense, the dilemma for Mr Major is acute and painful. He wanted to put Britain at the heart of Europe; but last December he demanded the right to choose the slow speed in a two-speed Europe. His wish has been granted. As Oscar Wilde said: 'There are two tragedies in life. One is not to get your heart's desire. The other is to get it.'

First appeared 21 September 1992

December 1995 Madrid summit – *EU leaders cross their fingers on Emu*

LIONEL BARBER

EU leaders crossed their fingers at the Madrid summit and took the minimum steps necessary to preserve the credibility of monetary union. The ultimate fate of Emu hangs as much on events in France as on the slowdown in the European economy. But the Madrid agreement on a name for the single currency and a blueprint for its launch on 1 January 1999 makes it harder to doubt the political commitment to the project.

A dramatic opening exchange showed how Emu is drawing a line between a wavering Britain, a committed German-led hard currency bloc, and a huddled rump who hope to squeeze through the door when EU leaders decide in early 1998 on which countries qualify for membership.

Mr John Major, British prime minister, highlighted the political difficulties inherent in Emu. He spoke of countries forming elitist groupings, the risks of trade wars, and huge budgetary transfers likely to be needed to cope with the strains of a fixed currency regime, both for those inside and outside Emu. Chancellor Helmut Kohl immediately weighed in. Half-jokingly, he chided Mr Major for being a pessimist. Then he called on colleagues to draw inspiration from the leaders of Serbia, Croatia and Bosnia-Herzegovina, who, just the day before in Paris, had buried their doubts and reached agreement in the broader interests of peace. Monetary union is a necessary step towards Europe's eventual political union, said Mr Kohl, adding that 'political union is about freedom and peace'. This is the chancellor's big pitch, the antidote to resurgent nationalism, American isolationism, and Russian collapse. In the words of one EU diplomat present: 'Kohl blew Major away.' But another diplomat was less harsh. 'Major's presentation was calm and reasonable. Many people agreed with him about the problems (with Emu) but the trouble is that he isn't offering any solutions.'

Mr Major's hands are tied because of his ever-dwindling majority in the House of Commons. Yet on the admittedly minor matter of the new name for the currency, several delegations said 'florin' could have triumphed over the uninspiring 'euro' had Britain been able to press its merits; but to have done so would have provoked uproar in the Tory party. The question is whether British prevarication is worsening the political vacuum inside the EU, created by weak governments from Austria and France to Greece, Italy and Spain. Once again, French indecision and unpredictability were a summit feature. President Jacques Chirac first campaigned for the Ecu and finally gambled on an EU-wide poll for a name. Mr Kohl replied that eighty million Germans 'and a few sympathizers' in other countries would simply vote for the D-Mark. Mr Chirac is also merrily continuing his feud with Mr Lamberto Dini, the Italian prime minister.

This time his *bête noire* was not the weak lira, just the matter of Italy's vote at the United Nations, along with nine other EU members, condemning French nuclear tests. Other countries appear prisoners of national domestic pressures. The Dutch spent much of the summit complaining about the size of their budget contributions. The Danes and the Swedes spoke up on enlargement, but otherwise they had one eye on their euro-sceptic publics. The political vacuum accentuates the German vision on the future shape of Europe, because no other country has such a clear view. 'There is only one other leader who has a truly European outlook,' says a veteran EU diplomat, 'and that is Jean-Luc Dehaene of Belgium.'

In this sense, Mr Kohl's criticism of the European Commission was not an attack on the institution as such, but on its effectiveness under the benign stewardship of Mr Jacques Santer. However much Mr Kohl shares British concerns about intrusive and unnecessary EU legislation, he, unlike Mr Major, would like to reinforce the authority of the Commission president. Not everything, however, went Mr Kohl's way. On enlargement, the chancellor's hopes of pencilling in Poland, the Czech Republic and Hungary as members of the first wave of applicants foundered on objections from the Nordics and France.

Eastern enlargement remains a strategic priority for Germany, particularly Poland's membership. It is integral to Mr Kohl's vision of Germany bedded down in a united Europe. The smart money in Madrid was that, at some point, it will be linked, however informally, to Germany's terms for monetary union.

First appeared 18 December 1995

December 1996 Dublin summit *– A compromise on stability: deft Irish handling of the EU summit ensured that economic and monetary union remains on track*

LIONEL BARBER

The European Union summit in Dublin flirted briefly with failure, but ended at the weekend on a mood of relief and self-congratulation. Thanks to deft Irish chairmanship, ably supported by Luxembourg, a crisis between France and Germany over the terms of economic and monetary union was averted. Emu remains on track, a message reinforced with the long-awaited publication of the design of the new euro banknotes.

Yet behind the smiles, the future looks uncertain. Dublin barely addressed the reform of EU institutions and decision-making required by the intergovernmental conference (IGC), which is reviewing the Maastricht treaty. Meanwhile the final communiqué devoted only one paragraph to the Union's planned enlargement to central and eastern Europe. The impression is that Emu is absorbing all of the EU's energies, especially after the seventeen-hour-long negotiations on the German-driven budget-stability pact. The final compromise left all sides proclaiming victory, but it could not dispel the feelings of mistrust between the French and the Germans.

In a narrow sense, the stability-pact dispute turned on a definition of the circumstances in which countries joining the euro zone can avoid being penalized for running a deficit in excess of 3 per cent of gross domestic product, the limit prescribed in the Maastricht treaty. The dispute quickly developed into a matter of principle: the conflict between German demands for a 'stability culture', enforceable through numerical targets buttressed by an independent European Central Bank; and French counter-demands for maximum ministerial discretion in the imposition of penalties, under the slogan of 'national sovereignty'. Time and again, Mr Theo Waigel, the German finance minister, accused Mr Jean Arthuis, his French counterpart, of retreating from what he saw as the spirit of Maastricht. The Frenchman wobbled, but refused to budge. 'I have never seen Theo get so angry with Jean,' said one senior EU diplomat. 'He thought the French were trying to pull the wool over his eyes.' A German diplomat adds: 'The problem was that both the French and the Germans could argue that they had the treaty on their side.'

In the end, the Germans settled. But only because Mr Helmut Kohl, the German chancellor, had decided several days before that the risks of delaying a deal were too high. He had one eye on the financial markets which have become increasingly positive about the prospect of the single currency going ahead on schedule on 1 January 1999, but his other worry was the likely damage to relations with Paris.

As Mr Kohl acknowledged in a news conference on Saturday afternoon: the Gaullist coalition government is in trouble, weakened by slow growth, high unemployment, and a political class split over the merits of the single currency which it sees as a recipe for deflation and austerity. But why did it take Bonn so long to sense the shift in French mood?

One explanation is that the German government was so concerned about its own fragile public support for surrendering the D-Mark that it lost sight of its own partner's predicament. 'The Germans could have secured an even tougher stability pact three months ago,' says a Benelux diplomat, 'but they delayed in the hope they could obtain better terms.'

The final Irish compromise on the stability pact is based on a Belgian proposal; it provides for a two-tier approach which Mr Kenneth Clarke, the UK chancellor, described as an 'ingenious' solution. Thus, member states which experience a fall in gross domestic product of at least 2 per cent over a year will qualify automatically for 'exceptional' status, while a country suffering a fall in GDP or 0.75 per cent or lower may plead a special case to the Council of Ministers. In a gesture to President Jacques

Chirac of France, EU leaders agreed to rechristen the agreement the 'stability and growth pact'.

The deal may prove more important in terms of psychology than economic logic. The stability pact's fines, which move on a sliding scale from 0.2 per cent of GDP to a ceiling of 0.5 per cent of GDP, are intended primarily as a deterrent; few expect the penalties to be applied in practice because of the explosive political consequences. Yet Germans can be reassured that the principle of fiscal discipline in the future euro zone is enshrined in regulations and a political declaration.

Mr Carlo Ciampi, Italy's veteran treasury minister, drew a broader conclusion from the negotiations, citing the need for a balance between technocrats and politicians in the future monetary union. His view was echoed by Mr Chirac who again called for a political counterweight to the future European Central Bank, perhaps through a new 'stability council' comprised of ministers from Emu countries.

The question which Dublin failed to answer is how the Emu debate relates to the IGC, which is supposed to be wrapped up by June 1997 at the Amsterdam summit but which could well slip to October because of uncertainty over the timing of the UK general election and the fate of the increasingly Euro-sceptic Tory government.

What is striking is the sheer amount of detail in the blueprint for Emu compared to the draft text of the Maastricht II treaty which the Irish presented at the summit. The Dublin agreement on Emu contains not just the stability pact, but also a deal on a new 'hub and spokes' exchange-rate mechanism which will provide currency discipline between Emu 'outs' and Emu 'ins' built around the euro; and texts on the legal status of the single currency. The 140-page Irish draft for Maastricht II is clear and readable, but leaves the most difficult questions to the incoming Dutch presidency. This was no more than was asked of the Irish; but it does not address seriously the balance of power between smaller and larger countries, the extension of majority voting, as well as 'flexibility' allowing countries to co-operate more closely without being held back by recalcitrant members. Mr John Bruton, the Irish prime minister, was only half exaggerating when he declared: 'Over the next six months we are going to need the sort of inspiration of those who framed the Declaration of Independence – a large sense of vision.'

France, in particular, has grumbled about the slow pace of the IGC, warning that failure to reform EU institutions will leave the Union incapable of taking in new members from central and eastern Europe, a view shared by almost all countries with the exception of the UK. Yet one EU official involved in the Maastricht II conference says Paris is still uncertain about how far and how fast to surrender national sovereignty in areas ranging from border controls, immigration, and asylum to the common foreign and security policy. 'The French cannot make up their mind. They are split in terms of personalities and parties.'

France's refusal to show its full hand in the IGC is one of the causes of the strains with Germany. One senior German official likened Mr Chirac to an 'eel' after last week's inconclusive Franco-German summit in Nuremberg which ended with a nine-page document which drew faint praise in Dublin. Yet Dublin did offer some clues as to the course of events in the next few months as the pressure for a deal on Maastricht II grows, if only to keep the talks separate from Emu and enlargement.

The first incident occurred on Friday afternoon, towards the climax of the stability-pact negotiations, when Mr Ruairi Quinn, the Irish finance minister, convened an informal group of ministers. Present were Mr Waigel, Mr Jurgen Stark, his deputy, Mr Arthuis, and the ministers of the next two presidencies: Mr Gerrit Zalm, the Dutch finance minister, and Mr Jean-Claude Juncker, prime minister and finance minister of Luxembourg. Mr Kenneth Clarke, the UK chancellor, was not on the privileged list but proceeded to invite himself. The fact that he was welcome is a tribute to his standing, but as one participant noted: 'It does not set a precedent for the future if Britain stays out of monetary union.'

The second development was the intervention of Mr Juncker whose skills in French, German and English, as well as his command of the Maastricht treaty, drew all-round praise. Mr Juncker's virtuoso performance looks like a declaration of intent on behalf of the smaller states that they are not going to be sidelined or steamrollered by the bigger countries. It is all the more significant as the next two EU presidencies fall to the Netherlands and Luxembourg. 'Juncker's intervention was strategic,' says an EU diplomat.

Mr Juncker happens to be a Christian Democrat protégé of Mr Kohl who remains as determined as ever to make monetary union the defining force in a united Europe in which Germany finds its secure place. According to one German diplomat, Mr Kohl spelt this out in stark terms to Mr Chirac on Friday. 'I could retire tomorrow. Everybody expects me to retire,' Mr Kohl is quoted as saying, 'but I am not going to retire. I'm staying on because I want to make sure the single currency goes ahead.'

First appeared 16 December 1996

***May 1997 Germany revalues its gold** – In storm-tossed waters: Helmut Kohl's determined pursuit of Emu has brought him into bitter conflict with the Bundesbank*

PETER NORMAN

It was a glittering occasion. The 65th-birthday celebrations last August for Mr Hans Tietmeyer, the Bundesbank president, saw Germany's political and financial elite converge on the nation's central bank in Frankfurt. Especially gratifying for Mr Tietmeyer was the speech of the guest of honour, Mr Helmut Kohl, Germany's chancellor. He departed from his prepared text to pledge that Bonn would allow 'no rotten compromises' on the road to European economic and monetary union.

Nearly nine months later, on 15 May 1997, Mr Theo Waigel, Germany's finance minister, is making a flying visit by helicopter to a meeting of the Bundesbank's central council in Frankfurt. His mission is to broach the idea of a change to the Bundesbank law to revalue Germany's 95 million ounces of gold reserves and use some of the DM40 billion (£23.5 billion) of extraordinary profits that would accrue to the bank to meet the Maastricht treaty criteria for Emu. If Mr Waigel can place the proceeds of the revaluation in an existing government 'redemption account for historic burdens' this year, he will be sure Germany has a public deficit below 3 per cent of gross domestic product. Total public debt will be close to the 60 per cent of GDP specified for countries joining the planned European single currency. The next day, in a packed Bundestag, Mr Kohl airily sweeps aside angry opposition complaints that the government is guilty of 'creative accounting' of the sort it has so often criticized in other EU nations.

These are three snapshots en route to a bust-up that has put the Bonn government and the Bundesbank on a collision course and spawned serious doubts about the single currency and the stability of German politics. The fury of this week's row between Bonn and Bundesbank over Mr Waigel's plan to revalue Germany's gold reserves this year to help Germany qualify for Emu is not without precedent. But the conflict is more than usually flammable because the two institutions ranged against each other – Mr Kohl and the Bundesbank – are desperate to secure their place in history. The row comes in a bad week for Emu. Opinion polls suggesting a win by the French left in the final round of the national assembly elections on Sunday have increased uncertainty surrounding France's ability to qualify for the single currency.

In Germany, a complaint to stop Emu has been lodged with the constitutional court and opinion polls continue to show two-thirds of the population opposing the single currency. Although the Bundesbank is not opposed to Emu, its accusation that the government's action would undermine the credibility and sustainability of the planned single currency has for the first time provided a respectable focus for those who want to keep the D-Mark. Until now Chancellor Kohl has been able to prey on people's fears of appearing unpatriotic or extremist should they refuse to support this drive for ever closer European integration.

The Bundesbank's charge that the government is threatening its independence has also turned the dispute into a highly political affair. The central bank is one of Germany's few revered institutions and the idea that its independence can guarantee monetary stability is strongly rooted. The danger facing Mr Kohl is that the scheduled loss of the D-Mark and the replacement of the Bundesbank by the European Central Bank from 1999 could trigger a powerful political backlash among an electorate already unnerved by high unemployment, shrinking welfare benefits and the widely perceived threat of higher taxes. If voters now have grounds to fear that the euro will be a soft, inflation-prone currency, the chances of Mr Kohl winning a fifth general election victory term in September next year could nosedive.

In these circumstances, it does not matter that the Bundesbank agrees with the government that the gold will have to be revalued at some point as part of the procedure of starting the euro-area from 1 January 1999. The finance ministry promises that only about half of the expected DM40bn gain from the gold revaluation will be channelled to Bonn are falling on deaf ears. The Bundesbank has won the moral high ground with its rejection of the government plan. The few daily newspapers that appeared yesterday – a public holiday in much of Germany – were unanimous in their condemnation of Bonn and fully supportive of the central bank.

To a large extent the government has itself to blame for the mess. It emerged this week that Mr Tietmeyer had warned against a gold revaluation at a closed meeting of the Bundestag budget committee on 19 March, arguing that it could cast doubt on the credibility and solidity of financial policy and generate turbulence on financial markets. On 17 April Mr Tietmeyer aired some of his concerns in public, telling a press conference that gold revaluation was a matter for the governing council of the European Central Bank after it was appointed next year. That Mr Waigel forged ahead with his plans shows how achieving Emu has become Mr Kohl's paramount objective. This was also apparent at a meeting of the Christian Democrat and Bavarian Christian Social MPs of Mr Kohl's coalition immediately after the minister's mid-May dash to Frankfurt. Although Mr Waigel reported unanimous support for his plans, participants later spoke of a tense meeting in which few details were provided, questions were discouraged and the discussion ended without a formal vote. Yet it is these MPs, with colleagues from the small Free Democrat party, who will determine whether the government can revalue the gold and bring the proceeds to Bonn.

Mr Kohl has a Bundestag majority of only ten votes. If his troops stay true to form, they will loyally pass the changes to the Bundesbank law. The fact that Wednesday's government statement rebutting the Bundesbank's objections was issued by Mr Kohl, the other coalition party chairmen and the leaders of the parties in parliament, suggests that the pressure to support the move will be huge.

But German politics has moved into a new and uncertain phase in which old loyalties may buckle. Even if Mr Kohl pushes a new Bundesbank law through the Bundestag and secures the proceeds of the gold – and with that the future of Emu – the events of this extraordinary week may still be felt in sixteen months in the German general election.

First appeared 30 May 1997

Emu's broody hen – *The German chancellor whose dogged pursuit of European integration has led to the birth of the euro*

PETER NORMAN

It should be Helmut Kohl's day of triumph, a second peak in a political career that has already united Germany. The German chancellor will be the only European Union leader to have held power continually from the conception to birth of economic and monetary union. Without his dogged pursuit of European integration it is difficult – perhaps impossible – to imagine that today's gathering of EU leaders could have launched the single European currency. This is a project that Mr Kohl told Germany's parliament in April 1998 was the most important decision for Germans and Europeans since the unification of Germany. A decision indeed that was one of the most important of the entire century.

But, as is often the case in matters European, the party could be spoiled by a family spat: the bitter squabble between France and the rest, including Germany, over the presidency of the European Central Bank. And in a strange way, that is fitting. For a combination of high ideals and raw power politics has been the story of Mr Kohl's involvement with Emu since it reappeared on the agenda more than ten years ago.

Mr Kohl is not the father of the euro. That honour must go to the late François Mitterrand of France. He revived the idea in 1987 from the limbo into which it had fallen after an earlier attempt failed in the 1970s. Documentary evidence and an account of the period by Gerhard Stoltenberg, the German finance minister in the 1980s, indicates that Mr Kohl was in no hurry to press ahead with Emu before the collapse of communism and the fall of the Berlin Wall.

According to Mr Stoltenberg, it was in December 1989, a month after the fall of the Berlin Wall, that Mr Kohl bowed to President Mitterrand's demands for speedier progress to Emu as the price for French backing of German unification.

In all this, Mitterrand's motives were hardly in Germany's best interest. He wanted a single currency as a way of controlling the Bundesbank's power over monetary policy in Europe after crisis devaluations of the French franc in 1986 and early 1987.

But since the launch of the project, at the June 1988 European summit in Hanover, Mr Kohl has pursued Emu with increasing conviction and determination. Undeterred by a wary Bundesbank, unflustered by a cool or hostile German public reaction, and unconcerned by a sceptical Britain, Mr Kohl has cajoled and bullied successive European summits and countless European governments. And all this to bring to fruition a project that will mean the end of Germany's most potent post-war symbol – the D-Mark. Why? Euro-idealism is undoubtedly part of the explanation. Now sixty-eight, Mr Kohl belongs to a dwindling band of European politicians to have known at first hand the horrors of the second world war. The death in army service of his elder brother in 1944 and his own march, during his teens at the end of the war, from the Bavarian Alps to his destroyed home town of Ludwigshafen near the French border, left an indelible impression. These youthful experiences turned him into a passionate supporter of Franco-German reconciliation and European integration. The creation of a euro area with an economic power that may come to rival the US owes much to the attitudes and ideals that fired Mr Kohl, as a young man, to demonstrate and tear down frontier barriers between Germany and France.

His early career reinforced his European ideals. As a rising politician in the West German Christian Democratic Union, he cosied up to Konrad Adenauer, the federal republic's first chancellor. It was under Adenauer that Germany embarked on the process of European integration as a founder member of the European Coal and Steel Community in 1951 and the European Economic Community in 1957.

But why Emu? Mr Kohl is no policy obsessive. His lack of interest in (and knowledge of) economics is manifest when he refers to statistics in a speech. His real interest has been political union in the EU – which he hoped originally would develop in parallel to Emu.

In the face of a Europe-wide public backlash, he has dropped that idea, or at least the rhetoric of it. The words United States of Europe no longer appear in his speeches. Instead, he has concentrated on incorporating Germanic views on economic stability into Emu. By dint of tough negotiation, Germany has been able to equip the project with Teutonic safeguards, such as a central bank with greater independence than the Bundesbank and a stability pact limiting budget deficits among member states. As other countries have come to see advantages in Emu, Europe has developed a sufficiently strong stability culture for the German Bundestag, the lower house of parliament, to accept Emu with eleven members last month by a massive majority.

After the struggles of Emu's ten-year gestation, Mr Kohl sounds lyrical about the euro and European union. It is a stroke of good fortune, he said before last month's crucial vote. Without European integration, it would have been impossible to have eradicated war in western Europe during the past fifty years or unify Germany, he declares.

When the weekend is over, Mr Kohl will be back in Germany fighting for his political life. Although a doughty campaigner who should never be written off, his chances of winning a fifth term of power in Germany's September general election look poor. Last weekend, at the state election in Saxony Anhalt, support for Mr Kohl's party plunged from 34.4 per cent to just 22 per cent. In nationwide opinion polls, the opposition Social Democrats lead by about 15 percentage points.

Yet, whatever the outcome of the national poll, Mr Kohl's contribution to European history will live on. The Emu, which will be hatched in Brussels today, is a progeny of compromise and improvisation. But if the other, younger EU leaders present show half Helmut Kohl's ingenuity and determination in support of the project, it will surely fly.

First appeared 2 May 1998

ECB presidency débâcle – *Single currency, multiple injuries: the race for the ECB presidency and the price of Chirac's insistence on a Frenchman*

LIONEL BARBER

On the evening of 3 November last year Jean-Claude Juncker, the youthful prime minister of Luxembourg, received an urgent telephone call from President Jacques Chirac of France. A European Union summit on employment was barely a fortnight away. Juncker, who would chair the meeting as holder of the rotating EU presidency, assumed that the call was related. He could not have been more wrong. Chirac announced that he was about to nominate Jean-Claude Trichet, governor of the Bank of France, as president of the future European Central Bank. The ECB was to be based in Frankfurt, Germany. It was 'normal' that the top job should go to a Frenchman.

Juncker was stunned. He had assumed the post of ECB president – the most powerful unelected job in the European economic and monetary union – would go to Wim Duisenberg, the Dutch central banker who enjoyed the support of fourteen EU governments. Juncker asked whether Chirac had informed Chancellor Helmut Kohl of Germany or Wim Kok, the Dutch prime minister. No, came the reply. Juncker requested that the Elysée contact Kok, who was travelling in New Zealand. He would deal with the Germans. The Luxembourgers were left open-mouthed by the French *démarche*, but the Dutch were outraged. Kok, woken up early in the morning on the other side of the world, took the call from Paris calmly but exploded in his next conversation with The Hague.

Duisenberg was equally amazed. He had just presided over an informal meeting of EU central bank governors in Frankfurt at which Trichet had been present. Not a word had been said. The next morning he received Trichet in his office. Why did you do this? he asked. Trichet explained that this was the way the French worked. When the president of France asks a civil servant to do something, there is no choice but to obey. So that is as far as the independence of the central bank goes, Duisenberg replied.

Coup d'état

Six months later, at the end of a momentous weekend summit in Brussels, the battle over the appointment of the first ECB president has ended in an uneasy compromise. Duisenberg has agreed 'voluntarily' to step down halfway through his eight-year term. The French have won a political commitment that Trichet will be his successor. Set against the genuinely historic decision to proceed with Emu, the battle over the ECB appointment looks a minor affair. But the story offers a rare insight into the manner in which Europe's leaders conduct business. It also reveals the tensions between elected politicians and unelected central bankers whose power has expanded exponentially in a world of monetary orthodoxy and liberalized capital. It is also a story about the decline of Helmut Kohl, Europe's premier statesman and one of the architects of Emu, and his uneasy relationship with Jacques Chirac, an unpredictable, impulsive character who has confounded allies at home and abroad with high-risk gambles which have never quite paid off.

The origins of the ECB row do not, however, lie in French or German politics. They go back to the spring of 1993 when EU leaders were casting around for a suitable candidate to head the European monetary institute (Emi), the body in Frankfurt charged with managing the transition to the single currency.

Most EU central bankers favoured Duisenberg. But he turned down the approach. A bon viveur with a weakness for strong cigarettes, he was comfortable as governor of the Dutch central bank. Colleagues suspected there was another reason: he shared their doubts about whether Emu would ever get off the ground. EU leaders were dismayed. The Maastricht treaty stipulated that the Emi had to start operations on 1 January 1994. In desperation, they turned to Alexandre Lamfalussy, the professorial former president of the Bank of International Settlements in Basle; but he, too, turned down the job. Lamfalussy said he was almost sixty-five, young enough to take on a three-year term at the Emi but too old to move on to the job of president of the ECB – a job which, he confessed, he would have killed for had he been a few years younger. However, the Belgian government eventually broke Lamfalussy's resistance. As holder of the rotating EU presidency, it needed to settle the Emi job and settle a long-running debate about where to locate the future ECB and a dozen other EU agencies.

The final deal was struck in October. At German insistence, the bank went to Frankfurt. Lamfalussy accepted the Emi job, but on two conditions: first, that he could leave early if things did not work out; and, second, that he would make no commitment to seek another three-year term. Lamfalussy feared that a delay in Emu beyond the target launch date of 1 January 1999 would leave him stuck at the Emi. But if Emu went ahead on schedule but EU leaders could not agree on an ECB president, he could find himself press-ganged into serving the full eight-year term mandated by the Maastricht treaty. Hence his insistence on a firm date for retirement to focus minds on a successor who would be well-placed to take over when the Emi metamorphosed into the ECB on 1 July 1998.

The idea of building a bridge between the Emi and ECB jobs was logical. The transition to the irrevocable fixing of exchange rates among Emu qualifiers on 1 January 1999 was a period of maximum uncertainty in the financial markets. The post of Emi/ECB president would be a point of continuity. Yet the economic logic of a seamless changeover was politically tricky. The Maastricht treaty stipulated that central bankers had the power to recommend a nominee for Emi president which EU heads of government would approve by unanimity. The ECB job was also subject to the same unanimity but, crucially, the right to recommend a nominee lay with EU finance ministers. In early 1996, Lamfalussy reminded his colleagues that he intended to leave by the end of the year.

He had several conversations with Hans Tietmeyer, president of the Bundesbank, who urged him to stay on. However, in late April, he received a call from Duisenberg who said he was ready to take the job. Tietmeyer had exerted pressure on him to take the job.

Duisenberg said he had to consult the Dutch central bank and his wife. In Washington, in the margins of the IMF–World Bank meeting, Tietmeyer had one question: 'Have you asked your wife?' At last, Duisenberg gave a clear commitment, albeit with two conditions. First, he did not want to move to Frankfurt until 1 July 1997 – six months later than scheduled. The Netherlands was due to take over the rotating EU presidency on 1 January 1997 and Duisenberg said he did not want to leave during this period – not least because the Amsterdam summit was due to be held in the Dutch central bank.

The second condition was even more important: Duisenberg wanted a reasonable assurance that he would move from the Emi to the ECB. His central bank colleagues agreed unanimously, and proceeded to sound out their national governments within an agreed ten-day deadline. All but two of the fifteen governments gave a positive response: France and Italy. The latter failure was understandable because the government of Lamberto Dini had fallen; but the silence from France was ominous. Trichet blamed his own poor relations with Chirac and the Gaullist-led government. Neither was enamoured with his tight monetary policy. As a sign of support, Trichet wrote a personal note of support for Duisenberg which the Dutchman later deposited in his personal safe.

On Monday 13 May, EU central bank governors blessed the deal. Lamfalussy agreed to stay on for another six months. Duisenberg was unanimously approved by his colleagues and the announcement came the next day. Jacques Santer, president of the European Commission, would later describe the attempt to engineer the ECB succession as a central bankers' '*coup d'état*'. There were grumbles at a meeting of EU finance ministers on the following Monday. But the man most outraged was Jacques Chirac.

Enter Monsieur Trichet

Chirac heard the official confirmation of the Duisenberg appointment on 14 May when he was attending an Anglo-French summit in London with John Major, the UK prime minister. Yves-Thibault de Silguy, EU monetary affairs commissioner, tracked down a top Chirac adviser in London: his advice was to torpedo Duisenberg on the grounds that it was a transparent attempt to engineer the ECB succession. But he was advised that central bankers were in line with the treaty. An internal Elysée memorandum drew up two options: either to veto Duisenberg or to accept with reservations, signalling that the Emi appointment in no way prejudiced the decision on the ECB presidency.

Chirac raised his concerns at the Dublin summit in December 1996. But the meeting was dominated by a titanic clash between the French and the Germans over the terms of the stability pact for enforcing budgetary discipline in the future euro zone, if necessary through draconian sanctions. Kohl and Chirac, their faces almost touching, tore into each other. After seventeen hours of negotiations, the stability pact was renamed the stability and growth pact to take account of French demands that more attention should be paid to job creation. When Chirac slipped in his reservations about the ECB succession, few took the gesture at face value.

Shortly afterwards, Chirac confided to de Silguy that he had a French candidate for the ECB job: Michel Camdessus, the managing director of the International Monetary Fund. Chirac dropped several hints about the ECB job but never explicitly asked Camdessus to leave Washington. When rumours appeared in the press, Camdessus, who had just been appointed to a third term at the IMF, made clear he preferred the world stage to Europe. The Asian financial crisis, which erupted last summer, killed off any lingering hopes of persuading Camdessus to move.

So Mr Chirac was left with two choices: Jacques de Larosière, the former head of the Bank of France and the IMF and soon to retire as head of the European Bank for Reconstruction and Development; and Jean-Claude Trichet. Neither was ideal.

De Larosière was nearing seventy and a well-deserved retirement. Trichet had impeccable credentials as a central banker; but his attachment to hard money and high interest rates had made him unpopular with both the left and right in Paris.

Chirac was searching for a means of reasserting his authority at home. In the spring he had gambled on early parliamentary elections, only to see his Gaullist–UDF government crushed by a Rainbow coalition led by the Socialists. What better ruse than to put Trichet up for the top ECB job, wrapped in the tricolour, and force Lionel Jospin, the new prime minister, to go along? When Jospin hesitated, Chirac warned him that he risked undermining the interests of France – a remark which some aides to the prime minister took as a threat to leak the matter to the press. So Jospin went along reluctantly, though he would later exact his revenge.

Dominique Strauss-Kahn, the powerful economics and finance minister, was even more dismayed. He knew the Germans would be infuriated by the Trichet nomination. He was more interested in winning Bonn's support for strengthening the euro-X club – the informal grouping of euro-zone finance ministers – as a political counterweight to the ECB. But Chirac prevailed. In mid-October Trichet was summoned secretly to the Elysée to see the president and to the Matignon to see Jospin. He accepted the nomination without reservation.

Denouement

Chirac announced his *démarche* on 4 November, the day before Kohl was due in Paris. French officials say Kohl was forewarned at the regular Franco-German summit in Alsace-Lorraine a fortnight before. German officials are less clear, though it seems that Kohl did not try to dissuade Chirac from plunging ahead. At the Luxembourg summit on employment, the chancellor expressed regret that the ECB presidency had turned into a matter of prestige and called for a wise compromise.

Enter Jean-Claude Juncker and the Luxembourg presidency of the EU. In Dublin, twelve months before, Juncker had played an invaluable role as mediator between Kohl and Chirac on the stability pact. He intended to try for a repeat performance. But he was diverted by two other EU rows: Turkey's bid for membership of the EU and Britain's demands for access to the euro-X club. At the Luxembourg summit, Tony Blair, the British prime minister, spent six hours wrangling with the French over euro-X. Tempers frayed. Chirac's officials bad-mouthed Blair as a Labour version of Margaret Thatcher. Juncker, who had hoped to produce a compromise involving early retirement for Duisenberg, kept the deal in his pocket.

Early in the New Year, at the instigation of Kohl, Juncker made a fresh effort to break the deadlock. One option was to introduce a mandatory age for retirement of the ECB president such as sixty-seven, mirroring similar rules at the Bundesbank. Another idea was to obtain an assurance from Duisenberg that he would leave halfway through his term to make way for Trichet. Chirac dug in. He knew Duisenberg's birthday by heart: 9 June 1935. A message came from Paris: surely the most elegant solution would be for him to retire on 9 June 2000, his 65th birthday.

Duisenberg grew frustrated. He had nothing against the French. He spoke the language and had a house in Provence. He had even been awarded the *Légion d'Honneur*, in recognition of his role in supporting the French franc during the wave of currency speculation in 1992–3. But he was also a proud man: he was not prepared to go on bended knee to the Elysée to win Chirac round. He saw that as an affront to his professional integrity and the independence of the future European Central Bank. He was also baffled by reports from Paris that Chirac's opposition was not personal but was largely linked to the French president's distaste for the Netherlands' soft drugs laws.

The battle over the ECB was to become a war of nerves between the French, Dutch and Germans. At this point, the British, who held the rotating EU presidency, began to become worried. On 1–3 May, the EU was due to select the founder members of Emu, the most important development in Europe since the fall of the Berlin wall. Failure to agree on the ECB presidency risked turning the Brussels summit into a fiasco which could unsettle the financial markets. Blair inquired whether Britain could act as honest broker, but was told politely that this was a matter between the Dutch, French and Germans. All would be sorted out.

The Brussels summit

Early on Saturday afternoon, 2 May, Blair formally convened the Brussels summit to decide the founder members of monetary union and the ECB presidency. But instead of starting with a lunch for all EU leaders, he broke off and convened a meeting between Chirac, Jospin, Kohl and Kok. British officials explained that Blair – with one eye on the recent breakthrough in the Northern Ireland peace talks – calculated that it would be impossible to settle differences with fifteen heads of government round one table.

Soon the differences between the Dutch, French and Germans emerged. Chirac was adamant that Duisenberg should be out of the ECB by 1 January 2002. Kok held firm. Kohl was uneasy. Blair telephoned Duisenberg. The Dutchman repeated earlier private assurances that he would step down early but at a time of his own choosing.

As the meeting dragged on, other EU leaders began to feel left out. Juncker made a couple of acid remarks. Jean-Luc Dehaene, the Belgian prime minister, threatened to convene a separate lunch in central Brussels. By late afternoon, Kohl, Kok and Chirac appeared to be coming round to June 2002, the final date for the switch-over from national currencies to euro notes and coins. Blair checked with Duisenberg who said he was happy, subject to a text. Kohl appealed for a reasonable solution.

Then something went wrong. Duisenberg, who had reportedly had contacts with Tietmeyer, stiffened his opposition to a precise date. Gerrit Zalm, the Dutch finance minister, also urged Kok not to accept a date. He was worried about how a fudge would appear in the Dutch general election on 6 May. But the most surprising shift came within the German delegation which included Kohl, Klaus Kinkel, foreign minister, Theo Waigel, finance minister, and Tietmeyer. 'Kohl was turned over,' says one insider. German disarray emerged during a one-hour meeting with the Dutch delegation. By the time Blair spoke again to Duisenberg in person, French demands for a firm departure date had run into a dyke of resistance.

Pressure on Chirac to strike a deal was mounting. Jospin had left for

New Caledonia, in effect daring Chirac to veto Duisenberg and provoke a Dutch veto of Trichet which would have wrecked the summit. Blair warned Chirac that the search for a third candidate would create uncertainty. Finally, Blair came up with a formula which EU lawyers had devised some time before: Duisenberg would make a personal, voluntary statement that he would take early retirement. He would read out the statement to EU leaders in the summit conference room.

It was a memorable moment – nothing as dramatic as the birth of the euro but a reminder that the new central bank would be accountable to the politicians. Chirac had made his point – and he had secured a commitment that the next ECB president would be French. Yet Chirac had pressed the French cause with scant attention to the re-election interests of a hard-pressed Helmut Kohl, nominally his closest ally and the man who has made a career of subjugating German national interests in the name of Europe. It was a high price.

First appeared 5 May 1998

3 The macroeconomics of Emu

The launch of the euro is a landmark in Europe's search for currency stability, a nominally irreversible step which advocates hope will help to preserve Europe's economic standing alongside the US, Japan and China in the twenty-first century.

Whether Emu succeeds or fails depends ultimately on whether countries inside the euro zone can sustain the macroeconomic policies which they have pursued, with some success, in the run-up to the launch of the euro. This chapter offers a closer look at the current state of 'convergence' and future prospects once Emu gets under way.

As Peter Martin explains, Emu changes everything. The introduction of a single currency alongside the single market will force business and consumers to think more in terms of a market on the scale of the US. The elimination of exchange rates offers advantages; but it will also deliver a competitive shock to the European economy, exposing rigidities and forcing weaker businesses to the wall.

The European Central Bank will have a crucial role to play. Wolfgang Münchau, the *FT*'s ECB watcher in Frankfurt, offers an inside guide to the new institution in 'Teething troubles in store'. As a separate series of articles on monetary policy under Emu shows, there are no easy answers when it comes to devising suitable targets for the eleven members of the euro zone. How much weight to the orthodox monetary targeting favoured by the Bundesbank? How much attention to inflation targeting favoured by the Bank of England? In practice, says Wolfgang Münchau, there may have to be a subtle combination of the two.

The relationship between the ECB and EU finance ministers meeting in the Ecofin council (and the new French-inspired euro-11 forum for euro-zone members) will also be decisive in the formulation of macroeconomic policy. If the ECB feels that member states are retreating from their commitment to medium-term budget balance, it might be tempted to tighten monetary policy prematurely. Equally, some finance ministers are unlikely to welcome an excessively cautious monetary policy at the expense of economic growth and jobs.

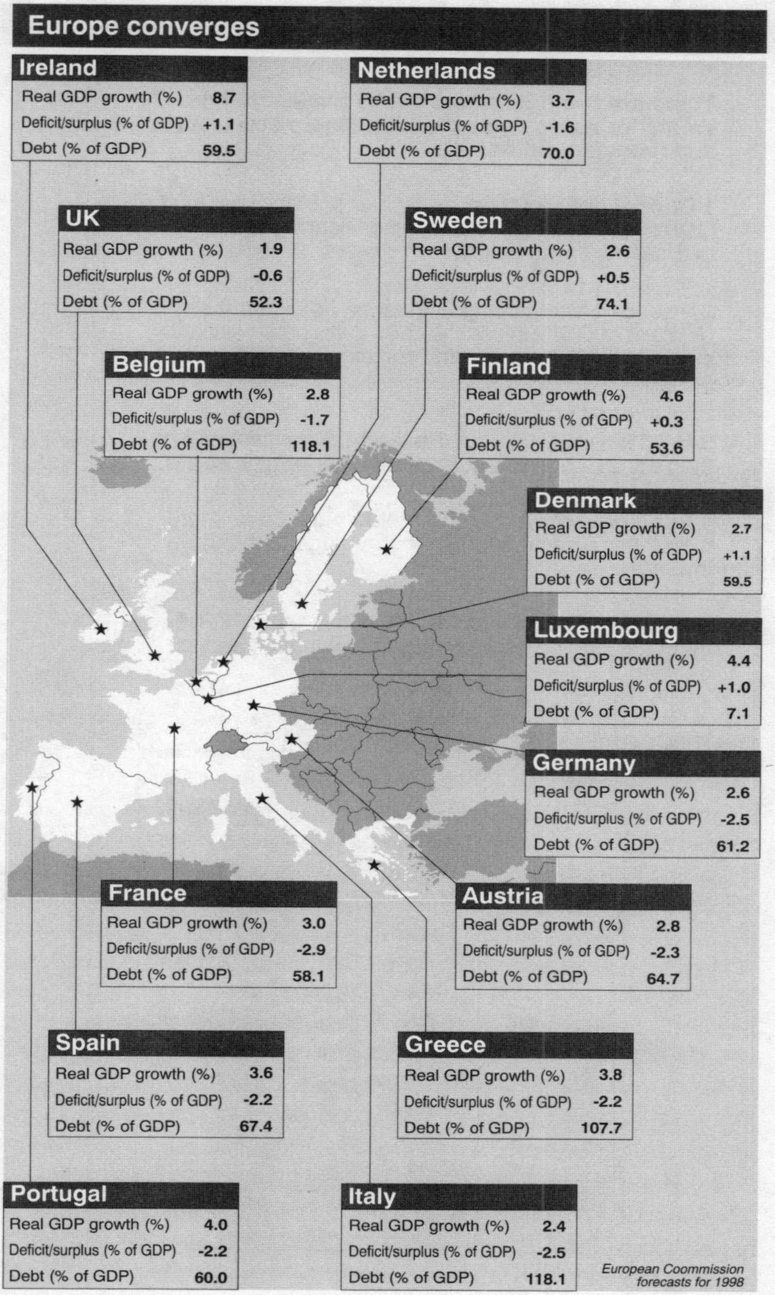

Europe converges

Ireland

Real GDP growth (%)	8.7
Deficit/surplus (% of GDP)	+1.1
Debt (% of GDP)	59.5

Netherlands

Real GDP growth (%)	3.7
Deficit/surplus (% of GDP)	-1.6
Debt (% of GDP)	70.0

UK

Real GDP growth (%)	1.9
Deficit/surplus (% of GDP)	-0.6
Debt (% of GDP)	52.3

Sweden

Real GDP growth (%)	2.6
Deficit/surplus (% of GDP)	+0.5
Debt (% of GDP)	74.1

Belgium

Real GDP growth (%)	2.8
Deficit/surplus (% of GDP)	-1.7
Debt (% of GDP)	118.1

Finland

Real GDP growth (%)	4.6
Deficit/surplus (% of GDP)	+0.3
Debt (% of GDP)	53.6

Denmark

Real GDP growth (%)	2.7
Deficit/surplus (% of GDP)	+1.1
Debt (% of GDP)	59.5

Luxembourg

Real GDP growth (%)	4.4
Deficit/surplus (% of GDP)	+1.0
Debt (% of GDP)	7.1

Germany

Real GDP growth (%)	2.6
Deficit/surplus (% of GDP)	-2.5
Debt (% of GDP)	61.2

France

Real GDP growth (%)	3.0
Deficit/surplus (% of GDP)	-2.9
Debt (% of GDP)	58.1

Austria

Real GDP growth (%)	2.8
Deficit/surplus (% of GDP)	-2.3
Debt (% of GDP)	64.7

Spain

Real GDP growth (%)	3.6
Deficit/surplus (% of GDP)	-2.2
Debt (% of GDP)	67.4

Greece

Real GDP growth (%)	3.8
Deficit/surplus (% of GDP)	-2.2
Debt (% of GDP)	107.7

Portugal

Real GDP growth (%)	4.0
Deficit/surplus (% of GDP)	-2.2
Debt (% of GDP)	60.0

Italy

Real GDP growth (%)	2.4
Deficit/surplus (% of GDP)	-2.5
Debt (% of GDP)	118.1

European Coommission forecasts for 1998

Hitting the targets

There are five criteria set out by the Maastricht Treaty for assessing suitability to join economic and monetary union:

1 Budget deficits must be no higher than 3 per cent of GDP unless the rate is falling significantly and is close to 3 per cent (see below).

2 Public debt outstanding must be no higher than 60 per cent of GDP unless the ratio is falling significantly and is approaching the limit sufficiently quickly (see below).

3 Inflation must be no more than 1.5 per cent higher than the average of the three best performing states.

4 Long government bond yields must be no more than 2 per cent higher than the average of the three lowest.

5 Exchange rates must be within the normal ERM band for two years before membership elegibility is decided.

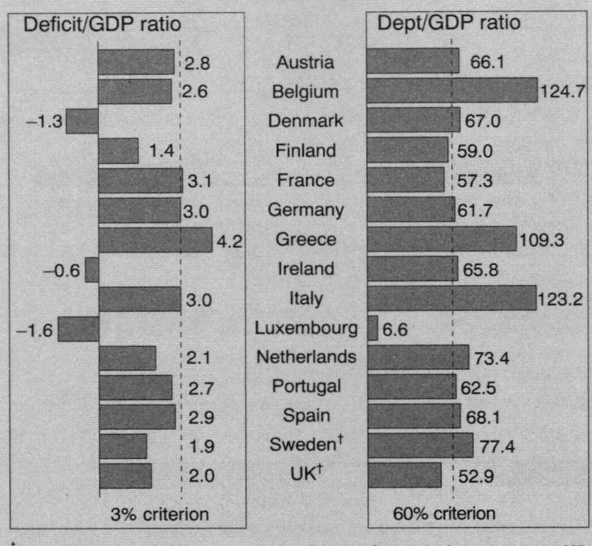

†Not current members of ERM

Source: European Commission forecasts, autumn 1997

Euro exchange-rate policy also features in the debate. Will the euro be a hard or soft currency vis à vis the dollar or yen? How big is the temptation to give European exporters a competitive advantage measured against a strong currency to tame inflation? Where does the balance of power lie between the ECB and finance ministers in the general orientation of exchange-rate policy?

The Maastricht treaty offers some answers, but as our writers explain, some of the trickier decisions will only become clear once the ECB and the single currency is up and running. Rudi Dornbusch, a professor at MIT, has few doubts about his preference in his personal column: 'In praise of hard money'.

For those who are occasionally confused by the myriad acronyms and committees which are involved in the formulation and execution of macroeconomic policy, this chapter offers a layman's guide to the various institutions. Look for 'Lines of Power in the Emu structure'.

LIONEL BARBER

A The overall economic implications of Emu

Predictions of widespread risk and reward: *Emu carries deep structural implications for Europe's economies*

WOLFGANG MÜNCHAU

There are not many historic parallels that measure up in significance to Emu. The most obvious is the German Zollverein in 1834, the customs union of German states that gave rise first to a fixed-exchange-rate system between the gulden, the southern German currency, and the thaler, the northern German currency, which merged into the mark in 1873. Historians still disagree over whether customs union and monetary union gave rise to political union, but the parallels to current-day Europe are evident.

Emu is without doubt the most important economic event in post-war European history, and it may turn out to have been the most important economic event in most of our lifetimes. At the same time, Emu is fraught with immeasurable risks, and could still turn out to be an economic disaster. This is precisely because it carries deep structural implications for Europe's economies, for Europe's companies and employees, and for competition in general.

Bilateral conversion rates for currencies of countries adopting the euro

	100 BFr/Lfr	100 French franc	100 D-Mark	1 Irish punt	100 Guilder	100 Escudo	100 Peseta	100 Shilling	100 Markka	1000 Lira
Belgium/Lux	-	614.977	2062.55	51.2210	1830.55	20.1214	24.2447	293.162	678.468	20.8338
France	16.2608	-	335.386	8.32893	297.661	3.27189	3.94237	47.6704	110.324	3.38773
Germany	4.84837	29.8164	-	2.48338	88.7517	0.975559	1.17547	14.2136	32.8947	1.0101
Ireland	1.95232	12.0063	40.2676	-	35.7382	0.392834	0.473335	5.72347	13.2459	0.406743
Netherlands	5.46285	33.5953	112.674	2.79812	-	1.09920	1.32445	16.0150	37.0637	1.13812
Portugal	496.984	3056.34	10250.5	254.56	9097.53	-	120.492	1456.97	3371.88	103.541
Spain	412.462	2536.54	8507.22	211.267	7550.3	82.9929	-	1209.18	2798.42	85.9313
Austria	34.1108	209.774	703.552	17.4719	624.415	6.86357	8.27006	-	231.431	7.10657
Finland	14.7391	90.6420	304.001	7.54951	269.806	2.96571	3.57345	43.2094	-	3.07071
Italy	4799.90	29518.3	99000.2	2458.56	87864.4	965.805	1163.72	14071.5	32565.8	-

Source: Bank of England

Contrary to widespread belief, Emu is not about lower transaction costs in cross-border operations, or about lower hedging costs, and all the other relatively petty reasons that have been invoked in its defence. Its introduction is likely to have a real economic impact, producing changes, some foreseeable, some less easily so. Some companies will go bust as a direct result of Emu. Others could find windfall gains. There will be employees who will lose their jobs as a result of Emu. There will be many winners and many losers, but their national, regional and sector distribution is impossible to forecast. This is where the political risks set in.

The pure macroeconomic effects of Emu, by contrast, are somewhat easier to assess, with the usual caveat that applies to all economic forecasting. The first prediction is that Emu will lead to a significant redistribution of wealth in the EU. This is not necessarily a redistribution from poor to rich or vice versa, but more likely a redistribution across the board. The single currency will hit many sectors of the economy unevenly. Many industrial companies have warned that they will consolidate the number of their EU-based factories. Surveys suggest that many companies will consolidate their banking relations – the result being a likely haemorrhage of small banks.

Big international companies hope to benefit strongly from the euro; mid-sized companies are more lukewarm, while many small companies fear that the euro will bring only cost, but no benefits and perhaps even danger. Some economists even suggest that governments could find Emu acting as a wealth tax on the black economy, which is after all a cash-based economy. Under Emu, black marketeers would at one point have to transfer their ill-gotten D-Marks – the currency of choice in the EU's black economy – into euros, thereby putting themselves at considerable risk. This could be a popular move, but given the size of the black economy in some parts of Europe, it could instead turn out to be a highly unpopular move.

Much of this enhanced competition and the ensuing redistribution of wealth and income should have come as a direct result of the single European market. But this did not happen because the residual exchange-rate risk left much of the single market's economic potential untapped. A single currency will make prices not just comparable across nations but also more transparent. It will mean a far greater degree of price arbitrage across the EU, for example on the part of mail-order companies, which can be relied upon to exploit price differentials with ruthless efficiency. The euro economy is likely to react to price signals far more efficiently than nationally based economies.

Independently of Emu, the single market is likely to grow in importance in any case, because several key sectors of the economy, such as telecommunications and energy, are currently in the process of privatization and deregulation across the EU.

This brings us to our second prediction: with margins, profits and prices coming under pressure, Emu will be highly anti-inflationary, possibly even deflationary. Another more familiar reason is the way one can reasonably expect the future European Central Bank (ECB) to conduct economic policy. As one of the most independent central banks in the world, the ECB may seek to establish credibility early on. Since successful monetary policy is not a precise science, but a mixture of economic analysis, judgement and a dose of good luck, the ECB will probably choose to err on the side of caution. This in turn implies that real interest rates will be high initially and may fall only in the long run. This assessment makes one crucial assumption, which may well turn out to be wrong: that the new central bank will act in the way in which the Bundesbank, its constitutional and institutional role model, acted in the past. Yet it is conceivable that the ECB may look for inspiration elsewhere, for example the Federal Reserve, probably the world's most successful central bank in the 1990s.

In an interview early in 1997, Mr Alexandre Lamfalussy, then the outgoing president of the European Monetary Institute (Emi), recalled that hardline monetarism is relatively young, having emerged only from what he referred to as a 'cultural revolution' in the 1970s. Few revolutions succeed, and even fewer last. But given the prevailing mindset among EU central bankers, one suspects that this particular revolution is not quite finished yet.

This brings us to our third prediction: Emu will probably have a positive effect on economic growth in the long run, but could have a negative effect on some economies in the short term. This outcome is probably the least certain of all. There will be increased competition, both from Emu directly and from the single market. The need for tight fiscal policy may accelerate reform of public finances – and already has done in several EU countries – and if this were to coincide with reforms of social security systems, it could in time take some pressure off the labour markets. The result could be a series of mutually reinforcing virtuous mechanisms.

The negative-growth implications in the short term would stem directly from an overtight monetary policy. This would be reinforced by a tight fiscal policy on the basis of the stability pacts, signed by EU leaders. If the combination of a tight fiscal and monetary stance were to lead to an overvalued exchange rate and a slump in exports, Emu could easily trigger an economic downturn. If the downturn became a recession early on, Emu itself would be at great political risk.

This leads us to the fourth and perhaps most depressing prediction: unemployment will remain significantly above levels considered necessary for price stability for some time to come. High EU unemployment is not only the result of malfunctioning labour markets but of malfunctioning social security systems, which are financed not through general taxation but through levies on the labour market directly.

Most EU countries have yet to take fundamental steps in reforming these systems, which constitute a significant tax on jobs. In Germany, indirect wage costs account for well over 40 per cent of total wage costs, the reason for Germany's top position in the international league tables of wage costs. Most experts agree that it makes no economic sense to place the entire welfare burden on the labour market at a time of record unemployment. But most European governments have failed to push through more than cosmetic reforms.

The final prediction about the macroeconomic effects of Emu is that the euro will become a large reserve currency to rival the dollar. The development is entirely benign, because it would make the international financial system – and the international financial institutions, such as the International Monetary Fund and the World Bank – less lopsided. Many central banks, especially in Asia, are expected to switch over some of their reserves into euros, to achieve a more balanced portfolio that is more in tune with their trade flows. Reserve currency status for the euro will have some consequences for monetary policy, and could lead to greater exchange-rate volatilities than would otherwise be the case – a potential problem for exporters.

Taken together, the economic consequences of the euro are likely to be more immense than any policy decision taken for decades. Yet the introduction of the euro was decided primarily on political grounds – to provide a further impetus for European integration, which supplanted the economic argument that a single market requires a single currency to be fully effective. This contradiction has plagued the preparation period significantly, and is posing a great dilemma for countries, such as the UK, Denmark and Sweden, which are sceptical about further political integration, and yet they fear that they may suffer economic disadvantage by staying outside the euro zone. But a currency is not just a medium of exchange, a store of value, and a unit of account as the textbooks suggest. It also forms part of a country's constitutional and political fabric.

Looking at the economy as a whole, the long-term consequences of Emu could turn out to be benign as long as the promised efficiency gains come about and as long as the sharp tools of monetary policy are used with restraint. But this depends to a great extent on the wisdom of the governing council of the independent ECB. If it lacks political sensitivity, the result could be very different.

First appeared 28 May 1997

A market on the scale of the US: *the euro will help to create an integrated European economy, operating – like the US – on a continental scale*

PETER MARTIN

The euro changes everything. Its introduction in January 1999 will be a watershed for European business, as the wave of pan-European bids and mergers confirms. Most of the discussion about the single currency has been conducted in national terms. Which countries will qualify? Which economies will gain or lose from a one-size-fits-all monetary policy? Which nations' politicians will have most influence on the board of the new European Central Bank? But to think of the single-currency project in those terms is to miss the point. The essence of the project is to erase the national boundaries that still govern most people's thinking. In many countries, the debate over the euro has focused on its suitability as a replacement national currency. A slightly more sophisticated level of discussion has seen the single currency as merely another variant of fixed exchange rates.

To the business people who must cope with its consequences, however, monetary union is something far more significant. It removes a crucial – arguably the most crucial – barrier to the creation of a fully integrated European economy, operating on a continental scale like the US. What are the reasons for the sweeping nature of this change? And what are the consequences for business?

The answers to the first question are not, at first, obvious. After all, there have been currency unions before – between Britain and Ireland, or Belgium and Luxembourg, or the Latin monetary union of the mid-nineteenth century. Few of these justify such portentous language. And though the Bretton Woods system, which governed international monetary relations for the quarter-century after the second world war, was not a currency union, it did impose fixed exchange rates on the whole of the developed world. So why should European business be transformed now by a reversion to such rates?

There are three reasons for seeing the euro as a watershed. First, the creation of the single currency will mark the climax of a sustained effort to create a genuinely single market in Europe, dating back at least to the

Treaty of Rome in 1957. A great deal of progress has been made, but the single market still awaits the final, symbolic step: the setting of all prices in a single currency. Overnight – in 2002 when euro notes and coins replace national denominations rather than in 1999 – prices in one country will be instantly comparable with those in its neighbour. Goods and services which have increasingly become homogeneous in packaging and content will now be subject to a common set of pricing disciplines.

Second, monetary policy in the euro region will be set with reference to economic conditions in the whole of the area. Though 'core Europe' – today's D-Mark bloc plus France – will strongly influence the decisions of the new central bank, monetary policy will still be less attuned to any country's domestic economic conditions than is currently the case. The nation will be even less relevant as a unit of economic activity. This, of course, is what opponents of the single currency, both economists and politicians, object to.

Third, the introduction of the new currency is taking place at a time when technology and globalization of markets are freeing companies from their historic national roots. Individual European governments have much less ability to force companies into line. Again, a national frame of reference becomes less relevant.

So what will the consequences be for business? Some will be practical, others more sweeping and distant. In the short term, companies will need to cope with the consequences of greater cross-border price transparency. They will almost certainly need to move towards a common European price-list, with some regional variation. This will be a big shift from the current pattern of separate national prices, influenced heavily by custom and much more lightly by the desire for euro-consistency. Similar nagging practical matters – already widely recognized – will arise over handling the new notes and coins, switching to euros for accounting, issuing new share certificates in euros and so on.

Though these issues will consume millions of hours of work, they are not the central ones. As the merger wave indicates, companies are already trying to scale themselves up to cope with a number of bigger, longer-term trends. The most obvious of these is that physically transportable products, especially ones where there is little difference in national tastes, will become commodities traded in Europe-wide markets by a relatively small number of companies operating on a continental scale.

Money is the most easily transportable product of all, transmissible at the touch of a switch. So it is not surprising that many cross-border mergers are taking place in financial services. When all banks and insurance companies are providing services in a single currency, the biggest remaining national barriers in this industry will have fallen. There will still be barriers of information, of course. Consumers will be ignorant about non-local suppliers of financial services. Banks will be ignorant about unfamiliar credit risks; insurers about local patterns of health and behaviour. And, despite the EU's single passport for financial firms, there will be local regulatory barriers to foreign firms. But it will be only a matter of time before all these obstacles fall away. In financial services, as in other highly transportable businesses, the winners will be those competitors that most rapidly – and most cost-effectively – develop trusted Europe-wide brands. These may not, of course, be European-owned.

A second big theme affecting companies is the impact of changes in the capital markets. In most European countries, interest rates will fall to historically low levels. They may also – though this is a more controversial point – be more stable, as they shift from following the vagaries of national economic cycles to tracking the larger and more diffuse European one. Certainly, a huge, liquid pan-European bond market will emerge, providing a cheaper, more plentiful source of long-term borrowing. This will change the competitive picture in capital-intensive businesses, and in those industries where mid-sized competitors have previously had limited access to long-term money. Similar changes may also make equity finance more widely available, as investors react to the absence of currency risk by diversifying their portfolios across national borders.

Across Europe, entrepreneurs will rush to use these new financial opportunities in order to assemble hasty, ambitious business empires. As is usually the case in eras of financial innovation, many of these 'first flush' empires will not survive in their initial form. But from their ashes a smaller number of well-run pan-European businesses will arise – companies that would not have come into being without the excesses of their founders. A third theme of the euro era has already been foreshadowed. Governments will lose influence, and the national frame of reference will become less useful. Companies will think increasingly of non-national target markets: regions, linguistic groups, demographic cohorts, cross-border pools of people with similar aspirations and tastes. As they do so, and as they become larger, pan-European entities, they will come to realize that individual national governments influence them in only a handful of ways – and each of these can be avoided. National governments set tax rates; they establish labour regulations; and they influence the framework for corporate governance.

Increasingly, however, companies have discretion in the extent to which they are subject to these influences. They can shift production abroad; they can move their tax burden round the world; and they can transfer their corporate entities to other stock exchanges and other legal jurisdictions. An integrated European economy will make it ever easier for companies to circumvent national European jurisdictions, undermining the power of governments further.

Paradoxically, companies' ability to escape will make governments keener to exact tribute from those that do not, or cannot, threaten to make use of their greater mobility. As the levers of monetary control slip out of governments' hands, and as the fiscal autonomy of euro member states becomes limited both by the 'stability pact' governing members' fiscal policy and by the limits of public tolerance for taxation, the battleground shifts. The 35-hour week promises in France and Italy are a reflection of this trend. In the long run, companies can escape them by moving operations abroad; in the short run, they reflect a lingering desire on the part of governments and voters to re-establish the national frameworks that are crumbling everywhere. Such developments indicate the severe political tests that the single currency will have to undergo in the early years of the next century. It may not survive. But if it does, European business people will have to adjust to a completely different environment.

The question of whether monetary union is a good thing for Germany or a bad thing for Britain will come to seem obsolete. Some companies in every country will prosper from its consequences; others will suffer. The members of each group will have more in common with fellow beneficiaries – or sufferers – across Europe's vanishing borders than they will with compatriots in the other camp. National identity will remain relevant in some areas – culture, law, education, infrastructure. In other areas of life, especially those that influence purchasing decisions, other identities will prevail: local, linguistic, group, or Europe-wide. For 21st-century European business, this second category will be the crucial one.

The introduction of Europe's single currency is only one of the forces which are bringing about this shift. But in years to come, we shall see it as the moment at which the balance tipped.

First appeared 16 October 1997

B Macroeconomics of Emu

Some Emu surprises: *the run-up to European economic and monetary union has been nearly the opposite to what many had expected*

SAMUEL BRITTAN

Instead of banging on about the Maastricht conditions and the stability pact, German financial officials would have done better to have remembered the verse from St Matthew which says: 'But many that are first shall be last: and the last shall be first.'

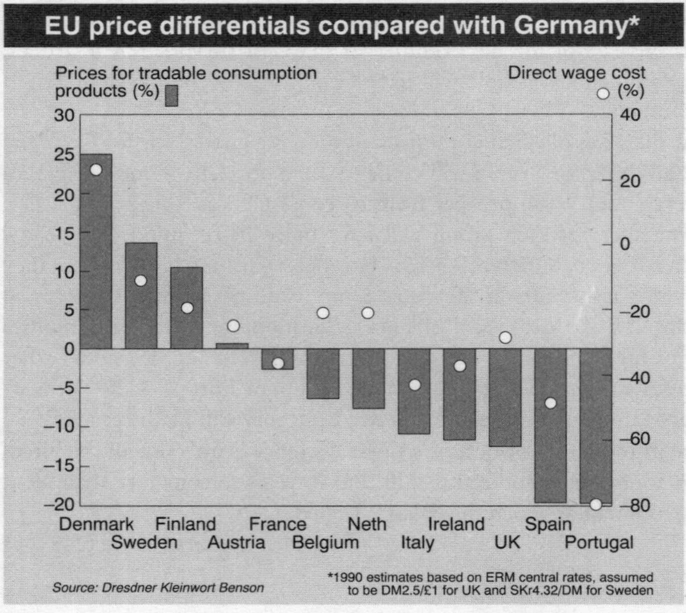

About a year ago German political and business opinion was strongly opposed to starting Emu with a wide membership. The preference was for beginning with a small northern nucleus consisting mainly of France, Germany, Austria and the Benelux countries. But once Theo Waigel, the German finance minister, announced his abortive plan to use foreign exchange profits of the Bundesbank cosmetically to reduce the German budget deficit, any possibility of keeping out the non-core countries vanished. Germany was no longer in a position to lecture on the use of clever accounting devices.

Emu is almost certain to start on time in 1999 on a wide basis, with eleven EU countries. Moreover, the problems caused by this membership are almost the opposite of what had been feared. Even the old formulation in terms of northern versus 'Mediterranean' countries has proved mistaken – unless Finland and Ireland are regarded as Mediterranean. The contrast is now between the hard central core and peripheral countries. Far from proving embarrassing laggards, the peripherals have been the best performers among the eleven. The most rapidly growing countries have been, in ascending order, Spain, the UK, Portugal, Finland and Ireland – with Ireland winning all the prizes. Unfortunately Italy now counts as a core country, doing slightly less well than Germany and France.

The rapid growth of the peripherals has been going on for several years and accompanied by an inflation performance either as good as, or better than, the EU average or even Germany. When it comes to price levels, as distinct from rates of change, the contrast is even greater. The chart on p. 106, which has been prepared by Julian Callow of Dresdner Kleinwort Benson, shows prices of tradable consumer products in EU countries, compared with those in Germany. (Goods heavily influenced by differential indirect taxes, such as drinks and tobacco, have been removed.)

The likely peripheral members, excluding Finland, have much lower prices than Germany or France. So prices and profit margins in France, Germany and surrounding countries should come under severe pressure. On the other hand, they should rise in Spain, Portugal, Ireland and perhaps Italy. This prospect should not be attributed to Emu alone. If the single market works as intended, prices in tradable products should converge (apart from transport costs). But a single currency will promote 'transparency' and thus hasten the process.

The main financial effect of prospective EU membership so far has been convergence of bond rates. Nominal short-term interest rates are still up to 1½ percentage points higher in the peripheral countries than in Germany. But the gap will have to narrow as the end of the year approaches. This convergence has been foreseen, perhaps instinctively, by international companies, which have directed much of their overseas investment towards the periphery.

Asian experience shows, however, that one can have too much of a good thing – even growth. If this continues at recent rates, some of these countries are liable to run into domestic overheating. The obvious case is Ireland, which cannot sustain recent growth rates of 7 to 10 per cent for year after year. The pressures are already showing up in asset price inflation, especially in the Dublin property market. Yet far from being able to raise interest rates in a pre-emptive move, the Irish central bank is having to prepare to reduce them as EU membership looms.

Thus some peripheral countries are liable to suffer from excess demand in the early years of Emu. Here indeed is the main economic reason advanced by officials in Britain – which can be regarded as a non-joining peripheral – for staying out of the first wave. Does this mean that such membership is a mistake for peripheral countries? Not necessarily.

A reason the east Asian crisis has been so severe has been the plunge in exchange rates, which has made all dollar-denominated debts almost impossible to service. Once Emu occurs, such an undershooting of exchange rates is by definition impossible. What is likely to happen is something more equivalent to a localized boom in a region of the US, for example a Californian land rush.

The basic question, quite reasonably raised by Eddie George, governor of the Bank of England, concerns not just the peripherals, but also whether unemployment levels in the core countries are an obstacle to successful monetary union. At first sight Germany and France seem pretty much in the same boat: a vessel in dire condition. The all-German unemployment rate is not much lower than the French one of 12½ per cent and it has been rising more rapidly. If, however, the eastern Länder are excluded, west Germany emerges with an unemployment rate 2½ percentage points less than France. How far this adds up to a case for a devaluation of the franc against the D-Mark I am far from sure. Recent events have strengthened the sceptics' case. The most important development has been not in recorded numbers, but rather in the advent to power of an old-fashioned socialist government in France. This is trying to fight unemployment by measures – such as reductions in working hours without adjustment in wages – that are bound to increase labour costs.

If France had a genuinely free-market government (which it did not have even before the 1997 parliamentary elections), there might be a case for a temporary downward float of the franc to ease the adjustment of labour costs. If the Jospin administration were to do a U-turn on Emu and devalue the franc, I could only see continuing devaluation and inflation for the country, which would throw away all the hard-won gains of the 1980s and 1990s. The present French government could not undertake a credible non-Emu policy.

There is scant prospect of tackling European structural unemployment by overall financial policy without tackling its roots in the labour market. It is customary to put the blame on lack of 'flexibility'. But what does this mean? In the words of one candidate for the presidency of the European Central Bank – and not the one whom you would think – the main problem is excessive labour costs. And these are all labour costs and not merely the non-wage ones arising from social security taxes, which it is fashionable to emphasize.

If labour costs can be made more responsive to market conditions, Emu will work. If labour market problems are left to fester, Emu will not work. But nor will anything else.

First appeared 5 February 1998

Emu's hard edges: *fears that the euro will lead to a boom–bust cycle in the 'peripheral' countries of the European Union, such as Spain and Italy, have been exaggerated*

RICCARDO BARBIERI

Over the past six months, the debate on the implications of 'peripheral' countries joining European economic and monetary union has changed dramatically. To begin with, the focus was on the risk that early membership in the euro zone of Italy, Spain and Portugal would force the Bundesbank, and later the European Central Bank, to push interest rates way above what would be appropriate for 'core' Europe (basically France and Germany). The upshot would be a deflationary bias to the whole euro zone. More recently, the debate has focused on the opposite risk: that euro-zone interest rates will be too low for the peripherals. According to this line of thought, excessively low interest rates would condemn Italy and, even more, Spain and Portugal, to severe overheating and a boom–bust economic cycle.

The overheating argument runs as follows: the ECB is likely to set monetary policy on the basis of the weighted average of inflation rates across Emu, not of their simple average. That is, in setting European interest rates, it will give full weight to the big economies, especially Germany and France. Given that the peripheral countries – including Italy and Ireland – account for just over a third of the euro-zone gross domestic product, a monetary policy strongly influenced by the low-inflation big countries would produce interest rate cuts to, perhaps, 4 per cent for the peripherals – too low to restrain inflation (Italian one-month rates are 5.8 per cent, Spain's 4.5 per cent). The peripherals would experience a strong pick-up in growth, and then a surge in inflation that would erode their competitiveness and lead to stagflation and rising unemployment. They would not be able to devalue within Emu, nor would they be able to significantly ease fiscal policy without incurring the sanctions of the stability pact. Hence they would be limited in their ability to do anything to stop unemployment short of leaving Emu altogether.

There is an element of truth in this argument. But it seems to me that the risk of overheating is moderate, and would be outweighed by the economic benefits of a broad Emu. There are four reasons for this view. First, while lower interest rates will undoubtedly boost growth, they will do so less than is usually thought. Moreover, the inflation fallout is also likely to be smaller. The reason is that, if exchange rates are fixed, low interest rates have a more modest – and different – macroeconomic impact than they do in small open economies with independent monetary policies. A fall in rates tends to stress investment growth rather than private consumption.

To see the effects, consider Italy. Simulations carried out by the Bank of Italy on its econometric model suggest that under Emu for each 100 basis-point decline in interest rates (for two years), real GDP rises by 0.31 per cent in the second year and 0.24 per cent in the third. Private consumption rises only modestly (0.12 per cent by the third year), while investment responds strongly (1.8 per cent). Inflation rises by only 0.09 per cent. If – outside the Emu – the exchange rate were allowed to respond to the change in interest rates, inflation would rise by 0.5 per cent – five times more than under a fixed exchange rate.

The small response of private consumption to lower interest rates is explained by Italian households having large holdings of financial and real assets, and little debt: at the end of 1996, their financial assets were equal to almost fifteen times their liabilities. Furthermore, Italians still hold most of their financial wealth in the form of short-term instruments and floating-rate notes. As a result, lower rates will cut income from such deposits, outweighing the positive 'wealth' effects caused by the drop in interest rates. This is not unique to Italy. Similar considerations apply to Spain, the other large Mediterranean economy.

Second, there are structural reasons for thinking the inflationary potential will be lowered: Emu is likely to bring about more competition and an increasing sense of economic insecurity. A single currency will make it easier for companies to move into other euro-zone markets. Industries so far protected from international competition (such as banking) will undergo massive restructuring which entails substantial job losses. And public confidence in public pension systems is likely to decline further. These factors suggest not only that a boom in private consumption is unlikely, but that retail margins may remain under pressure for a while.

Third, the overall stance of fiscal policy in the peripheral countries is likely to remain restrictive, hampering the possibility of a boom–bust cycle starting. The Emu dividend of lower interest rates will free up resources in government budgets (especially in Italy), but they will be largely used to replace the one-off revenue-raising measures implemented in 1997 and, to a lesser extent, 1998. As a result, it will probably take at least two years before a real easing of the fiscal stance is observed (as measured by cyclically-adjusted budget balances excluding the one-offs).

Fourth, increased emphasis is likely to be put on keeping wage growth in line with low official inflation targets via so-called 'incomes policies'. The expectation of wage moderation relies not only on the achievements of the past few years, but also on the fact that, if Emu goes ahead, Italian and Spanish companies will have to hold the line on wages much more firmly than has been the case in the past. The trade unions, on their part, will have to realize that excessive wage growth in a single market with a single currency moderation in wages and prices does not mean that a return to growth after years of stagnation will not entail some inflation in service and asset prices, notably property. However, the available indicators suggest that since 1992 property prices in Italy (and to a lesser extent Spain) have declined sharply in real terms. A recovery, to the extent that it does not turn into a bubble, would not signal a serious inflation problem. Overall, if interest rates drop further in the run-up to Emu and stay reasonably low afterwards, Spain and Portugal should have more years of economic expansion ahead, and Italy will return to healthy rates of economic growth after a decade of stagnation.

Stronger growth and wage moderation should make for greater company profitability, especially in the non-traded sector. Core Europe should also benefit from the easing in monetary conditions and the return to growth in the so-called periphery, as the latter is currently its largest export market. As a result, overall euro-zone economic growth and stock market performance should improve. A broad Emu may not be immune from risks, but it increasingly looks like Europe's best chance to return to healthier economic growth.

First appeared 19 March 1998

Leader: fiscal policy under Emu

Many critics of the European Union's economic and monetary union consider fiscal policy to be its Achilles' heel. Some argue that combining a centralized monetary policy with a decentralized fiscal policy is simply unworkable. That is wrong. But the task will be tricky.

There are three chief areas of debate: first, whether bigger internal transfers will be needed to deal with country-specific shocks; second, whether the Emu zone can generate a sensible overall fiscal stance; and third, how far controls on the fiscal policies of member states can eliminate the interest-rate costs induced by the fear of public-sector bankruptcies.

The EU is not the US. For many, this means the single currency cannot work, because of the absence of the automatic transfers generated by the US federal budget. This argument is false: the EU's differences offer advantages, as well as disadvantages. The EU does lack internal labour mobility and federal taxation. For these reasons, however, member states will be able to sustain high taxes on labour income.

Within Emu, the ideal response to an adverse country-specific shock is for the affected country to run a larger fiscal deficit. Provided underlying fiscal positions are strong, member states can do so. They will be able to achieve this, under the stability and growth pact which limits fiscal deficit to 3 per cent of gross domestic product, as long as they run balanced budgets over the cycle.

This sensible answer to the concern about country-specific shocks raises a second worry: if member states balance their budgets over the cycle, they will automatically determine the overall fiscal stance of the Emu zone. Sometimes, however, that outcome will be unfortunate. Monetary policy may, for example, be unable to offset an EU-wide fiscal policy that proves too contractionary. Alternatively, economic activity may be sustained by a weak exchange rate and a destabilizingly large current account surplus. Either way, aggregate fiscal policy may need to be changed. The question then is whether needed agreement can be achieved.

Finally, the principal focus of fiscal discipline has been on deficits, rather than the debt. Yet if a country with negligible public debt were to run sizeable deficits for a few years, little problem would be created. A large problem might be created, however, by a modest increase in the deficit of the country with a big debt overhang.

If there were also doubt about the ability of other member states, or the European Central Bank, not to rescue the profligate state, Emu-wide interest rates would rise. Moreover, the need for a credibly tight constraint on borrowing by countries with large debts will be still more important if Italy does join in the first wave. It is far from clear, however, whether the available constraints are tough enough.

The combination of a decentralized, but rule-governed, fiscal policy with a centralized monetary policy should work, most of the time. But for Emu to work all the time, there will need to be just the right combination of flexibility, discipline and co-operation – for ever.

First appeared 6 February 1998

Economic and monetary turmoil: *as Emu is launched, Europe will become more prone to the sort of financial disturbances that have rocked east Asia*

PAUL DE GRAUWE

Can a financial crisis similar to the one in Asia erupt in Europe? At first glance, the answer appears to be 'no'. Such disturbing financial upheavals occur in 'emerging' markets, not in the bastions of stability found in Europe. The conditions that led to the financial crisis in Asia are just not present there. But the question should not be brushed aside too lightly. From Asia's financial débâcle we have learned the following about the conditions that can lead to financial instability. First, when capital markets are liberalized, they create the potential for vast international movements of financial assets. Second, when countries keep their exchange rates pegged, they create the perception that there is little risk involved in moving funds from one market to the other. Third, problems can occur when the monetary regime (including the system of regulatory control) is not adapted to the new regime of liberal capital markets.

These three factors were present in Asia and also in Latin America during the 1970s and 1980s. Of course, they do not always lead to disaster. There are examples of countries that have avoided financial disturbances even though they went through the same liberalization process. Nevertheless it is fair to conclude that these three factors substantially increase the probability of problems.

And Europe? The conditions for financial turmoil might emerge with the introduction of economic and monetary union. Emu will dramatically increase the degree of capital mobility within the euro area. Today European capital markets are still relatively closed. Financial institutions and insurance companies in Germany, France and Italy hold an overwhelming share of their total portfolio (often more than 90 per cent) in domestic assets. The complete elimination of foreign exchange risk following the introduction of the euro and the disappearance of regulatory constraints on the holdings of 'foreign' euro assets will change all that. Financial institutions will sharply increase their holdings of euro assets. The result will be to open up financial markets in Europe in a more profound way than in the 1980s, when most European countries eliminated capital controls. The amount of funds moving within the euro area will make a quantum jump.

Against the background of this dramatic liberalization, the regulatory and institutional environment will not be adapted. Prudential control will still be done at the national level. This will handicap regulators in assessing the risk of the institutions under their jurisdiction. In addition, financial institutions in each country of the euro area will, at least initially, be overwhelmingly national. This segmentation will make it difficult efficiently to spread the risk of asymmetric economic shocks – that is economic shocks occurring in one country and not in others. The future euro area will therefore theoretically be prone to financial disturbances, at least during its initial phase when institutions have not yet adapted to the new environment. This does not mean crises will occur inevitably. In order to gauge the risk, let us analyse a particular scenario.

Suppose a country, which we arbitrarily call Spain, experiences a boom stronger than in the rest of the euro area. As a result of the boom, output and prices grow faster in Spain than in the other euro countries. This also leads to a property boom and general asset inflation in Spain. Since the European Central Bank looks at euro-wide data, it cannot do anything to restrain the boom. In fact, monetary union is likely to intensify Spain's asset inflation. Unhindered by exchange risk, vast amounts of capital is attracted from the rest of the euro area. Spanish banks, which still dominate the Spanish markets, increase their lending. They are driven by the high rates of return produced by ever-increasing Spanish asset prices, and by the fact that, in a monetary union, they can borrow funds at the same interest rate as banks in Germany or France. After the boom comes the bust. Asset prices collapse, creating a crisis in the Spanish banking system – or any system in which the initial conditions apply.

Is this too far-fetched? The U S monetary union provides many examples of such local booms and busts followed by financial crises that lead to large-scale bailouts. Scenarios like the one described will almost certainly happen in the future euro area. The essential ingredient triggering such crises is the regional differences in rates of return on assets coupled with the fact that banks will be able to borrow at the same interest rates. These future euro financial crises will, however, differ from the Asian financial crisis in one crucial respect. They will not lead to speculative crises in the foreign exchange markets. Thus, if Spain is confronted by a banking crisis, it will not spill over into the Spanish foreign exchange market. There will be no such market. That source of further destabilization will, therefore, be absent.

The founders of Emu have taken extraordinary measures to reduce the risk of debt default by governments. Maastricht convergence criteria and a stability pact have been introduced to guard Emu from the risk of excessive government debt accumulation. But the Asian financial débâcle shows that excessive private debt accumulation can be equally, if not more, risky. In the meantime the Emu-clock is ticking. The institutions that should guard Emu from financial and banking crises have still to be put into place.

First appeared 20 February 1998

C Monetary policy under Emu – six-part series by WOLFGANG MÜNCHAU

Monetary versus inflation targeting: *European central bankers face a dilemma in deciding monetary policy*

One of the few unresolved questions about the European Central Bank is the choice of monetary policy instrument. Two alternatives are on offer: monetary targeting, used by the Bundesbank and several other European central banks, and direct inflation targeting, used by the Bank of England and the Swedish Riksbank.

There are two broad schools of thought among European central bankers. One says it does not matter. In practice, monetary policy tends to be far more judgemental than most observers, especially financial market economists and journalists, believe. Targets may serve as a useful input, but policy makers tend to 'look at everything' when they set interest rates. This is known by economists as the 'discretionary' approach. The other school firmly believes in targets – whether inflation targets or monetary targets. The main argument for targeting is consistency. Target followers still look at everything. But they may look first at M3, a broad measure of money supply, and then at various forward-looking indicators of inflation and other economic variables.

The German model is still seen as likely to prevail in the medium-to-long term, but senior officials now acknowledge the need for some flexibility in the ECB's early years. At a *Financial Times* conference, Hervé Hannoun, deputy governor of the Bank of France, admitted to having doubts. He still came out in favour of monetary targeting, but he did so 'with a caveat'. As it turned out, the caveat was more revealing than other well-rehearsed reasons in favour of monetary targeting.

Listing all the known arguments for monetary targeting – transparency, consistency – he warns that the strategy hinges on the stability of money demand, by which he means the relationship between the amount of money in an economy and the price level. 'Preliminary research has shown that EU-wide money equations often perform better than comparable national equations. Nonetheless this may provide no safe guidance for the starting period of Emu in so far as the move constitutes a change of regime which might lead to breakdowns in empirical relationships,' he said.

Otmar Issing, one of the most influential members of the Bundesbank's decision-making council, has given the most explicit acknowledgement of the need for mixed targeting so far: 'Because of the great uncertainties at the beginning of economic and monetary union, a monetary target should be complemented by – as I would call it – an inflation forecast.' Here, leading central bankers warn that the monetary policy that Europe's central banks have been using for more than twenty years may no longer work.

The Bundesbank has operated monetary targeting since 1975, but has met its self-imposed monetary targets only 12 times in the last 22 years. Under inflation targeting, the central bank targets an inflation indicator, using a mix of economic and monetary data. The UK, Sweden and Finland use this method. The European Monetary Institute, the forerunner of the ECB, has left the choice open. Monetary targeting was seen as the hot favourite until recently, but central bankers have become more open-minded. When presenting the Bundesbank's monetary targets for 1998 in November, Hans Tietmeyer, Bundesbank president, merely insisted that monetary targeting should play 'an important role' under Emu.

Mr Issing's concession is partly an acknowledgement of the Lucas critique, named after Robert Lucas, the 1995 Nobel Prize winner in economics, who is famous for the observation that a change in policy systematically alters the structure of econometric models. Applied to Emu, the Lucas critique says statistical relationships that appear reliable on a national level before Emu may no longer be reliable on a European level after Emu. Mr Issing remains, however, a strong defender of monetary targeting. In an article from 1997 (Otmar Issing, 'Monetary targeting in Germany: the stability of monetary policy and of the monetary system', *Journal of Monetary Economics, 39*) he writes that 'the Lucas critique does not imply that economic relationships will be unstable' if the authorities behave consistently.

Ivo Arnold, a monetary economist at Nijenrode University in the Netherlands, observes ('Monetary targeting in the Emu: lessons from the United States', *Kredit und Kapital*, Duncker & Humblot, Berlin, 1997, Heft 3) that it was the success of the Bundesbank that gave credibility to monetary targeting, and not the other way round. His own research has indicated that the demand for money could be far more unstable under Emu than was widely thought. Like many monetary economists, he has argued that inflation targeting is a more appropriate instrument for a new central bank that has yet to build up its own credibility. 'The bottom line is that the Bundesbank can afford to regularly miss its monetary targets, the ECB not (yet)', he writes. The growing scepticism about monetary targeting is influenced by forecasts that Emu might lead to upheavals in the financial sector. Experts are forecasting an increase in bank mergers, and greater use of electronic money. Some economists argue that the choice of instrument does not matter, since central banks tend to be pragmatic under any system. The opposite view holds that the choice of target still affects expectations in financial markets, and this could reverberate on the decision-making process itself.

Adapted from two articles which first appeared 25 November 1997 and 23 December 1997

The policy mix: *the ECB must decide how to mix fiscal and monetary policy in the new Europe*

The success or failure of European monetary union will depend to a large extent on how politicians and central bankers manage the so-called 'fiscal–monetary mix', a term describing the interaction between fiscal and monetary policy. The mix, which incorporates the combined policy stance of an economic area and is generally counter-cyclical, is the subject of intense interest among economists and central bankers gearing up for Emu. It is a complex and speculative area, with an almost endless number of scenarios.

What makes Emu potentially complicated is the degree to which EU-wide fiscal policy remains decentralized. To set an appropriate fiscal–monetary mix, the European Central Bank will have to co-ordinate with eleven member-governments and the European Commission, which administers the EU's own budget. This degree of decentralization could give rise to a 'free-rider' problem. Any single country's unilateral fiscal action would have little impact on the Emu-wide average. As a result, governments – especially in small countries – have an incentive to run the highest permissible budget deficits.

Of course, if everyone acted this way, Emu-wide fiscal policy could err permanently on the side of high deficits, and this could quickly become intolerable. Besides, individual government action is limited by a ceiling set by the stability and growth pact, agreed at the EU summit in Amsterdam last June. The ceiling stands at 3 per cent of gross domestic product. The ECB might decide to counter excessive fiscal deficits with a relatively tight monetary policy. If it compensated fully, interest rates would be permanently higher than they would be under perfectly symmetric conditions. The euro, the future single currency, might then rise against other currencies, the terms of trade for the entire Emu area would worsen, and economic growth would settle at sub-optimal levels.

However, for political reasons, the ECB's monetary policy might be able to compensate only partly for fiscal laxity. In that case, inflation would be higher than under a perfectly co-ordinated policy. Either outcome would be seen as economically inefficient, socially undesirable and politically unstable.

In a recent discussion paper ('Options for the future exchange rate policy of the Emu', Occasional Paper No. 17), the London-based Centre for Economic Policy Research notes that the rigid ceiling imposed by the stability and growth pact could perversely end up damaging the ECB's credibility. It considers a case in which all except one or two Emu countries are in recession. Faced with such a situation, the ECB would run a loose monetary policy. But this stance would be inappropriate in the one or two countries not in recession.

'A better policy would call for a smaller monetary expansion, accompanied by a fiscal stimulus in those countries where the recession is deeper', according to the paper. The 3 per cent deficit ceiling 'will put the ECB under pressure to opt for a tight fiscal–easy money policy mix. It will therefore impede rather than assist the ECB. Nor could the ECB argue for a lax application of the stability and growth pact, for fear of losing its own credibility.'

This is one of many scenarios under which Emu could face strains. The authors make the point that the pact is not sufficiently flexible. Fiscal policy flexibility would, however, be extremely important in dealing with asymmetric shocks or asynchronous business cycles. As long as business cycles are convergent and fiscal policy well co-ordinated, monetary policy may face few obstacles. But it is impossible to know whether some sudden crisis may blow up in the future, forcing a change in arrangements.

This is why the current institutional and constitutional framework of Emu may not be carved in stone. The CEPR researchers conclude that the stability and growth pact is untenable in its present inflexible form, and will need to be replaced by more supple rules. 'Such a reform, however, should be accompanied by procedures designed to foster the co-ordination of fiscal policies among national governments, and of monetary and fiscal policies between Ecofin (EU economics and finance ministers) and the ECB.'

This would imply what 'Emu-minimalists' have been keen to avoid: the overall stance of fiscal policy will not just become a subject of common concern, as is already the case, but subject to common rule. This means an unprecedented degree of economic government.

First appeared 13 January 1998

One size fits all? *Will one monetary policy fit all? EU members differ and so do the effects of a rate change*

Central bankers and economists are becoming increasingly troubled by the consequences of a 'one-size-fits-all' monetary policy. A group of researchers at the International Monetary Fund are, at the time of writing, the latest to warn that monetary policy under Emu may not work as smoothly as widely believed. At issue are the so-called transmission mechanisms – the channels through which monetary policy feeds through to the real world of economic growth and jobs.

Central bankers know that a rise in short-term interest rates or other forms of monetary tightening will ultimately affect the rate of economic growth. In most countries, they have a rough idea about the time-lag between the two events. But they do not always understand the precise route through which a rise in interest rates feeds through the system.

According to an IMF working paper (Ramaswamy, R. and Sloek, T., 'The Real Effects of Monetary Policy in the European Union: What Are the Differences?', International Monetary Fund, Working Paper 97/160, December 1997), EU countries can be divided into two groups, according to the speed and extent with which they react to interest rate changes. A slow-response group is made up of Germany, the UK, Netherlands, Austria, Belgium and Finland; while a fast-response group is made up of Denmark, France, Italy, Portugal, Spain and Sweden. The result is surprising because, as the authors point out, the two groups do not correspond to the conventional distinction between 'core' and 'none-core' EU countries. France and Germany are on different sides of the divide, with France falling in a group with several countries generally perceived as non-core. The UK and Finland, by contrast, fall into the core category.

Output in the countries in the first group bottoms out eleven to twelve quarters after a sudden monetary tightening, while in the second group it takes only five to six quarters. However, the economic effects are almost twice as strong in the first group compared with the second. According to the IMF, a monetary shock would reduce economic growth in the first group by 0.7 to 0.9 percentage points, against 0.4 to 0.6 percentage points for the second. A tightening of monetary policy under Emu would take time to make its full extent felt in Germany, but would be strongly felt in the economy. It would affect France much faster, but with less impact. Monetary policy affects the real economy in several ways. Generally, a rise in interest rates increases the cost of capital and damps demand. In a small open economy, however, exchange rates might be more important: higher interest rates can trigger an appreciation in the nominal and real exchange rate and a subsequent fall in exports.

Other potential transmission mechanisms are asset prices, which might fall after a rise in interest rates, and credit, since higher rates can lead to a decline in bank lending. The European Commission has also acknowledged that the different transmission mechanisms in EU countries might pose risks for Emu. In a wide-ranging report on the economic consequences of Emu (European Commission, Directorate General 2, 'Economic policy in Emu, Part B', Economic Papers, No. 125), the Commission argues that structural differences in the financial systems are partly responsible for variations between countries' transmission mechanisms. Such economic differences include the degree of competition between banks, the share of bank credit in total financing, ownership structures, the degree of internationalization of the banking system, and foreign currency holdings.

The Commission's paper adds two mitigating factors. Members of the exchange-rate mechanism may have already made significant adjustments in recent years. In addition, the transition to Emu itself could trigger further harmonization. 'Emu will represent a fundamental regime change which will inevitably modify the structural parameters of national economic systems and, hence, the differences across countries. However, while some of the differences are bound to disappear as soon as a single currency becomes a reality, others will only vanish in the long run, while others will be permanent.' In view of the uncertainties about transmission mechanisms, experts are hesitant to recommend concrete policy action.

The Commission's paper concludes cautiously: 'Any reform aiming at increasing the efficiency of monetary and credit markets goes in the right direction, but further research is needed to single out more specific interventions.' The IMF paper concedes that the structural differences might narrow after the launch of Emu. But it ends on a cautionary note. 'The task of conducting monetary policy at the EU-wide level is likely to be a challenging one in the initial years of the monetary union.'

First appeared 30 December 1997

Exchange-rate policy under Emu *– Euro exchange-rate policy is still the big uncertainty: currency interplay may be very different from that of the past*

The exchange-rate policy that will govern the future single currency remains uncertain. Europe's exchange-rate relations with the rest of the world are sure to undergo change as the euro's introduction reshapes the region's economy. The interplay between European and other currencies may turn out to be very different from what it was in the past.

Yet exchange-rate policy after 1 January 1999 remains a largely unresolved issue. While the European Union's Maastricht treaty stipulates that the European Central Bank (ECB) should be concerned primarily with internal stability, there remains significant room for interpretation about the need to secure external stability, especially concerning the euro/dollar exchange rate. The question of future exchange-rate policy is the subject of a detailed discussion paper (Begg, D., Giavazzi, F. and Wyplosz C., 'Options for the future exchange-rate policy of the Emu', Occasional Paper No. 17) by the Centre for Economic Policy Research in London. The paper makes the point that Emu will transform a group of small open economies into a large closed economy, similar in some respects to that of the US. This will change the importance of the exchange rate for domestic policy.

Under Emu, the export share of gross domestic product will be about 10 per cent, similar to prevailing levels in the US, but significantly lower than current levels in all the EU economies. The reason is that trade between two EU members is now accounted for as foreign trade, while it will become 'domestic' trade under Emu. 'In a closed economy, monetary policy operates through interest rates and asset prices, including housing. In an open economy, the exchange rate assumes paramount importance', the paper notes. A relatively closed economy, such as the US, has more monetary independence than a small open economy such as the UK, where monetary policy is severely constrained by the exchange rate.

The paper argues that this difference becomes important once the central bank faces a policy dilemma. The Federal Reserve, for example, would invariably focus on the internal objectives, if faced with a conflict between internal and external stability. 'For these reasons, it is natural to expect the ECB will devote less attention to the exchange rate than has been the case with European central banks so far.' With an exchange-rate policy of 'benign neglect', the exchange rate will become a policy issue only under extreme economic circumstances or under extreme exchange-rate volatility.

Is extreme exchange-rate volatility more or less likely under Emu? The paper gives no conclusive evidence, but points out that Emu will remove one stabilizing factor. At present, when the dollar weakens against the D-Mark, other European currencies also weaken against the D-Mark. As a result, the dollar's overall rate against a basket of European and other international currencies weakens by less than the dollar/D-Mark rate would suggest. Under Emu, that buffer would no longer be there.

Other factors could add to volatility. 'Each major currency has its fringe of hangers-on and the euro will be no exception', the authors note. This is a reference to the post-1999 exchange-rate mechanism, a voluntary exchange-rate system to link the currencies of non-participating EU countries, such as Demnark, to the euro. Some eastern European countries might also maintain links, such as the currency board operated by Estonia, which at present ties the kroon to the D-Mark. But where no formal exchange-rate links exist, the result could be increased volatility in intra-European exchange rates, for example between the euro and the pound.

'Extreme caution will be required to avoid trade friction from boiling over into political tensions on suspicions of beggar-thy-neighbour policies', the authors note. Under a policy of benign neglect towards the exchange rate, in both the US and the EU, close policy co-operation in international organizations such as the International Monetary Fund and the Group of Eight industrialized countries could in times of need become critical.

But the report argues that formal exchange-rate systems, such as the Bretton Woods system in the 1950s and 1960s or the ERM, are unrealistic, because they work only if one currency acts as an anchor. Given the relatively equal economic weight of the US and the Emu zone, the conditions for this are unlikely to apply. Policy co-operation would therefore have to be voluntary and geared to 'informal and ad hoc exchange-rate arrangements', on lines similar to the exchange-rate accords of the 1980s. So far, relatively little attention has been paid by EU officials and central bankers to how such policy co-operation would work in practice.

First appeared 6 January 1998

The euro – a strong or a weak currency? *The new European currency could surprise sceptics with its strength*

Nowhere is the herd instinct in financial markets as pronounced as in the belief that the euro is doomed to permanent weakness. The stress is on 'permanent'. Currency analysts and several politicians have adopted the notion of a weak euro as one of the great certainties of our time. US fund managers are so dismissive of the future European currency that they rank it somewhere between the Albanian lek and the Thai baht. The D-Mark's weakness against the dollar is the clearest symptom of the euro's questionable reputation.

The myth of a weak euro rests on three assumptions. The first and least questionable is that European economic and monetary union will start on time in 1999 with a large membership base, including Italy, Spain and Portugal. Second, it assumes that these three countries – and maybe others – would return to inflationary fiscal policies the minute they are admitted to Emu. Third, European Union unemployment would remain high because of 'inflexible' labour markets – a catch-all argument to explain Europe's recent economic failures.

Whatever the merits of these assumptions, this forecast misjudges two important recent trends. European economic growth is at last picking up, and the Bundesbank, the German central bank, appears determined to counteract EU-wide inflationary expectations. The role of the Bundesbank is critical. Until recently, the consensus was that short-term interest rates in Germany would remain at 3 per cent until the start of Emu. From a purely German standpoint, that rate does not seem entirely unreasonable, as Hans Tietmeyer, president of the Bundesbank, explained last week. But the current rates are less appropriate for the Netherlands, Spain or Ireland, whose economies are ahead in the economic cycle and have been growing much more strongly than that of Germany. Yet the domestic interest rates of each of these countries closely mirrors German rates. Averaging out, the combined interest rates in the prospective member states of Emu are probably lower than they would normally be at the current stage in the cycle.

The idea that a rise in German interest rates could be helpful for Emu would have been laughed out of court only a few weeks ago. It seems much less laughable now. The Bundesbank insists on orienting monetary policy purely towards the needs of the domestic German economy. With Emu so close, the goal has remained the same, but the means are becoming more complex. Any build-up of inflation outside Germany will invariably spill over into Germany after 1999. To fulfil its legal obligation of ensuring price stability, the Bundesbank must therefore take into account the whole of the EU, and not just Germany.

In some respects it may even be easier to formulate a pan-EU monetary policy than a purely national one. The chart below shows that M3, the broad measure of money and the Bundesbank's policy barometer, has behaved much better for the EU as a whole than for Germany alone during most of the 1990s. So what does all this mean for the euro? First of all, the Bundesbank's determination to counteract inflationary expectations is bound to be matched by the European Central Bank.

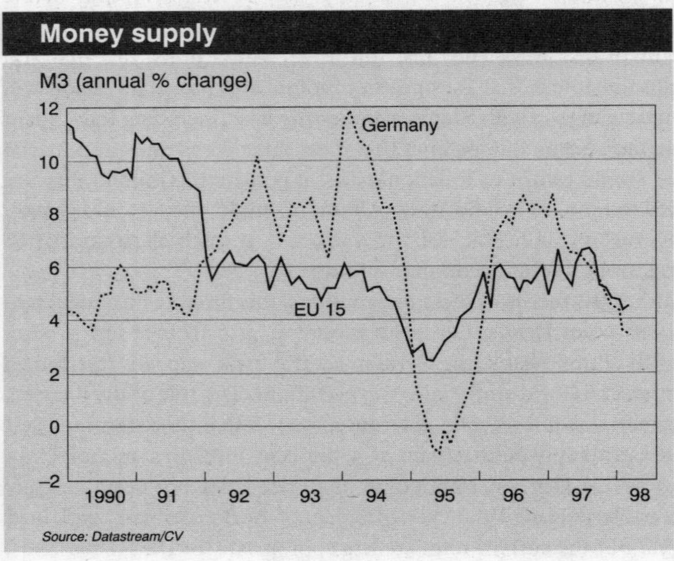

As a central bank, the ECB will be more independent than the Bundesbank, since its independence is rooted in the European treaties, and not merely in ordinary law as in the case of the German central bank. The Bundesbank has to support the economic policies of the German government, while the ECB operates under no such constraint. As a new central bank, the ECB will be keen to establish credibility early on. Given the continued anti-inflationary hawkishness among the EU's central banking establishment, combined with wage moderation and competitive markets, there is little risk of a sustained inflationary surge.

EU central bankers are aware that inflation would pose the biggest political risk for the new currency. Since it is the ECB's primary objective to ensure price stability, its board of governors can be relied on to choose a monetary policy that errs on the side of caution. If the ECB failed in achieving its primary objective, it would not only put its own independence at risk, it may also jeopardize the entire Emu project. Yet, if the ECB succeeds in its primary objective – as one might expect – the euro would strengthen, unless of course the Emu zone were to languish in permanent recession. Judging by the latest economic statistics, the prospects of permanent recession seem remote.

The long-awaited economic upturn may even have started during the second quarter of 1997, with an EU-wide annualized growth rate of 5.2 per cent, according to a J. P. Morgan estimate. The EU's forecast current account surplus is estimated at $114 billion (£70 billion) in 1997, much higher than Japan's. Admittedly, the economic upturn is export-driven, helped by the recent devaluation of EU currencies. But this is the early stage of a cycle. It is not inconceivable that the EU economy might be growing at a sustained annualized rate of more than 3 per cent in 1999, the year Emu is due to be launched.

If the euro is associated with a booming economy, it might become popular among the general public, contrary to what opinion polls currently suggest. By contrast, most Europeans would remember the 1990s as a decade of austerity and low growth. The euro's popularity might only be a temporary phenomenon but it might help sustain the currency politically in its early years.

If the Emu environment is characterized by low inflation, accelerating growth, and a hefty current account surplus, it is difficult to see how the euro could be permanently weak. It is, of course, possible that the currency may be temporarily weak. Currency markets fluctuate, and they may fluctuate even more in the future, as some forecasters suggest. The euro might, for example, trade at a temporary discount against the dollar until the ECB has established credibility with the markets.

But such fluctuations are largely irrelevant in the long run. At issue here is permanent – structural – weakness. There is little sign of that happening. If anything, there is a greater risk of a more familiar problem. Far from being too weak, the euro may end up being too strong.

First appeared 1 September 1997

Sustainability: *glue binding Emu members likely to hold*

Sceptics are certain that European economic and monetary union will at some point go wrong and then collapse like a house of cards. It is an appealing argument: after all, economic cycles can and do diverge, and a 'one-size-fits-all' policy may end up fitting nobody. Yet even for the most confirmed sceptic, this is not the worst imaginable outcome. Imagine if Emu were to go wrong, but nevertheless survived. Some recent economic research suggests that this is precisely what may happen. Sceptics may be underestimating the political and economic glue that will hold the Emu countries together, almost irrespective of how successfully or otherwise Emu is seen to operate.

If a country ever wanted to leave Emu, its government would not simply have to calculate the economic costs and benefits of keeping the euro versus those of re-introducing a national currency. It would also have to evaluate the economic consequences of the decision itself. A withdrawal would undoubtedly cause transitional disruption, but might also do permanent damage.

The question of sustainability has been the subject of a long and detailed report by the Association for the Monetary Union of Europe, a Paris-based think-tank (Stefan Collignon, 'The sustainability of monetary stability', pp. 6–24, The Sustainability Report, Association for the Monetary Union of Europe, Paris, February 1998). It arrives at two main conclusions about the sustainability of monetary policy in particular.

- The greater the uncertainty about the costs and benefits of leaving Emu, the less the extent to which countries will be inclined to take the plunge – unless the benefits of leaving Emu are perceived to be overwhelming. However, a situation in which countries would even consider opting out of Emu is bound to be a situation marked by high uncertainty.
- Pursuit of price stability is not only a necessary but a sufficient condition for the sustainability of Emu. Countries would not have an obvious, and, most importantly, a calculable incentive to leave Euroland unless Emu resulted in higher inflation – compared with previously prevailing national inflation rates.

Stefan Collignon, economist at the Association for the Monetary Union of Europe, argues that the second result – the sufficiency of price stability for the sustainability of Emu – is not as obvious as appears at first sight. Of course, it holds as a matter of definition, if one believes in the monetarist orthodoxy of the 'neutrality of money'. This says that money does not affect the real economy of economic output and jobs, and it does not cause long-term unemployment. But Collignon says it holds even if one takes the Keynesian view that there is a trade-off between inflation and unemployment. It boils down to the observation that if such a trade-off exists, it is not stable but varies with the average level of inflation. The higher the rate of inflation, the lower the trade-off. 'It could also mean that the instruments of monetary policy (the exchange rate and interest rates) are sharper in a low-inflation environment, so that output stabilization becomes easier. Emu may have greater real effects than previous discussions have suggested', he writes.

In other words, active economic demand management works, but only once a strong degree of price stability has been achieved. 'Therefore, in a stable monetary union, the supposed advantage of flexible exchange rates has been replaced by the much more tangible advantage of more efficient monetary policies', he argues.

As long as the European Central Bank achieves price stability, monetary policy remains a potent tool for output stabilization, he argues. It loses its edge once inflation rises. This is an argument also cited by Otmar Issing, a senior member of the Bundesbank's directorate, who is now a member of the ECB's executive board. He cited evidence (Otmar Issing, 'The European Central Bank as a new institution and the problem of accountability', paper delivered at a symposium on the global economy, Kiel, 20 March 1998) that independent central banks not only achieve greater stability of prices but also greater stability of output variation. Their economic cycles are smoother, compared with countries where the central banks are not independent.

But Mr Issing warns that the ECB's chances of success are far from guaranteed, and argues that there is everything to play for at this point. Whatever the EU's Maastricht treaty may stipulate about central bank independence and the primacy of price stability, the ECB's success will depend on its policies, the economic environment in which it operates and, of course, the quality of its central bankers. Mr Issing argues that if the ECB operates in an environment in which it came under persistent political pressure, it will not be able to withstand that pressure for ever. 'The independence of the central bank is a necessary, but not sufficient, condition', he says.

What about unemployment? Could high and rising levels of unemployment lead to the collapse of Emu? Collignon argues that the main adjustment has already occurred, when countries consolidated their fiscal policies to qualify for Emu. Emu itself is unlikely to make matters much worse. On the contrary, for most countries Emu implies lower long-term and short-term interest rates, compared with the levels of the 1980s or early 1990s. But even if electorates were to blame Emu for high unemployment, it is not immediately apparent that leaving Emu would solve the problem. For that to occur, a country would need to achieve a real devaluation of its new currency against the euro – after accounting for inflation both at home and in the euro zone.

But it is far from clear that the remaining Emu rump would tolerate a real devaluation of a trading partner in a single European market. As a result, if the ECB fails to achieve price stability, its failure will be apparent, and the benefits of leaving will be evident. If, however, the ECB delivers 'too much' price stability, with low economic growth and high unemployment, the benefits of leaving Emu will be highly uncertain. It is therefore a game stacked heavily in favour of Emu's survival – except under conditions of persistently high inflation.

First appeared 30 April 1998

D Europe's new economic institutions

Teething troubles in store: *the European Central Bank faces a difficult early life as it combats uncertainties over statistics, policy, and relations with national central bankers and politicians*

WOLFGANG MÜNCHAU

The launch of the European Central Bank marks the start of the biggest experiment in central banking since the second world war. Outwardly, not much will happen. The nameplate at the Euro Tower building in the centre of Frankfurt may change, and so will the letterheads. Otherwise, the ECB will take over directly where the European Monetary Institute, its secretive forerunner, left off.

This outward calm belies the frantic activity that lies ahead for Wim Duisenberg, the first European Central Bank governor, and his 400 staff. The ECB will take over policy decisions from the central banks of the eleven founder members of European monetary union and insiders say there is not much time to complete the necessary preparations to get the single currency off to a safe start on 1 January 1999. Some staff were told to cancel their summer holidays – almost unprecedented for a European institution. Almost forgotten is the bitter aftertaste left by Mr Duisenberg's nomination at the European Union summit in Brussels on 2 May, where he was forced to declare 'voluntarily' that he would retire early from his eight-year term. Fears that his humiliating statement would damage the credibility of the ECB – which seemed plausible at the time – now look distinctly wide of the mark.

The nomination of the six executive board directors – Mr Duisenberg, Christian Noyer as vice-president, plus Otmar Issing, Tommaso Padoa-Schioppa, Eugenio Domingo Solans and Sirrka Hämäläinen – was well received by the financial markets. The six central bankers have been working together in the Emi for years, and are mostly on first-name terms. But credibility and internal harmony are not the only qualities needed to make a successful central bank. One essential ingredient is transparency. Respected central banks are relatively transparent, not in the sense that the markets can predict their every interest-rate move, but in the sense that the outside world understands how and why they act as they do. At present, perceptions of ECB policy priorities are confused, even though the Maastricht treaty is clear on the ECB's mandate – the relentless pursuit of price stability.

Many analysts believe that the bank will focus on the weakest countries in recognition of the member states' uneven economic performance and because political pressure may force it to do so. This view would suggest that the ECB might tolerate permanently high levels of inflation – but this is unlikely.

Uncertainties abound. Mr Issing, formerly of the Bundesbank and most likely to take over as the ECB's chief economist, recently acknowledged that the quality of Euro-wide statistics may not be as good as it should be. Monetary statistics – one of the most important data series for central banks – could turn out to be misleading, at least initially. One senior German central banker said: 'On the whole I am quite optimistic about the ECB, though I am a little surprised that they have not made any more progress on this matter.' The data, such as M3, a measure of broad money, will be available from summer 1998, but nobody will know how reliable they are. Top ECB officials have therefore decided to adopt initially two complementary policies: German-style monetary combined with a UK-style inflation forecast.

At his confirmation hearings in the European Parliament in May 1998, Mr Duisenberg admitted this mixed bag was not ideal. He said: 'That makes the explanation of the policies you are pursuing more complicated and more difficult. It makes it more complicated to see through, but it has to be done.'

Also undecided is whether the ECB will adopt minimum reserve requirements – deposits that banks must place at the central bank to reflect the size of outstanding loans. Minimum reserves are a potentially divisive issue. Many central bankers favour them because they tie commercial banks to the central bank and temper their loan policies. But the requirement can drive business away from financial centres because commercial banks in general do not earn interest on the deposits.

London, where there are no minimum reserve requirements, has benefited from their absence as business has transferred from Frankfurt. If and when the UK enters Emu, the playing-field will be level again from a continental perspective. But business could leave the euro zone altogether. A compromise could be to compensate banks for any losses by paying market interest rates on the deposits.

A third uncertainty concerns the relationship between the ECB and the national central banks. Power will be more dispersed between the centre and periphery than in other central banking systems and it is not clear who will prevail. While the ECB will be responsible for setting policy, the national central banks will conduct the bulk of money market operations and foreign exchange intervention.

The ECB's policy-making council, which will decide interest rates, will consist of its executive board (based at its headquarters) and the heads of national central banks. At Germany's Bundesbank, on which the ECB is modelled, eight executive directors face nine regional central bank chiefs. At the ECB, the relationship is six against eleven – and as more countries join Emu, the majority of the outsiders will become larger. The national central banks will also retain much larger staffs than the ECB. The Bundesbank and the Bank of France both have more than 10,000 staff, while the ECB will only increase its employees to about 500 by the end of the year. Many of the national bank employees are involved in humdrum processing and logistics, while the ECB employees will be largely decision-makers. But the statisticians and economists retained by the banks may play a significant role in the intelligence-gathering behind policy formulation. For example, at the Bundesbank Mr Issing oversaw a department of about sixty economists. When he moves to the ECB – presumably in the same function – his team will probably be smaller.

Daniel Gros, director of the Centre for European Policy Studies, a Brussels-based think-tank, is concerned that the national bank 'outsiders' could gang up on the insiders by forming coalitions. This could impede efforts to gear policy towards the euro area as a whole, with a group of countries pushing their own self-interest. A counterweight to this concern is the observation that European central bankers have a long history of co-operaton and in most cases a tradition of central bank independence. Whatever their perceived national priorities, their interests lie in making sure the ECB is a success.

The central bankers themselves are reasonably optimistic. The economic outlook for Europe is benign. Growth is finally picking up without any signs of inflationary pressures. The member states of Emu have also shown a surprisingly high degree of economic convergence in fiscal and monetary policy. The real test will come when the worlds of politics and central banking collide. Will the ECB be able to stand up to EU finance ministers? The euro-11, the group of finance ministers of Emu member countries, may ultimately develop into an effective counterpart to the ECB but this, too, may take time. Yet unlike national central banks operating in national political systems, the ECB has no direct counterpart in politics at present.

Support from Europe's citizens will be critical. The Bundesbank has benefited from people's support for its role as the guardian of the D-Mark. Winning over the public requires a consistent approach to communication and information by ECB top officials. Here lies the greatest risk for the ECB. Central bankers are not by nature the most assiduous of communicators, although the US Federal Reserve and the Bundesbank have often been run by central bankers with fine-tuned political antennae, such as Alan Greenspan and Karl Otto Pöhl. This is a skill that Mr Duisenberg will need to demonstrate. At his confirmation hearings, Mr Duisenberg ruled out the publication of minutes of the council meetings – a practice common in the US and the UK. Instead the ECB will run a cabinet-style system. Every member is expected to represent the central bank's agreed line to the outside. The Bundesbank pursued its information mandate through endless visits and speeches, in which officials explained policy to many sections of society. The diverse power structures of the EU will make communication more difficult for the ECB.

Mr Duisenberg said the launch of the single currency would mark 'a new age' for Europe, not just for its economy but also for its politics. The ECB may be independent of politicians but to succeed it will have to be acutely politically sensitive or risk a confrontation that it may not win.

First appeared 1 June 1998

In praise of hard money: *over the past fifty years, the Bundesbank has written the central banking textbook. The European Central Bank should study it*

RUDI DORNBUSCH

Fifty years ago, on 20 June 1948, German monetary reform put an end to the Reichsmark and economic repression. As hard money celebrates its fiftieth anniversary in Germany this Saturday, it is also the end of the Bundesbank as Europe's monetary leader; step forward the European Central Bank. Europe is at a crossroads just as significant as the events that gave rise to the D-Mark and the Bundesbank.

Nobody knew in 1948 what the bold removal of price controls and the introduction of a new money would mean, except that it could not be worse than the prevailing state of affairs: a war economy with controls and black marketeering, pervasive shortages, and collapsing production. Deregulation and monetary reform were an act of faith. Who could be sure that hyperinflation would not emerge, as it had in the 1920s? US General Cassius Clay told the then economics minister Ludwig Erhard: 'Mr Erhard, my advisers tell me your plans are crazy.' And Erhard replied: 'General, my advisers say the same.' The rest is history: an economic miracle built on free market economics and on five decades of uncompromising pursuit of price stability.

No other central bank has sustained price stability like the Bundesbank. While the D-Mark's purchasing power is down to just one-quarter of what it was in 1948, that of the dollar is only 15 cents. Britain, Italy and France have done much worse. The Bundesbank has been so good at public relations it is tempting to overstate its success. Inflation has been between zero and 2 per cent in only fifteen of the past fifty years, though no one else has fared nearly as well. Yet over the past fifty years, German inflation averaged 2.7 per cent, exceeding its goal of 1 or 1.5 per cent. There has always been an explanation: fixed exchange rates on the dollar in a world of over-expansion in the 1960s, two oil shocks in the 1970s, and the unification shock at the beginning of the 1990s – each a good reason for higher inflation. In each case, the Bundesbank put out the fire. Could it have done better? No doubt. But not without even higher unemployment. Sheer toughness would not have paid off in higher credibility, and hence better results.

The fact that, even with a determined central bank, there has not been unqualified success has surely to do with unions and the welfare state. The Bundesbank sets its money growth, while the welfare state and the unions determine the split. It always comes out as too much inflation and too little economic growth. One of the lessons of the Bundesbank must be that it takes two to foster credibility and performance: a tough central bank and a competitive economy. Nonetheless, few would dispute that, over the past fifty years, the Bundesbank has written the central banking textbook. Three central points emerge:

- A commitment to price stability, not necessarily day to day, but clearly as a trend;
- The easily verifiable targeting of monetary aggregates as the key commitment to price stability;
- Reiterating to the German public the bank's promise of 'price stability', but not necessarily of full employment, high growth and quick prosperity.

The ECB would do well to avoid monetary targeting – even the Bundesbank could barely hold up the myth of a stable relationship between money and prices. Economic and monetary union does not guarantee stable aggregates, particularly as the process of financial restructuring creates quite different monetary instruments. Like everywhere else, inflation targeting should be the framework and interest rates the key instrument.

By contrast, the ECB should learn from the Bundesbank that political independence can be gained only if the public trusts the central bank more than the politicians (remember when the Bundesbank stared down poor Theo Waigel, the finance minister, on the gold issue). The Bundesbank achieved that trust through decades of thoughtful communication, keeping close to the public – from savers to bankers to scholars – and building a constituency in support of hard money. It was a traumatic monetary history that gave the Bundesbank the backdrop against which to invoke the fears of inflation, but that does not diminish the accomplishment.

The precedent will be hard to match: just about everyone in Germany, from economics professors to housewives, the aged and the clergy, is distressed by the introduction of the euro. Emu has been achieved by haggling and compromise. It is a political ambition rather than a good idea in support of hard money. As a result, the ECB is starting off with a credibility deficit. It needs to make its case to the people; it cannot be satisfied just with making decisions and keeping quiet.

More will be celebrated in Frankfurt next Saturday than half a century of hard money in Germany. There is cause to celebrate too the worldwide acceptance, at least by central banks, that inflation is no answer to unemployment, even in the short term. There is no European or American central banker who has not at some time been driven to near despair by the Bundesbank's insistence on staying its course. Yet they have all come on board. What better message to send to the ECB?

But those who will be present at the ceremony, from Helmut Kohl, the chancellor, to SPD leaders Gerhard Schröder and Oskar Lafontaine, badly need another message from the same history book. Central banks are easily overburdened. A heavy dose of competition and deregulation would work miracles for price stability and growth, as it did in 1948.

First published 18 June 1998

France's wish for more co-operation across the euro zone would not limit the ECB's independence

DOMINIQUE STRAUSS-KAHN

Since the European Council of Amsterdam in June 1997, the French government has insisted on a closer co-ordination of economic policies among the future participants in the European economic and monetary union. This idea was initially received with scepticism, but significant progress has been made since June, as evidenced by a series of bilateral meetings I had with my colleagues, and by the agreement I have reached with Theo Waigel, the German finance minister, on this issue. I am confident that further progress will be made in the run-up to the European Council of December where I hope to reach a final agreement.

The reasons why the French government is keen on this issue have not always been understood. Let me clarify. We have no intention of putting pressure on the European Central Bank, whose independence is enshrined in the treaty and which will not take instructions from any European or national body. Central bank independence is now part of French legislation, and widely accepted at home.

We do not intend either to form an exclusive club, whose members would *de jure* or *de facto* deprive other EU members from participating in decision-making. The Council's prerogatives are also part of the treaty and we do not mean to challenge them. The case for a closer co-ordination within the euro zone rests on two arguments: one political, the other economic. The political argument is that, in the absence of a visible and legitimate political body, the ECB might soon be regarded by the public as the only institution responsible for macroeconomic policy.

In the absence of a counterpart, citizens in the euro zone might soon make the bank responsible for growth, employment, or even unemployment, whereas its mandate is to focus on the narrower objective of price stability. This discrepancy between the legal mandate of the ECB and its perception by European citizens would ultimately limit its room to manoeuvre. In this respect, emphasizing the collective responsibility of the ministers of the euro zone could in fact protect the bank from misplaced pressures. The economic argument is no less compelling. Emu will transform the relationship between participating countries: whatever the current degree of integration through goods and capital markets, the single currency will represent a qualitative leap. The need to match increased monetary interdependence with closer economic and budgetary co-operation was recognized in the Maastricht treaty.

But subsequent developments – notably in the stability and growth pact – have put more emphasis on co-ordinating national policies through rules (for example, the no bail-out clause) and disciplinary provisions (sanctions for excessive deficits) than through common diagnosis and joint action. My view is that, though useful for preventing excessive deficits, the stability pact will only provide limited information when deficits do not exceed or approach the 3 per cent threshold.

Let me give an example. Assume that in five or ten years, fiscal deficits in the euro zone are below 3 per cent, but are nevertheless deemed excessive, and that national governments intend to reduce them. If the governments act in an unco-ordinated fashion, the ECB will not be in a position to make an accurate assessment of the evolution of public deficits. It will then have to keep monetary policy on hold and will only be able to reduce interest rates after budgetary decisions have actually been implemented and started to deliver tangible results. In view of the lags in the transmission of monetary policy, budgetary adjustments could therefore prove more painful than actually needed.

If, on the other hand, governments were able to co-ordinate and to commit to a policy, the ECB would be able to loosen monetary policy in time (obviously, if it could do so without endangering price stability). Co-ordination could therefore help solve the informational problem arising from the coexistence of one monetary authority and several fiscal authorities.

Exchange-rate policy is another reason why consultation among euro-zone participants will be needed. In virtually all countries with a flexible exchange-rate regime, the government monitors exchange-rate developments and, when it is appropriate, talks to the markets, especially when rates deviate from what is considered a level corresponding to economic fundamentals. It may adjust domestic macroeconomic policy in response to exchange-rate developments.

I think the euro group should be able to do just that, while remaining careful not to conflict with the ECB's objective of price stability. Whatever the strength of Europe's commitment to stable money, we cannot anticipate with precision how markets will initially respond to the introduction of a new currency. And after its quality as a store of value is demonstrated, it will surely be demanded by asset holders worldwide, which could trigger an appreciation. We therefore cannot rely entirely on the euro's internal stability to deliver external stability. This is why Emu must be equipped with an ability to monitor exchange-rate developments, and, if needed, to react in co-operation with our Group of Seven partners.

In short, Emu participants will have several reasons to exchange information, to develop close consultation and to co-ordinate policy in budgetary and other areas. Together with Germany and several other partners,

France is proposing that EU members create an informal, but legitimate, body to meet before each Ecofin meeting of EU finance ministers to discuss matters relating to the operation of Emu, and exchange views on decisions to be taken in the Ecofin.

As Gordon Brown, the UK chancellor, rightly emphasizes, the single currency is a venture in the success of which all EU members have a stake. I am convinced this body (which, needless to say, will open its doors to all future participants in the single currency) will prove to be a positive contribution to the EU policy system, to the benefit of the euro participants and of the other EU members.

First appeared 27 November 1997

Lines of power in the Emu structure

European Central Bank

The ECB stands at the heart of Emu. it is the central bank for the Emu zone and the sole issuer of the euro, the new currency. The ECB will be based in Frankfurt, where it is expected to take over physically and legally from from the European Monetary Institute, its precursor.

The ECB will be headed by a president, who is appointed by EU heads of state and government. The first president is Wim Duisenberg. The executive committee of the ECB will consist of a president, vice-president and four other members drawn from countries that participate in Emu. Their term of office is eight years, non-renewable, but there are different transitional arrangements for the first set of executives. The term of the first vice-president, for example, will be only four years.

The ECB's main objective, as defined in the Maastricht Treaty, is to ensure price stability. Like other central banks, it will set short-term interest rates with a view to achieving its objective. The level of interest rates will be set by its governing council, which consists of the executive committee and the governors of the national central banks.

Under the Treaty, all members of the council must be independent from political interference. It is one of the strongest legal forms of independence ever devised for a central bank.

National central banks

Contrary to popular perception, national central banks will continue to exist and will play an important role under emu. Together, the ECB and national central banks will form the European System of Central Banks (ESCB). Similar to the federal central bank systems in the US and Germany, the operations of the ESCB will be highly decentralized.

While the ECB's governing council determines the overall stance of policy, national central banks will retain operational responsibility. The precise share-out, however, has yet to be established. There are also different views among EU central bankers about the desired degree of decentralization.

It is likely that large national central banks, such as the Bundesbank and the Bank of France, will play an important role in money market operations for example, by conducting regular securities repurchase tenders. With the help of these so-called repos the ESCB will supply the financial system with liquidity, and fine tune the level of interest rates within the parameters set by the ECB's governing council.

Intervention in foreign exchange markets will be conducted by national central banks, if such action is deemed appropriate.

Ecofin

This is the prime decision-making forum on macro-economic policy comprising finance ministers of all 15 member states. Meetings take place every month. They have grown in importance as the blueprint for the single currency has taken shape, and many observers believe Ecofin amounts to an economic government by any other name.

In the post-emu world, Ecofin will be responsible for general economic guidelines, continuing the use of peer pressure to encourage budgetary rectitude. But only euro zone members will have the right to vote on sanctions against fiscal backsliders and on external exchange rate policy for the euro. Also, Ecofin faces a potential rival body–the euro-X–the informal grouping of members of the single currency zone.

Euro-X

It remains unclear how the euro-X will work in practice, but France is determined that it will play a central role in defining the common interests of the euro zone. It could have a permanent rather than a rotating chairman. On policy, it could shape the EU's response to short-term shocks or market turbulence. It could also define the common position of the majority of EU members in the international institutions such as the G7 or the International Monetary Fund. Some observers believe euro-X is also likely to be the forum for new EU-wide initiatives in key areas such as taxation.

Economic and financial committee

This new body will replace the secretive EU monetary committee which prepares Ecofin meetings. However, the composition of members will be the same: national treasury officials, central bankers and two members of the European Commission. If anything, it is likely to become even more powerful if the trend toward smaller, informal meetings of ministers continues. Its composition shows that the central bankers will still exert powerful behind-the-scenes influence, despite French-led efforts to make Ecofin the political counterweight to the central bank.

European Commission

Fighting hard to preserve its role at the centre of coordination of economic policy. The Commission will continue to prepare recommendations on broad macroeconomic guidelines, monitoring member states' performance, and if necessary drawing attention to slippage. It monitors the stability and growth pact as well as analyzing member states' (convergence) programmes, preparing recommendations, including possible fines.

The Commission has successfully carved out a role for itself in coordination of employment policy, but is struggling to exercise its influence in external representation of the euro in G7 and the IMF.

European Parliament

Slowly raising its profile in preparation for the post-Emu world. MEPs debated the recommendations of the European Commission on which countries qualified for Emu. They grilled the nominees to the executive board of the Central Bank. Maastricht also requires the ECB president to present the bank's annual report to Parliament which can hold a general debate. The treaty also provides for regular contacts between the ECB and Parliamentary committees. The model falls short of the Federal Reserve-US Congress, but it will evolve.

4 The microeconomics of Emu: reforming Europe's labour markets

One of the factors essential to the success of the single currency is its impact on labour and product markets. This chapter looks at how governments, the 'social partners' and consumers will respond to the changes Emu will bring.

Perhaps most critical is whether Europe proves able to tackle its mass unemployment and reform its increasingly costly social security systems. Proponents of Emu claim that stable, low interest rates, low inflation and increased trade resulting from the transparency of markets will allow for more investment and job creation. Opponents point to Europe's inflexible labour markets and say that without the monetary tools and fiscal leeway to deal with shocks, a recession will produce huge job losses and social unrest. Some fear that Emu could endanger the European social model, and its characteristic combination of a free market system and a welfare state.

Robert Taylor, the *FT*'s employment editor, outlines EU initiatives to combat unemployment, and the new emphasis on training and flexibility. He argues that Emu will be a tough test for Europe's labour markets. A unified labour market may remain a long way off given the huge social disparities that are likely to exist across the single currency zone. Giorgio La Malfa, leader of Italy's Republican party, and Franco Modigliani, the Nobel prize-winning economist, challenge the dominant view that European unemployment is primarily due to labour market rigidities.

Peter Norman, the *FT*'s Bonn correspondent, focuses on social policy in his article 'The welfare trap'. He argues that Emu will increase the competitive pressure on employers who are already carrying a heavy burden in social security contributions. Martin Wolf contends that large divergences in labour productivity mean that social security costs in different countries must remain different and wage-setting must continue to be decentralized.

Many people believe Emu will have a huge impact on product markets, creating a paradise for shoppers. Guy de Jonquières examines this argument and the contrary view that Emu will not lead to rapid price harmonization. Those who hold this view argue that 60 per cent of trade between France and Germany is actually intra-company trade. Price transparency will only bring lower prices in the least sophisticated parts of the market.

WOLFGANG MÜNCHAU

Employment moves up the agenda: *training and flexibility are high priorities as the EU tries to step up job creation*

ROBERT TAYLOR

The creation of economic and monetary union is going to test the effectiveness of European labour markets in creating and developing job opportunities at a time of continuing mass unemployment. But unless the level of open unemployment starts to fall significantly over the next few years, many observers believe governments inside Emu will have difficulty in holding down their deficits and curbing their spending programmes in line with the fiscal restraints imposed by the Maastricht treaty and the stability pact. They also fear that the level of social unrest could grow and undermine current efforts to develop more flexible and less regulated labour markets, which many regard as a necessary prerequisite for future employment creation.

In 1997 the EU treaty of Amsterdam set out – for the first time – the promotion of employment as 'a matter of common concern' requiring co-ordinated action. The employment chapter indicates a much more sustained effort will have to be made over the next few years in improving the effectiveness of labour markets. This is no mere repetition of grandiloquent promises of European-wide action. Instead, the emphasis is on the creation and implementation of national employment plans drawn up by member states which will set out specific targets capable of achievement. The aim is not to impose some big plan from on high on a diverse range of European labour markets but to accept, in the words of the declaration of the Luxembourg jobs summit in November 1997, 'differing solutions and emphases in line with individual situations'.

However, these developments will occur within a framework of EU-agreed employment guidelines for the next five years covering the transition to Emu. Improving the employability of the young and long-term jobless is the top priority. Here, countries are expected to review their existing benefit and training systems and shift the emphasis from passive measures of income maintenance for the employed to more active moves into the labour market. This involves offering those without a job training or a similar measure, with the aim that all the EU states will achieve, in participation, the average of the three most successful or at least 20 per cent of the unemployed.

Measures are also promised to 'ease the transition from school to work' through a more sustained effort to ensure young people are better qualified for the labour market than in the past. The social partners – employers and trade unions – are expected to play their part by developing closer relations, especially in removing obstacles to traineeships and work experience.

The European Commission, under the imaginative direction of Allan Larsson, director-general at the social affairs directorate, is urging member states to utilize new technologies and innovations in local labour markets and in the social economies to create jobs that link needs to new work.

There is also an emphasis on reforming the tax systems of member states to make them more 'employment-friendly'. At present non-wage labour costs in EU states average 42 per cent, compared with 35 per cent in 1980. In the countdown to the single currency, member governments are being set targets that mean reducing overall tax burdens, especially on the unskilled and low-paid, although – in the EU's words – not doing so in ways that would jeopardize 'the recovery of public finances or the financial equilibrium of social security schemes'.

The modernization of work organization is high on the new EU labour market agenda. This will involve the encouragement of negotiated agreements to introduce greater flexible working into enterprises and sectors without undermining security. The Luxembourg summit communiqué suggests this might involve the calculation of working time on an annualized rather than weekly or monthly basis, an actual cut in the number of hours worked by an employee without reductions in the use of overtime, as well as the development of part-time employment, lifelong training and career breaks.

The Commission is keen to encourage the creation of more adaptable forms of fixed-term contracts which ensure those who work them enjoy 'adequate security and higher occupational status compatible with the needs of business'. Action is also expected on strengthening equal opportunity policies in the labour market, with more active measures to facilitate the employment of women through moves to reconcile work and family life. In addition, measures are to be encouraged that can remove tax obstacles to investment in human resources and in-company training.

All of this adds up to what is a new employment agenda for Europe that seeks more energetically than in the past to reconcile employment efficiencies with job security. It will be implemented within the framework of co-ordinated macroeconomic policies based on sound and prudent financial constraints and designed to contain any inflation threat as well as strengthen the euro on foreign exchange markets. Through sustained growth, it is hoped a 'new dynamism and climate of confidence' will emerge 'conducive to boosting employment'.

Padraig Flynn, the EU's social affairs commissioner, is convinced that such an approach should go a long way to re-energize European labour markets. 'There has been a growing realization that while economic policy weaknesses have been the root cause of Europe's unemployment, it has turned into long-term unemployment because a lack of emphasis on employability – against too much stress on unemployment insurance and income maintenance – has weakened our capacity to adjust', he argued in his latest annual EU employment report.

Mr Flynn envisages the new labour market approach as reflecting a set of priorities that shifts away from the 'old paradigm – of mass production and its assumptions – of mainly male, manual production processes, demanding single, functional skills, operating in traditional markets'. 'Our vision is of a Union moving towards a new model, of a more interdependent Europe, demanding different skills and competencies; producing new goods and services; adopting new working and living patterns', he argues.

The implementation of the new EU employment strategy with its aim of securing a 'high rate of net job creation' through the modernization of labour markets is seen in Brussels as crucial for Emu's success. But Mr Flynn and his colleagues acknowledge the difficulties that lie ahead. Regional disparities in employment opportunities, wage and non-wage labour costs and the incidence of youth and long-term worklessness, are considerable. Proposed EU structural funds alone are unlikely to ensure rapid convergence, especially with an expansion in the EU to include a growing number of countries in eastern Europe. Moreover, geographical labour mobility inside the euro zone seems unlikely to grow significantly, at least in its early years. Fewer than 5 per cent of people resident at present in member states originate elsewhere, with only a third coming from other EU countries.

Such problems are unlikely to undermine the new European social market model that is emerging to complement the single currency and Emu. A unified Emu-wide free labour market may remain a dream for some. But the huge social disparities that are likely to exist across the single currency zone – from Portugal to Finland, from Holland to Italy – for the foreseeable future are bound to affect the successful implementation of agreed labour market strategies. The outline of employment modernization is clear enough but its eventual success must remain problematic.

First appeared 30 April 1998

Social partners: working solution sought

ROBERT TAYLOR

The so-called social partners (the European Trade Union Confederation and the two European employer organizations Unice and Ceep) would like to play an increasingly important role in decision-making after the creation of economic and monetary union, at least in the development of industrial relations and employment strategies.

Their desire to gain an accepted legitimacy in the changing EU power structure reflects a widespread concern on both sides of industry that the arrival of Emu will strengthen the domination of the financial sector through co-ordinated monetary policies and the harmonization of member state budgets.

Although the social partners for the moment may lack a common agenda on how to pursue their mutual interests, recent events suggest this may still prove possible. The two sides appear to have accepted the value of bargaining at EU level on measures that provide a minimum framework of legal workplace rights. Agreements have been reached recently through this social dialogue approach on unpaid parental leave and atypical work. Many employers may have misgivings about negotiating with trade unions on such issues but they prefer their direct involvement in the process than leaving it to member state governments to decide what should be done through the establishment of legally enforced directives.

The social partners at EU level remain weak organizations, dependent on the willingness of their affiliate nation-state-based members to allow them the freedom to increase their power and influence. They have been under-equipped in staff levels and financial resources to strengthen their competences as genuinely representative organizations. For the most part, employers continue to wish to exclude most social issues from negotiation at EU level, stressing the need for subsidiarity. By contrast many trade unions have seen the value of strengthening their position at EU level to compensate for their weakening influence with national governments.

But it is widely recognized that moves to greater social integration inside the EU have lagged far behind the pace of convergence in economic and monetary affairs. Otto Jacobi, head of Laboratorium Europea, the German independent think tank, says he is concerned that the resulting imbalance has created a 'legitimation gap' over Emu which has encouraged popular scepticism towards the whole European project. However, employers and trade unions acknowledge it is going to prove difficult to ensure more power is devolved to the social partners in Brussels with the arrival of Emu, however sensible this might appear. Social issues have always encouraged an exaggerated hyperbole at EU level which has belied a more modest reality.

But former EU president Jacques Delors has warned of the dangers to Emu's success if the social dimension is either ignored or given a low priority. Under his initiative after 1988 a serious attempt was made to construct social partnership as a necessary counterweight to the creation of the EU single market with its concern to pull down obstacles to economic integration of goods, capital and services.

However, strengthening the power of social partnership in Brussels appears to conflict with a countervailing tendency towards a more decentralized approach to collective bargaining, stimulated in part by technological change in the workplace coupled with competitive pressures in the product market.

To some extent the social partners can be expected to build up the existing sector-based industrial federations as bodies where a co-ordinated approach is possible. The European works councils have also provided the first means for creating direct cross-border linkages at company level that may help to stimulate more substantial European-wide strategies once Emu has arrived.

Despite some aggressive rhetoric there are no signs for the moment that any of this has brought the prospect of European-wide collective bargaining any nearer. Bernt Keller, professor at Konstanz University, argues that monetary union makes such a development 'necessary and unavoidable', compelling nationally based trade unions into Europeanized strategies. But the barriers of language, tradition, different trade union and employer structures continue to slow the convergence dynamic.

Surprisingly the majority of trade union and employer organizations inside the EU support the move to economic and monetary union, despite the undoubted social and political strain this has provoked in France, Germany and Italy. As George Ross, professor of European affairs at Rutgers University explains, the European Trade Union Confederation has 'developed as an organizational player from the top rather than as a mass organization from the bottom. Perhaps this quite different model will open up into a different kind of transnational unionism in the next millennium. Or perhaps not.'

However, if social partnership is to make any impact on the development of Emu it will have to establish a more robust network of connections across different levels of decision-making than seems likely at present. Along with the European Parliament, it remains the best hope of constructing a check or balance in a system that may find it difficult to establish any democratic legitimacy with the peoples of Europe.

First published 23 March 1998

Industrial relations: new strategies called for

ROBERT TAYLOR

The creation of a grandiose European-wide industrial relations system seems unlikely to follow the arrival of the euro and economic and monetary union. Nor are existing structures of collective bargaining between employers and trade unions at national, sectoral and regional level going to be swept away with any rapid convergence of nominal wage rates, productivity performance and unit labour costs.

The principle of subsidiarity, hardened by tradition and common sense, will remain a strong impediment to a radical transformation of European industrial relations for the foreseeable future. But this does not mean Emu and the single currency will have no impact on the way trade unions and employers behave in their pay negotiations. David Soskice, employment relations director at the Wissenschaftszentrum in Berlin, believes there is likely to be a growth of what he calls 'focal point bargaining'. He expects the powerful IG Metall union in Germany to become a lead body in negotiating collective agreements that will have a wider influence on bargainers in Austria, Belgium, Italy and the Netherlands. Such a pattern is already emerging under the disciplinary pressures provided by the European exchange-rate mechanism.

'There are two possible scenarios,' Mr Soskice explains. 'It is possible the German deals will set the pace for others to catch up with, despite difficulties over differential productivity rates and diverse unit labour costs. On the other hand, it is also possible other bargainers outside Germany will seek to undercut German agreements to secure a competitive advantage.'

This is already happening in Belgium and the Netherlands, where collective deals are being made with nominal wage increases that are worth 20 per cent less than in Germany. Such competitiveness could undermine workplace stability. But it may take some time to emerge as a problem. What is already emerging, however, is a European pay area unplanned by the 'social partners' – employers and unions. As Otto Jacobi explains in an article in *Transfer*, the European trade union journal, national collective agreements are already 'displaying a surprisingly high degree of convergence' in pay, working hours and other working conditions. It runs in parallel to convergence of price stability, lower interest rates and limits on public deficits.

Mr Jacobi points to recent industrial relations developments in Belgium and Sweden, where agreements have stipulated that wage rises may not be higher than in surrounding European economies in order to avoid competitive disadvantages. This suggests that the pressures for cohesion and restraint are substantial. On the other hand, he says this could lead to sustained pay restraint and stimulate a 'form of social undercutting that could trigger a downward spiral in wage standards throughout Europe, at the end of which everybody will be worse off'.

Such a disastrous outcome is what trade unions and many employers are both anxious to avoid. Much will depend on how the social partners can construct mutually acceptable industrial relations strategies at European level that can prevent disintegration. The establishment of a minimum framework of agreed labour standards across the EU is already well advanced. Social dialogue between employers and trade unions is also likely to establish wide-ranging consultation rights in companies on a growing number of issues beyond wages and benefits.

A stronger network of power and influence between trade union sector federations and national bodies can also be expected over the next few years. Such developments may help to strengthen the legitimacy of trade unions, prevent a downward spiral in social conditions and protect employers against unfair competition. But this does not mean that the euro zone is going to be weighed down by an intricate industrial relations system that will add costly burdens to business and hold back productivity improvements and employment creation. The EU's Amsterdam treaty and the subsequent Luxembourg jobs summit suggested that trade unions and employers were ready to negotiate on a new, more flexible industrial relations agenda that went beyond traditional items of collective bargaining.

There is a new emphasis on how to protect the rights of workers who are part-time or temporary, to encourage small enterprises, to improve worker employability through training and education, and to ensure that workers embrace workplace reorganization in the name of efficiency and competitiveness.

Mr Jacobi sees this as a sign of pragmatism among the European trade unions that has been played down. But David Foden at the European Trade Union Institute warns that many trade unions have not yet begun to appreciate the significance of Emu and the euro for them. 'The need for labour markets to adjust to intensified competitive pressures without the safety valve of devaluation will cause considerable strain,' he admits. 'The watchwords will be "negotiating change", "adaptability", "flexibility" and "security". If the social partners do not rise to the challenges these concepts pose, then Emu is likely to have unpleasant consequences.'

But the EU is more than a single market and an economic and monetary arrangement. It is also a 'community of social values', argues Mr Jacobi. He believes this is why an industrial relations system will emerge that provides workers not only with employment protection rights but also co-determination and consultation rights in the enterprises where they are employed.

It is most unlikely that trade unions and employer associations are going to see their powers and authority enhanced automatically in the age of the euro despite their efforts to gain some direct influence over decision-making in the European Central Bank and between EU governments. On the other hand, nor are they going to be marginalized. It may mean a strengthening of legal regulation and a weakening in voluntary bargaining. As Paul Marginson, professor at Leeds University Business School, has argued, collective bargaining could become 'an empty shell to which employers and policy-makers pay lip service but little else'.

What we are likely to see in the euro zone is a bewildering but potentially fruitful network of co-ordination at all levels – from Brussels to the workplace. This will probably lack the strength to act as a countervailing influence to that of the banks and financial system on the making of Emu monetary policy. However, supporters and critics alike also believe a new legitimacy for industrial relations is vital if the EU is to narrow its democratic deficit and ensure the euro has popular support.

First published 30 April 1998

The welfare trap: *business is preparing for the single currency, but welfare has barely started*

PETER NORMAN

There is a growing realization in continental Europe that the euro will greatly toughen competition. But there are still big gaps in the awareness of policymakers about the likely pressure for change that will flow from the increased transparency that the planned single currency will bring to all aspects of economic and social life.

Industry and commerce have got the message. Mergers, divestitures and other manifestations of corporate restructuring in readiness for the euro have dominated business news in the run-up to the single currency. But this frenetic jockeying for position in the private sector has prompted little reaction among governments.

So far, there has been little thought given to the impact of the euro on social policy. Yet the introduction of a single currency is bound to have a profound impact on the conditions in which governments support the weak, the sick and the elderly and on state systems which in many cases are under serious strain after having ballooned in size and ambition over the past twenty-five years.

True, the euro's impact on social policy is creeping up the agenda. But if two recent conferences in Bonn are any guide, it is the private sector that is making the running on the issue. The scale of the challenge was summed up by Klaus-Dirk Henke, a professor of finance and health economics at the Technical University of Berlin. 'A single currency will increase competitive pressures and so increase the importance of other factors such as tax systems and social security systems as determinants of competitiveness,' he told an Anglo-German conference on welfare reform organized by the European Policy Forum, a cross-party London-based think tank, and the Frankfurter Institut, a pro-market research body.

What this might mean in practice had been outlined a few days earlier by Regine Matthijsen-Sebbel, deputy director for international industrial relations and social policy at Philips, the Netherlands-based multinational corporation, at the annual meeting of the BDA, the German employers' federation. Mrs Matthijsen-Sebbel forecast that the euro would put pressure on governments to equalize the big differences between gross and net incomes in the EU. Her prediction implied substantial change in social security contributions paid by employers and employees, with pressure on high contribution countries to cut both the levies charged and the services provided.

The problem appears especially acute in Germany where the overall social budget has soared to about DM1,250 billion (£425.1 billion) and accounts for more than a third of gross domestic product. The state system, which covers health, pensions, unemployment and long-term residential care, is in crisis. Benefits are being cut while contributions, paid half by employers and half by employees, reached a record 42 per cent of gross wages in 1996. The chart overleaf, based on BDA figures from 1996, shows how social security costs carried by employers in western Germany are higher than elsewhere in the EU. As a result, German labour costs averaged DM47 per hour and so were well above those of other EU states. Although serious now, the problem of Germany's non-wage labour costs looks sure to grow. The conventional world of work, encapsulated in traditional employer–employee relationships, is in relative decline and becoming less capable of sustaining social security systems.

So what is to be done? Mercifully, there seems to be no great support for a harmonization of social policies in Europe. Such a project would be near-impossible to implement because of the very great cultural, institutional and historical differences among the fifteen EU member states. It would be incompatible with the principle of subsidiarity.

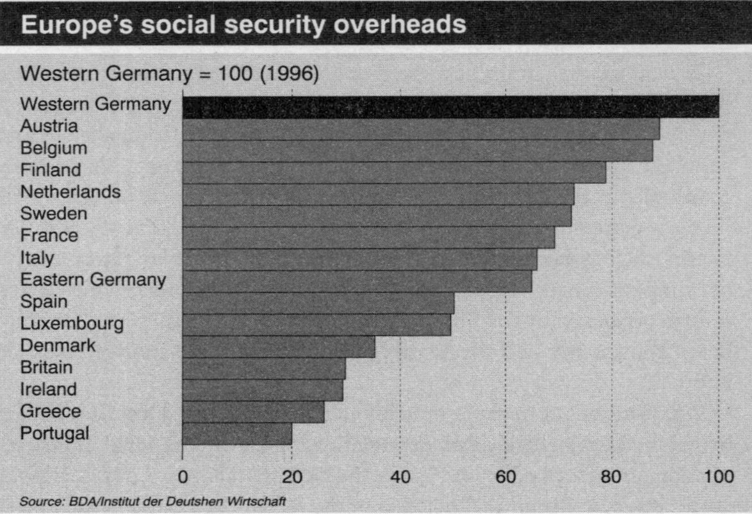

Harmonization would also create some alarmingly costly hostages to fortune in connection with the eastward enlargement of the EU.

On the other hand, continuing unchanged is hardly sustainable. A high-cost, high-benefit social security system as in Germany is unlikely to encourage investment in plant and full-time jobs when similarly qualified staff are readily available at lower cost in other parts of the euro area. In countries with high-cost, state-operated social security systems, it is easy to envisage a vicious circle of high and rising unemployment, lower social security contributions and benefit squeeze leading to social distress and disturbance.

The alternative is reform. At the BDA annual meeting, Dieter Hundt, the president of the employers' federation, called for a curtailing of state social security to a 'basic' level and reliance on private insurance for anything beyond that. To force the issue, he urged that the part of earnings on which social security contributions are levied should be frozen. Existing claims on the state system would be maintained but people wanting to increase their cover in line with growing wealth and inflation would have to take out additional private insurance. That would mark a step towards a partly funded system rather than one based entirely on pay-as-you-go.

Addressing the Anglo-German conference, Professor Henke also demanded a European 'middle way' that would retain some state social security provision while encouraging private provision. Otherwise, he warned, the state could find itself overstretched and destabilized.

Social policies in the UK have been moving down this path for some time. The need for change in Germany was illustrated by the Bonn parliament's decision to raise value added tax to 16 per cent from 15 per cent from April 1998 to prevent a jump in pension contributions to a politically unacceptable 21 per cent of gross salaries. That policy failure should be a signal for a review and reform of Europe's pay-as-you-go social security systems. For if politicians do not heed the message, the euro will be another factor forcing change.

First appeared 15 December 1997

Productivity study shows dangers of euro wage claims

PETER NORMAN

There is going to be no escaping the concept of subsidiarity in Europe over the next twelve months. But the idea that decisions should be taken as close to the citizen as possible has so far been linked mainly to efforts to reform the institutions of the European Union rather than economic and social policy.

This state of affairs may now change thanks to some pioneering work on labour productivity in the eleven-nation euro zone from Horst Siebert, head of the Kiel Institute of World Economics and one of five economics professors on the German government's council of economic advisers.

In a newly published Kiel working paper, Professor Siebert has produced what he claims are the first comparable figures on labour productivity among the eleven founders of Europe's economic and monetary union, using the bilateral central rates agreed in May 1998. The figures, summarized in the table, lead him to conclude that wage-setting and social security systems cannot be Europeanized. They will have to stay anchored in their present national structures for the foreseeable future.

Anyone who has dipped into the EU's Maastricht and Amsterdam treaties might be tempted to say: so what? Maastricht, while centralizing monetary policy, recognized that other aspects of economic management remained the responsibility of euro-zone members. The Amsterdam treaty made a similar point about social policy.

But the euro is proving a powerful force for further integration well before it is launched officially next January. According to Oskar Lafontaine, the leader of Germany's opposition Social Democratic party, trade unions have already recognized that they can't operate nationally and are beginning to develop activities across borders. Such initiatives, together with the enhanced transparency of prices and costs that the euro will

Labour productivity and labour costs in the euro zone, 1997

	Productivity[1] (%)	Costs[2] (%)	Jobless rate[3] (%)
Austria	90.9	89.5	4.4
Belgium	97.6	107.6	9.2
Finland	81.4	93.8	14.0
France	95.3	95.6	12.4
Germany	92.9	95.3	9.7
west	100.0	100.0	8.3
east	60.4	74.4	15.7
Ireland	69.5	71.8	10.2
Italy	85.3	79.9	12.1
Netherlands	85.4	94.4	5.2
Portugal	34.5	37.4	6.8
Spain	62.0	66.9	20.8
UK*	71.7	68.0	7.1

*Using actual central rate for sterling
[1]Nominal GDP per person employed as % of western Germany
[2]Gross compensation per employee as % of western Germany
[3]Standardized OECD rates with Kiel Institute calculations for eastern and western Germany

Source: Kiel Institute of World Economics

bring, could easily encourage calls for the same wage for the same type of work, Professor Siebert fears. This would be a grave error because of the divergent productivity levels in the euro zone. A Europeanization of wage formation would be sure to increase unemployment where it caused growth of costs to run ahead of productivity.

The table, which takes western Germany as 100, shows how much the productivity and labour costs of Emu member states differ. In the case of productivity, measured as nominal economic output per employed person, four territories (including Germany as a whole) come within 10 percentage points of the West German level. Three countries are between 81 and 86 per cent, and another three (including eastern Germany) between 60 and 70 per cent. Portugal is at 34.5 per cent.

Professor Siebert calculates UK labour productivity, which he includes for comparative reasons, at 71.7 per cent of the western German level. The middle column shows how labour costs, as gross income from employment per head, also vary. The data has to be treated with some caution, Professor Siebert says. The figures are a snapshot of just one year (1997). They take no account of varying unemployment rates (in column three), which make comparisons of underlying productivity and cost trends difficult. Data collection methods differ between countries. Italy's productivity figure could be swollen by the inclusion of an estimate of the black or informal economy in its GDP figures. The Netherlands, with its substantial part-time working, could understate productivity.

Caveats notwithstanding, Professor Siebert says the different productivity levels highlight the need for decentralized wage-setting, which should happen at the regional and company level rather than nationally or sectorally. His findings also have important implications for social policies, which in Europe are financed through levies on employment and are therefore ultimately determined by productivity.

The divergence in labour productivities makes clear that the costs of social security systems in the different countries must also be different, he says. This means social security benefit cannot be harmonized. As long as productivity varies widely among euro countries, the idea of a social union to accompany monetary union must remain a pipedream.

First appeared 7 July 1998

Perils of unemployment

GIORGIO LA MALFA AND FRANCO MODIGLIANI

We are on record as having supported Europe's economic and monetary union from the very beginning. We recognize its anticipated economic benefits stemming from eliminating currency transaction costs and exchange risks, thereby reducing interest rates. We value its contribution to a fuller integration of European economies and the leap it promises from national to European sovereignty. But lately we have developed some serious qualms about the way in which Emu is taking shape and the narrow definition of its responsibilities and objectives.

The root cause of our concern is unemployment. The average level in EU countries – 11 per cent – is gigantic compared with an average of 3 per cent in the 1960s and early 1970s. This, Europe's crucial economic and social problem, is threatening the future of the EU. And it is not the result of forces beyond the reach of economic policy, such as rapid technological progress, competition from low wage countries or a crisis of capitalism.

We know this because the steep rise in the jobless rate is absent not only in the US and Japan, but also in nearly all other industrial countries, including European ones not in the European Monetary System (such as Norway, Switzerland and to some extent the UK). Of course, many factors explain why some countries are doing better than others. But a big cause of the differential performance lies in the behaviour of aggregate demand spurred by investment.

Data indicate that the rise in unemployment in the European Union between the mid-1970s and 1997 has coincided with a reduction of the share of GDP going to investment by one-third. In countries where the ratio of investment to GDP has been relatively stable (such as the US), unemployment has not risen significantly, if at all. The lesson is clear. The EU must adopt policies to tackle unemployment through a big revival of investment. And it must do so promptly. Failure to do so may jeopardize Emu's future, as disgruntled countries may decide to withdraw unilaterally before the introduction of the euro in 2002.

Nothing in the Maastricht treaty or in the agreements reached during European summit meetings addresses this problem. Rather the reverse. The participants seem to have accepted the concept, repeated *ad nauseam* during the recent Luxembourg summit, that the level of employment is not a responsibility of the Union, but a task to be accomplished by each country separately.

At the same time they have taken away from the member countries all the tools of demand management. Fixed exchange rates and full capital mobility prevent central banks from setting interest rates. Narrow budget limits, as foreseen by the so-called 'stability pact', make fiscal policy impossible. The European Commission has no resources to spend on Union-wide investment projects and the European Central Bank is enjoined to aim exclusively at price stability.

The agreement to sterilize all demand policy tools seems to reflect in part the view that unemployment is due mainly to the malfunctioning of the labour market. We agree that labour rigidities may contribute to the unemployment problem in the EU and that they deserve attention. But they are certainly not the only cause and may not even be the main one. Removing the rigidities will not return unemployment to the level of the 1960s without a recovery of investment to corresponding levels.

A second ground for rejecting demand policies reflects a combination of callous disregard for the evils of unemployment and preoccupation with the idea that any policy directed towards raising employment might produce inflation. Such a preoccupation is unfounded. In 1997, inflation in all EU countries but two was below 3 per cent. Moreover, the five countries in the Union with the lowest levels of unemployment have below average inflation rates.

The time has come for a drastic change of policies for the third phase of Emu. A plan should be drawn at European level setting a target for employment to be pursued through a gradual but significant increase in total investment, private as well as public. Over time, this could be self-financing: the additional investment would be offset by saving the money that is currently wasted through spending on unemployment benefits. National governments ought to take responsibility for implementing this plan. It would be necessary to redefine the 'stability pact', making the balancing of current budget spending compulsory, but allowing the financing of investment expenditure through public debt, perhaps subject to authorization from the EU.

Even though we see no evidence for the concern that reducing unemployment means more inflation at the moment (although it could appear later once unemployment has fallen a lot), we suggest that it is still desirable to involve the 'social partners' (labour, employers and the government) in a compact aimed at ensuring price stability. This would free the monetary authorities to concentrate on the task of fulfilling the investment target. If any country tried to revive investment unilaterally, much of its impact would be dissipated to the benefit of other countries and it would soon run into unmanageable balance of payments problems. Finally, we would like to suggest that the so-called euro-X committee (the club for future Emu members), which was formally decided upon in Luxembourg, could best be suited to assume the role of decision-making body for this project.

We know that our opinions are shared by many politicians as well as by most economists, although few so far have dared to take a public stand in opposing the agreements underwritten by their governments. We hope that other voices will join ours in demanding feasible policies to ensure that Emu is not a straitjacket but an opportunity for a better Europe. Otherwise, there is a danger that the whole project might fail.

First appeared 16 January 1998

The need for realism about Emu: *radical labour market reforms are necessary if monetary union is to survive*

PETER NORMAN

Germany is beginning to wake up to the problems that will have to be tackled after the launch of the single currency. There has been a flurry of warnings that Emu will be born in a difficult environment and require radical economic adjustment among its member states.

Hans Tietmeyer, the Bundesbank president, reminded readers of *Die Woche*, a German newspaper, in the autumn of 1997 that the Maastricht treaty was taking Europe into uncharted territory and that his own country would have to change. 'In Europe, in contrast to other monetary unions, we will have neither a common tax system nor a common social security system', he said. 'Unlike most federal states, there will be no system of fiscal transfers. Europe will simply have a single monetary policy.' Germany, he said, 'must reform itself in such a way that business becomes more dynamic, invests more and employs more, and the public budgets and social security systems are once again placed on sustainable financial foundations'.

He pointed out that flexibility in the business sector and the labour market were essential for Emu to survive. Otherwise, the monetary union could produce conflicts, generate demands for fiscal transfers and prove 'very problematical'. A similar warning came from the International Monetary Fund which lamented the lack of economic reform in Germany, France and Italy. It suggested greater labour market flexibility was almost as important for the future of Emu as a sound fiscal policy in the member states. Without labour market reform, unemployment would rise and undermine public support for the single currency.

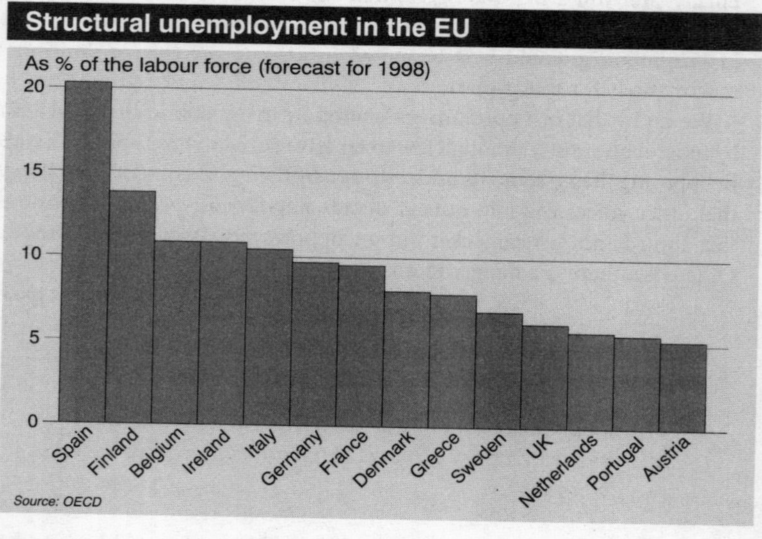

The need for action in much of Europe can be seen in the illustration showing recent forecasts of structural unemployment in 1998 by the Paris-based Organization for Economic Co-operation and Development (OECD). The OECD expects structural unemployment, which requires changed policies to be corrected, to be 10 per cent of the European Union labour force in 1998 – more than twelve times the 0.8 per cent cyclical jobless rate that might be expected to disappear with an economic upturn.

Concern about European structural problems and their implications for Emu was also apparent among academic economists and monetary officials attending the European Summer Institute conference in Berlin in September 1997 on the German economy and the EU. The need for reform of its tax systems was highlighted by two Italian economists, Francesco Daveri and Guido Tabellini, who demonstrated a strong link between high labour taxes and high unemployment in Europe. Manfred Neumann, professor of economic policy at Bonn University and chairman of the economics ministry's council of expert advisers, charged that 'close to nothing' had been done to reform Germany's labour market regulations, the public pension system or the tax system, although it was widely recognized that existing structures were 'seriously deficient and required major changes'.

Professor Neumann did not pull his punches. Fundamental reform of the labour market was 'not on the official agenda' and 'still taboo' in spite of unemployment of more than, at that time, 4.4 million. A mini-reform of Germany's pay-as-you-go pension system, designed by the government, might help for ten to fifteen years.

But official forecasts indicated that the number of people aged sixty-three and above was likely to jump from about 35 per cent of the population of working age in 2012 to 57 per cent by 2035. The implications of this large increase in Germany's elderly population after 2010 were 'essentially ignored'. Although it looked far into the future, Professor Neumann's address begged the question whether Germany and other launch members of Emu were fit for the euro. The demographic shift starting after 2010 is foreseeable today. In the absence of a policy response, it seems certain to have a profoundly negative effect on German business costs and the country's capacity to meet the Emu debt and deficit criteria in the long term. German politics, Professor Neumann complained, was 'hypnotized by the objective to qualify for Emu'.

Some of the closest political allies of Helmut Kohl, the German chancellor, subsequently showed that they also saw an agenda of structural reform in Emu. A policy statement produced under the auspices of Wolfgang Schäuble, the leader of Mr Kohl's Christian Democratic Union and its Bavarian sister party in the Bundestag, stated clearly for the first time that monetary union was aimed at 'a radical rehabilitation and modernization of Europe's economies'. The joint paper cast Emu in the role of a disciplinary agent on national governments rather than a vague guarantor of peace and freedom. The Maastricht treaty, it said, was designed to break the vicious circle of rising unemployment and the growing strain on public finances. Monetary union, it went on, offered a way forward to combat deficiencies such as excessively regulated labour markets, high and complex taxation, outdated education and training systems, imbalances in the old age pension system and the continuing rise in health care costs.

Mr Schäuble's paper recognized that Emu could be a problem for the government because the painful effects of economic adjustment would be felt long before the benefits accrued. Its publication at the start of twelve months of campaigning for the German general election in September 1998 was therefore a bold political step. But it will only mark a new realism about Emu if it is followed by action.

First appeared 22 September 1997

Prices: *what prospects of a paradise for shoppers?*

GUY DE JONQUIÈRES

As the single currency makes markets more transparent and competitive, prices will inexorably be driven down to the same level everywhere in the European Union. Once retailers display prices in euros, it is claimed, differences between them will be immediately apparent. That, and the elimination of foreign exchange costs, will encourage consumers to shop more aggressively across borders and release huge pressures for common EU-wide prices.

That, at any rate, is the prospect held out by many true believers in economic and monetary union, who see the promise of big consumer windfalls on the High Street as one of the plan's strongest popular selling points. But things may not work out quite that way.

The approach of the euro is spurring companies across the EU to review their marketing strategies. Most think it will reinforce the economic integration already triggered by the single market programme and fiercer global competition. But few expect the euro to bring dramatic price changes. Nor is it certain that all adjustments will be downwards. Many businessmen are sceptical of predictions that increased price transparency will suddenly transform consumer behaviour. Despite differing national currencies, many car buyers already know that prices vary widely across the EU. Cross-border bargain hunting has long been a way of life for residents of frontier regions.

Retailers question whether the euro will lead most shoppers to compare EU-wide prices more assiduously, or switch their custom abroad. Britain's Marks & Spencer, which has stores in ten other EU countries, sees no immediate need to standardize prices across Europe and says it will continue to be guided by local market conditions. Wide differences between European countries' consumer protection laws, which can make it hard to obtain redress for faulty products bought abroad, also deter cross-border shopping. Although EU experts are discussing proposals to harmonize rules, they are making slow progress.

Another reason why the euro's direct impact on consumers may be limited is that they are already enjoying some of the benefits that it is supposed to produce. In much of the EU, governments' efforts to stabilize exchange rates have sharply reduced the currency fluctuations which contribute to price differentials. Meanwhile, the advent of the single market has obliged manufacturers to tackle pricing anomalies, or risk seeing their marketing channels undermined by unauthorized 'parallel' imports from low-priced markets to high-priced ones.

These pressures have already caused wholesale prices of products, such as consumer electronics and domestic appliances, to converge. However, many companies say prices will never be uniform, because business costs and tax rates vary so widely across the EU. For most shoppers, the most immediate and visible impact of Emu will occur as retailers begin to display prices in euros as well as in national currencies. From 2002, prices in member states will be shown in euros only. Retailers are still wrestling with how to manage the switch. The trickiest problem is to convert from national currencies into euros the psychologically important 'price points', which shoppers use to compare the value of competing products.

Some retailers say they already plan to round prices down to the nearest convenient figure in euros, although that would mean cutting profit margins. But consumer organizations are sceptical. They fear retailers will instead use the transition to the euro to push through concealed price increases, and they want binding legislation to stop such abuses. For many consumers, car prices are likely to be the most telling benchmark of claims that the euro will be good for them. Car makers have been accused for years of maintaining big price differentials by preventing re-exports of vehicles between EU countries.

The European Commission has begun cracking down harder on such abuses. It recently fined Volkswagen Ecu102 million ($111 million/£66.5 million) for prohibiting Italian dealers from selling to customers in Austria and Germany, where its cars cost 30 per cent more. The euro will test claims, long advanced by car manufacturers, that price differentials reflect currency fluctuations. However, critics say competition will remain restricted while industry distribution arrangements are exempted from EU competition rules. They claim that, by allowing manufacturers to choose the dealers they sell through, the exemption makes it easy for them to rig the market.

Overall, the most important consequence of the increased transparency promised by the euro may be to throw more light on the underlying factors which shape competition and determine price levels in the EU. Where prices vary because explicit trade barriers are impeding the workings of the single market, Brussels and EU member governments may face stronger pressure to attack them. But when obstacles are rooted in consumer psychology, and the diversity of European culture and custom, the euro may make little difference.

First appeared 30 April 1998

5 Preparing for Emu

Emu will have a profound impact on the corporate sector, both at the operational level and in terms of strategy. Some companies have tried to steal a march on the competition, and have spent millions preparing for the euro. Others have not given the matter a moment of thought. This chapter examines the task of preparation and looks at how some businesses are going about it.

The rules of Emu are complicated, and much of the complexity is due to the arrangements of the transitional period, from 1999 to 2002, when the euro will coexist with national currencies. The term currency is misleading, because the national notes and coins will be mere denominations of the euro, in the way that the cent is a denomination of the dollar. From 1999 the euro will be the only currency in the eleven participating member states.

The overriding rule governing the transitional period is that companies or individuals will face 'no compulsion, no prohibition'. People can make transactions either in national denominations or in the euro. This means that companies will have to have systems in place to handle the dual-currency problem. But it is surprising how few companies have considered these problems in detail.

Mike Gardiner, a partner of Ernst & Young, the business consultants, provides a useful checklist. He argues that Emu will bring opportunities and threats so companies must plan carefully. And since the impact of Emu will be so broad it is essential that they prepare on a cross-departmental basis. Wolfgang Münchau, the *FT*'s economics correspondent, looks specifically at corporate treasurers, one of the business functions affected most by Emu. The establishment of a single and highly liquid currency will bring big changes to European capital markets. Developments, such as the accelerating process of securitization, could have a profound impact on the relationships between companies and their markets.

Andrew Fisher, the *FT*'s Frankfurt correspondent, investigates the competition between payment systems which channel money between financial institutions. Under Emu, systems have to be able to handle transactions across the euro zone. He looks at Target, the payment system operated by the European Central Bank, and two private sector competitors, the Frankfurt-based EA, and the Paris-based Euro Banking Association.

Jens Tartler writes about the effect of Emu on public administrations. Unlike private companies, the public sector has generally been slower in its preparations. The result is that even some national tax authorities will not allow taxes to be paid in euros when Emu starts next year.

One of the industries most profoundly affected by Emu is retailing. The new currency will affect the sector indirectly through more intense competition but also directly through the conversion of prices. Peggy Hollinger, the *FT*'s retail correspondent, takes a look at some of the issues, such as how attractive price points, such as DM9.99, can be converted into euros.

The chapter concludes with a series of case studies, detailing how eight companies – BMW, ICI, Siemens, Istituto San Paolo di Torino, Saint-Gobain, Chase Manhattan, Citibank and Unilever – have been preparing for Emu.

WOLFGANG MÜNCHAU

A General issues

Emu will bring opportunities and threats. Companies must plan carefully

MICHAEL GARDINER

Companies across Europe have been promised many benefits from European economic and monetary union. The single currency is meant to provide lower interest rates and more competitive economies. It is also meant to encourage better integration of national markets, simplified financial management and elimination of exchange transaction costs.

However, Emu carries with it significant risks for companies, and will require intensive preparation across all aspects of business activity. Companies can choose whether to make the minimum preparations necessary for Emu – or whether in addition to work to obtain advantages from the market changes which will follow. But ignoring Emu, and in particular ignoring the systems implications, is not an option.

Opportunities and threats

	Opportunities	Threats
Interim period	• Cost savings • Refining banking and treasury relationships	• Systems issues • Price transparency increases
Post 2002	• Consolidation and penetration of Euro market • Merger/alliance relationships	• Lack of co-ordinated European product process and systems strategies

Source: Emst & Young

This article provides a checklist of the major questions which companies should ask themselves in the run up to the 'paper' Emu in 1999 and the full single currency in 2002. Companies should define:

- their future vision of how they would operate in a euro environment;
- the opportunities and threats for each of their lines of business and countries of operation as shown in the diagram;
- how they would handle the transition phase.

Among issues to be considered by companies are:

Marketing and pricing

Assess each of your markets to identify the way in which they will operate after the single currency is introduced: the euro will bring existing national markets closer together and in some industries will result in market restructuring. Review your pricing strategy, because it may not be possible to maintain price differentials between existing national markets. Consider how your competitors will react to the single currency: will they rationalize their operations? Work with your customers to agree a switch to euro purchasing and your switch to euro pricing. Find out when your suppliers wish to change to euro pricing. If you publish price lists, consider how you will make the transition to the euro – for example, will you reassess prices to set them at appropriate euro values (e.g. 99 cents, rather than a straight rounding). Consider lead times for euro promotional material. Consider customer or supplier information programmes to deal with the changeover.

Systems and IT

Identify the operational systems to be changed to deal with the euro. You will need to assess each operational system and decide which to modify, and assess the risks of systems failure to your business. This is a major task and needs to be started quickly. Identify which systems need special changes for the period when you may have to deal with transactions in either euro or an old national currency. Confirm that systems can cope with currency conversion and rounding rules (6 significant figures, 3 decimal points). Identify cash-handling operations and consider what equipment and systems need to be changed. If you make use of electronic data interchange (EDI), find out what your trading partners are doing about Emu and ensure EDI systems can cope with the change. Identify all other external systems links involving currency transactions and ensure they are euro compatible. Obtain appropriate IT resources and consider putting together your euro systems project and your year 2000 project.

Finance and payroll

Decide when to change over your internal accounting to the euro. Decide when to change your payroll to euro (this is likely to be a year 2002 issue when coins and notes are available for retail use). Consider if your accounting will be affected by gains and losses between euro currencies which could crystallize in 1999. Identify when national and local governments will accept returns in euro (this is likely to be closer to 2002 than 1999). Consider an information and training programme inside your company.

Treasury and banking

Consider rationalizing banking relationships in the euro area (you may need only one bank for euro payments). Identify savings by the reduction of treasury operations, or by setting up some form of joint service organization for euro invoicing. Consider how the euro will affect your balance sheet and currency management in your balance sheet. Identify any issues on the redenomination of debt or securities in the rounding from old currencies to the euro.

Legal issues

Investigate contract continuity, particularly outside the EU where the EU regulations confirming contract continuity may not apply. Consider changes to your staff employment contracts and pension arrangements. Review contract terms and conditions to see that the euro is adequately covered.

Longer term

Review your operations to consider the advantages and threats of a single currency. For example, the existence of a large single currency area may lead you to consider relocating some operations there to avoid currency fluctuations. Consider operational changes such as rationalization of your supply chain to take advantage of a single currency.

The issues listed above show that the introduction of the euro will touch on all aspects of a company's business. To deal with these issues, many companies have put together a multi-disciplinary planning team. This team needs to address: a planning phase or impact assessment to agree the scope of the project; an options evaluation phase; obtaining agreement on the euro strategy; implementation of the preferred way forward. Companies will need to take account of the emerging experience of dealing with the euro, and of the advice being provided by industry working parties, the European Commission, the EMI and others. Good communication with customers, staff and suppliers is essential throughout. Time is now short for companies with operations in potential euro countries to begin planning their project and priority must be given to this issue.

First appeared 28 May 1997

A world turned upside down: *corporate treasurers will face fundamental changes in strategic areas*

WOLFGANG MÜNCHAU

No single area of business will be more affected by economic and monetary union than the corporate treasury departments, the interface between companies and the financial system. Not only will the way companies operate be affected, the changes could also fundamentally alter the structure of European financial markets. The three core areas through which Emu impacts on corporate treasurers are foreign exchange, cash flow management and corporate finance.

While transaction costs will come down, the savings generated are expected to be marginal. The real saving in foreign exchange operations is the elimination of foreign exchange risk. This trickles down the entire financial planning function. With Emu, financial planning across the EU is bound to become easier. Cash flow from a subsidiary based in one EU country can be input directly into the accounts of the parent company in another country without complicated risk adjustments.

Cash flow management is potentially highly significant. At the moment it can take up to five days for money to be transferred from one EU bank to another. The combination of Emu and various technical developments could drastically reduce transmission times. Under Emu, the settlement process will be fundamentally reformed. At the wholesale level, suitable for large transactions, banks will use the so-called Target system, a real-time payments system, which allows immediate settlements. Target stands for trans-European automated real-time gross settlement express transfer. The relatively high cost of the system will make it suitable for large-scale transactions such as those used in foreign exchange deals or large bond trades.

For smaller transactions, banks will have to rely on other complementary systems, such as the system operated by the Ecu Banking Association. The EBA system is currently a settlement system for the Ecu, the basket of European currencies, but will be extended to the euro from 1999 onwards. The system will have a higher capacity and lower charges than Target. But unlike Target – where settlement occurs real-time – the EBA system is a net system, under which accounts are settled only at the end of the day. There will be other ways in which money moves around after 1999. To transfer funds from France to Germany, the chain now goes from the debtor to a French commercial bank to the French central bank to the German central bank to the German commercial bank, before the money finally reaches the creditor. Post-Emu, the French bank could deal directly through a German subsidiary or associate bank.

Several opinion surveys suggest that large multinational companies will reduce the number of their banking relations post-Emu because they will no longer have to have banks in each EU country. There is a counter-argument though: central banks will still collect statistical information on cross-border payments. This extra administrative burden means banks may be charging higher costs for cross-border euro transactions than for domestic euro transactions. But this is unlikely to halt the trend towards greater concentration in the banking sector, according to experts.

Post-Emu, banks will be competing Europe-wide as opposed to nationwide. That means that lending margins, which vary considerably, will converge over time. Banks in Ireland, Spain and the Netherlands have among the highest lending margins, compared with those in Germany, France and Belgium, which have the lowest. The same will apply to other services offered by banks. Profit margin differentials are likely to converge, and most experts believe strong competition will force convergence at the lower end of the scale.

In present corporate management most European companies, and almost all small and mid-sized companies, use only one form of external debt finance – the traditional bank credit. In the US, bank loans only account for 38 per cent of total debt and it is not uncommon for even mid-sized companies to fund themselves through the capital market. The two segments of the capital market likely to strengthen are the commercial paper market and the corporate bond market. Commercial paper (short-term instruments) is not very common in many EU countries. Mr Atkin said money market funds are likely to become a much more potent force after Emu. In the US they have been the main buyers of commercial paper.

But the most significant change is the forecast boom in the corporate bond market. Big multinationals already use corporate bonds as a preferred method of external debt financing. But the market is virtually closed to small and mid-sized concerns. Under Emu, the European bond market will experience significant structural change. EU government bonds now carry triple-A ratings in national currency terms. Some will continue to carry the highest rating, but the ratings of other bonds will fall. This is because, under the Maastricht treaty, the European Central Bank cannot bail out a defaulting government, while national central banks at present can.

This means that, for the first time, companies can enjoy higher bond ratings than their governments. An institutional investor, who seeks a particular country exposure, might therefore choose a corporate bond for his portfolio instead of a government bond. Since investors no longer face foreign exchange risk, they might be able to accept higher risks in the bond market itself. This in turn could lead to the growth in the market for lower-grade high-risk bonds, better known as junk bonds. This would obviously have significant implications for the debt strategies of mid-sized companies which may suddenly find they have access to a bond market, where no such access existed before.

Commercial banks could be squeezed on two fronts. Not only will lending margins come down as a result of increasing cross-European competition, but the banks' traditional customers may use alternative finance options. These developments are extremely welcome to users of financial services, especially smaller and mid-sized companies.

Opinion surveys suggest that mid-sized businesses are not as well prepared as larger companies in the EU. Once the reality of Emu sinks in, however, the world of corporate treasurers will be turned upside down.

First appeared 21 November 1997

A host of new competition problems face bankers when Emu arrives

ANDREW FISHER

Most countries currently have their own electronic systems for settling cash, cheque and other transactions and this will not change with European monetary union – at least, not initially. But the systems will have to change profoundly to deal with the currency and pressures are likely to build up for fewer, more extensive payment systems.

The euro will start with far more payments systems than are really needed, says Eric Sepkes, a deputy chairman of the Euro Banking Association, which plans to be ready with a pan-European clearing system for euro transactions from the start of Emu.

National systems also intend to make payments in euros from the first day of the single currency. These include Chaps, the high-value payments system in the UK, although the country will not initially be an Emu member. In time, however, Mr Sepkes reckons competition – with big banks going where the deals are cheapest – will whittle down the number of rivals.

The Paris-based EBA, whose members include some fifty clearing banks from the European Union, the US, Japan and Switzerland, aims to grab around a third of the euro-based payments market, says Oliver Mas, its chairman. Its system, to be operated by Swift, the global payment message network, will be capable of handling 200,000 payments a day.

Although it is hard to estimate the volume of cross-border payments in euros after 1999, Mr Mas reckons this could be up to 450,000. Apart from the EBA, such large commercial, banking and official payments will also be carried by Target (which will link Emu central banks under the European Central Bank's supervision), domestic systems and two-way links between correspondent banks.

In Frankfurt, where the ECB is based, is one of the EBA's main future competitors, operated by Landeszentralbank in Hessen, the regional central bank that is part of the Bundesbank system. Called EAF, it handles around DM750 billion (£256 billion) worth of transactions a day and has grown by 30 per cent a year since its introduction seven years ago.

From January 1998 EAF was opened up for remote membership across Europe, not just in the euro zone. 'When the DM goes and the euro arrives, Frankfurt will no longer be the natural place (for routing payments to and from Germany) since settlement can be made in Paris, Frankfurt or elsewhere,' says Hans Georg Fabritius, the bank's deputy president. He believes EAF should carve out a sizeable share of the market. It is lengthening its hours of operation so as to overlap slightly with working times in the US and Japan.

For the banks handling big payments, however, it is a matter of indifference which system is used. They simply want to send and receive money with the minimum of fuss, delay and cost.

Volker Burghagen, heading euro preparations at Germany's Dresdner Bank, admits banks have some homework to do on this score. 'Our customers will tell us, when the single currency exists, that they do not see why a Frankfurt–Hamburg payment should cost less than Frankfurt–Paris in the same currency.'

In the medium term, therefore, banks will have to co-operate to ensure payments to France will be as cheap as those within Germany. The next step will be to develop a Europe-wide system for small retail payments, such as cheques and standing orders, which fall below the threshold of large-volume networks. When the euro comes, says Gilbert Lichter, the EBA's secretary general, 'we will not have an infrastructure for small payments that matches the European-wide logic of the single currency'.

The EBA could help bring national retail systems together under one umbrella. But it will take time to solve all the practical challenges posed by the single currency.

First appeared 16 December 1997

A golden opportunity for IT: *computer companies hope the euro currency will cause companies to rethink their entire business – and, with that, their computer systems*

NICK DENTON

Computer consultants and software companies are no slouches. Having warned that many elderly computer systems will read the year 2000 as 'year zero' and collapse, they have now found a new harbinger of doom: the euro.

In a deluge of alarming surveys and reports, the computer industry attacks complacency. IDC, for instance, highlights the gap in the number of European banks confident their computer systems will be ready for the advent of the euro – 91 per cent polled – and the proportion that have actually allocated a budget – just 15 per cent. PeopleSoft, the software company, is using language moderate for the industry when it claims European monetary union has 'the potential to make the systems fall over'.

The computer service companies, to which banks and other businesses are turning to prepare for the euro, have a vested interest in exaggerating the scale of the task. Steven Rogers, in charge of the monetary union issue for database company Oracle, admits: 'It is a huge opportunity for a software provider. It is the software equivalent of a natural disaster: customers have no choice.' But the introduction of the euro does pose a serious challenge to companies' computer systems.

The origins of the problem lie in the Maastricht treaty, by which European countries agreed to merge their currencies. It set a long crossover period to ease the euro into circulation, which complicates matters. As things stand, the euro will become legal tender from January 1999 in the countries which sign up to the new monetary bloc. But national currencies will co-exist with the euro for a further three and a half years.

From 1999 until the end of 2001, large companies will be required to report their accounts in both their domestic currency and the euro, which means their general ledger program must be able to handle at least two units of exchange. Payments and billing systems must also be adapted to give vendors and customers the choice to conduct business in either currency. And banks are worried about confusion between accounts during the crossover – 'get a million lire into a euro account, and you become rich overnight,' says Mr Alec Nacamuli, head of the financial services practice at IBM. In the subsequent phase, in the first six months of 2002, retailers must be able to accept both national and European currencies. If they have separate tills for euro and domestic currency transactions, they risk irritating customers who pick the wrong queue. And Emu participants may decide to speed the spread of the euro by insisting retailers give change in the new currency. That, unless retailers decide to supply their staff with special calculators, would require dual-currency tills.

If that was that, many would be able to navigate this transition just by tinkering with their computer systems. But the impact of the euro will be deeper. It will create a powerful new currency bloc which will affect companies outside the area as much as those within. A UK exporter, billing 20 per cent of its sales in French francs and another 20 per cent in D-Marks, might account for those sales in sterling and simply convert them at the point of sale into the customer's home currency. But if that UK company was selling 40 per cent of its production in euros, it might make sense to acquire invoicing software which was equally at home in sterling or in the new European currency.

Moreover, the introduction of the euro, the computer companies hope, will cause companies to rethink their entire business, and with that their computer systems. Banks will have to react to the loss of revenue from traditional foreign exchange business and overdraft charges. At the moment, if a client's D-Mark account goes into overdraft, the bank may levy charges even if the French franc account is in balance. If both these were in euro, that would be more difficult to justify. And the euro, like the single market reforms of the 1980s, may encourage companies to treat Europe as one market, which would require multi-currency software.

Mr Nacamuli of IBM says he always insists clients think about how the euro will affect their business, not just their computer systems, before deciding how to upgrade. 'The euro brings restructuring into focus,' he says. 'A lot of banks are seeing this as an opportunity to expand.'

So what are the options? The simplest solution, and one which is likely to be adopted by companies such as manufacturers with mainly local sales, is to convert all amounts at the start of one financial year during the transition into the new currency, find all national currency symbols in the software code and change them to the euro sign. If the company uses SAP payroll software, for instance, it can buy the conversion tools for this purpose from the enterprise software company. If the company is already accounting in euros, but has to sell in the national currency, it can convert bills manually or by using a small program plugged in to its main system. The second solution is to adapt existing software by introducing a new field – a new line in the computer form – for the euro. Or, third, and this is what many software companies are hoping, a company can decide this is the time to renew its computer systems.

'A major customer has two broad choices,' says Mr Rogers of Oracle. 'He changes what he has or goes and buys something new in the marketplace. The business case can go one way or the other.'

Whatever the solution, it means business for the computer service industry. BZW, the investment banking arm of Barclays Bank, believes the single currency is a far bigger boon to the sector than the year 2000. Its analysts estimate the cost of preparing computer systems for monetary union at $25 billion, of which about 50 per cent will be outsourced.

'This is a transition period that is going to last three years. Companies will not want to keep people on their payroll just for that,' says Mr Nacamuli. What is more, most of this spending, unlike that on the millennium bug, will be additional to existing information technology budgets. On this expectation, shares in computer service companies such as Cap Gemini have soared.

So it is no wonder that computer service companies are putting the bulk of their marketing efforts into solutions for European monetary union and deluging anyone who will listen with their thoughts on the subject. But their clients can be excused for taking their more extravagant doom-mongering with a pinch of salt.

First appeared 5 February 1997

Euro's impact reaches from high office to the corner store

JENS TARTLER

It is not just Europe's business sector that is readying itself for economic and monetary union. Public servants, from high-ranking eurocrats in Brussels to post-office clerks in the Austrian Alps, face similar problems in preparing themselves for life after national currencies.

Preparations in the member states are running at different speeds. Seven countries – Belgium, Ireland, Italy, Luxembourg, the Netherlands, Austria and Finland – have opted for the fastest and most comprehensive changeover scenarios.

These countries have issued transition plans or detailed statements of intent, with a full 'euro-option' for companies during the change-over phase from 1999–2002. During this time, the euro, the new single currency, can be used in parallel to the national currencies – but only for non-cash transactions, as euro coins and notes will not be introduced before 2002. In the transitional phase, state organizations, companies and individuals will operate under the principle of 'no compulsion – no prohibition' whereby they are allowed, but cannot be forced, to use the euro.

A full euro-option will permit companies to switch over to the euro in their accounts, tax declarations and tax payments from the 1999 financial year. Once companies have opted for the euro, they cannot revert to the national currency.

Belgium, Italy, Luxembourg, the Netherlands and Austria would also permit tax declarations and payments in euros for the public at large, a European Commission official said. In Finland, only self-employed people who earn more than 50 per cent of their income in euros will be able to take this option. In Ireland, it will only be possible if the taxpayer's employer is paying taxes in euros as well.

In France, the current position is that companies will have to pay taxes in French francs during the transition phase, although a final government decision on whether to allow euro payments is expected soon. In Germany agreement was delayed because a consensus is required as the Länder execute federal tax laws. Business is pushing for a changeover in 1999 as most of the big and some of the smaller companies will then switch their accounting to euros. Spain will permit company accounting and reporting in the euro for 1999 and onwards. Decisions on taxes, fees and social security payments are expected to be taken during coming months. Sweden and the UK have established task forces to handle this issue. The UK has recently launched a high-level standing committee to look into all practical aspects of Emu, but UK entry is too distant for comprehensive preparations at this stage.

Another crucial point is software development. The cities will bear the biggest share of the burden as they will have the closest contact with the public. Administrations will have to order systems for accounting, budgeting and payments as soon as possible to avoid shortages and price rises. Frankfurt and Munich announced they will start running their finances both in euro and D-Marks in 1999. A huge part of the technical equipment – such as parking meters, vending and postage machines, cash-desks and counting machines – needs to be newly programed or completely changed. Cities will have to update large sections of their paperwork to accommodate the new currency.

Another problem is the calculation of euro prices. Prices such as E1.57 instead of L3,000 for a parking space, or E8.36 instead of DM16 for a weekend bus ticket might not find acceptance among the public. The problem of rounding-up abounds. Many people, including the German association of taxpayers, fear administrations will not resist the temptation to raise charges.

In October 1997, the Commission urged member countries to launch their national information campaigns without delay and deliver their transition plans by the end of the year, including their positions in regard to accounting and tax declarations. But it is up to the public administrations in member states to carry out the transition itself.

Ironically, for the main European Union institutions, the amount of specific changeover legislation is relatively limited. It is confined to a few specific areas, such as the internal market, customs, indirect taxation and agricultural subsidies. But at lower governmental levels throughout the EU, the change will be momentous.

First appeared 4 November 1997

The conversion to the euro begins on the shop floor: *retailers are already planning how to prepare their customers for the single currency*

PEGGY HOLLINGER

For retailers, the introduction of a single currency will mean radical changes in the products they offer, the prices they charge and the way they present themselves to the consumer – whether or not the UK takes part. Retailers have already begun lobbying the European Commission about issues such as the target date for the launch of the euro. There can be few in favour of the current deadline – 1 January 1999 – New Year's Day being the hottest sales day of the year.

They are also beginning to tackle issues closer to home by setting up teams to dissect their businesses in preparation for the introduction of the notes and coins in 2002. They will examine, for example, supplier relationships – whether to invoice in euros or local currency – staff training, computer systems and financial reporting.

Marks & Spencer has even begun introducing a new computer system as part of its normal refit, which means that from 1998 customers would theoretically be able to use euros in any of its shops worldwide. Although there will be no notes and coins for another four years, for M&S, at least, it is worth the investment, even in the UK where monetary union is unlikely to take place before 2002. According to Paul Smith, head of the M&S euro project team, building awareness of the euro now is vital to the company's strategic success. 'There are not many parts of the business which are not impacted by the euro in some way,' he says. Introducing the till system is almost the easiest part. The software to accept foreign currencies – which is essentially what the euro will be until it is integrated – has been available for several years.

But the euro could affect things as basic as the size and design of a product. For example, how does a retailer price a dress which in sterling sells for £49.99? Simply translating it into euros could create a price consumers find hard to accept psychologically – say 55.57 euros – according to Elizabeth Stanton Jones of the British Retail Consortium. Rounding the price down in euros will affect profit margins; rounding up risks reviving suspicions among consumers that retailers are profiteering from conversion, a widespread feeling after the decimalization of sterling in 1971. To achieve an acceptable price point, retailers may have to ask suppliers to alter the way the product is manufactured – extra frills, for example, or fewer buttons.

M&S also maintains that retailers should be preparing to introduce dual pricing in local currency and the euro up to three years before notes and coins become a reality. This will help consumers form a sense of value in the new currency.

'If we are to retain the customer's confidence, we must retain their sense of value,' says Robert Colville, M&S finance director. Meanwhile, there are those UK retailers which have so far resolutely held back from investing anything, even time, in preparing for the euro because of uncertainty about the government's position. 'It will cost us millions in lost productivity if we get this wrong,' says Bill Hamilton, public affairs director for Safeway, the supermarket group.

On the other hand, for those who get the process right, the introduction of a single currency for Europe could make life much easier. 'Potentially there are ten fewer currencies to deal with,' says Ms Stanton Jones of BRC. 'So once the adjustment is made it should be a simplification. But this is still a profound change which needs a lot of thought and care.'

First appeared 13 November 1997

The euro will mean a huge upheaval for coin-handling machines

PETER MARSH

Early next century the seventy or so different coins circulating throughout the nations of the European Union will be replaced by just eight new euro coins of different denominations – a prospect to focus the mind of any manager involved with automatic coin handling. European monetary union could herald a huge upheaval for the operators of the seven million or so mechanisms around Europe that rely on coins to make them work. The costs in altering existing mechanisms, spare parts and training could be Ecu 15 billion (£11 billion), the industry estimates.

Of the seven million machines, roughly half are vending machines dispensing food, drink and other consumer items such as cigarettes. The rest include pay phones and ticketing and gaming machines. Furthest ahead in their planning for the switch are manufacturers of vending systems, which generally handle a wider range of coins and dispense a greater variety of items than the other types of machine. Companies in the vending industry are used to handling alterations in the shapes and sizes of coins in purely national currencies. For instance, UK operators have adjusted their machines for the new £2 and 50p pieces which became legal tender this year. But a change to a large number of leading European national currencies, all squeezed into a short time, would present the industry with an unprecedented challenge.

'It could be a logistical nightmare,' says Mr David Orton, managing director of Coin Controls, a British company which is one of three businesses dominating the $200 million (£119.7 million) a year industry in Europe of selling coin recognition systems, the essential 'brains' to a vending system.

The recognition systems normally work by a combination of optical and inductive sensors controlled electronically. The other two leaders in this equipment in Europe are Mars Electronics International and National Rejectors, both US-owned.

Counting only the vending machines, Mr Moritz Rottinger, secretary-general of the European Vending Association, a trade body for the industry, thinks it will cost about Ecu 10 billion to change over the systems to the euro, with most of the cost borne by his association's members. Including all types of coin-controlled systems, the cost estimate rises to some Ecu 15 billion. 'The euro is a big headache for most of us – I can't see much good coming out of it,' Mr Rottinger says.

According to the association, the European vending industry accounts for annual sales of some Ecu 13 billion, including both equipment sales and rental fees plus the value of the consumer items dispensed from the machinery. For many in the industry, a crunch point will come in 1998 when prototypes of the eight denominations of euro coin, valued at between 0.01 euro and 2 euros, are due to be unveiled. On current reckoning, the coins will become legal tender during 2002.

Options for the shapes and sizes of the new coins are being thrashed out in discussions involving the European Commission, the European Monetary Institute (the forerunner of the proposed European Central Bank), and national minting agencies, together with business representatives from industries such as banking, retailing and vending systems. Mr Gunter Kuhl, European sales manager for National Rejectors, says his company, like others in the industry, should be able to handle the switch to the new coins fairly easily – but only if operators give them enough time to avoid bunching of work on converting old machines. 'If it all has to be done in the last year before the switch to the euro in 2002, it will be too late,' he said.

While most people in the vending equipment sector fret about the things that could go wrong with the changes, some are more confident. Mr Hans Are, financial manager at Jede, a Swedish maker of vending systems, says he is sure large-scale problems will be avoided through the industry acting in collaboration in time. Mr Luis Ruiz de Galarreta, international customer services manager at Azkoyen, a Spanish vending equipment supplier, is determined to look on the bright side. His company is hard at work on new systems that recognize the euro along with existing national currencies. 'It will be an opportunity to sell new and better machines,' he declares.

First appeared 28 January 1997

The travel industry is looking for a boost from the euro: *greater price stability and the removal of exchange rate risks are two of the benefits foreseen*

SCHEHERAZADE DANESHKHU

Long-haul visitors to Europe are faced with several obstacles when they travel to more than one country within the continent. The visa requirements, the problems of communicating in a variety of languages and the need for so many different currencies can be off-putting. The European Union's travel industry believes that, by eliminating one of these irritants, Emu will lead to an increase in travel to and within Europe. Business travel volumes would also be likely to increase. 'The travel industry is in favour of the euro, because we expect it to boost tourism and therefore increase the turnover of local agents,' says Mr Michel de Blust, secretary-general of Ectaa, the Brussels-based European association of travel agents and tour operators.

Emu should also lead to greater price stability by removing exchange rate risks and fluctuations. This is particularly welcomed by tour operators, which book hotel rooms without knowing what the conversion rate of the local currency will be when they come to set package holiday prices some months later. They are obliged to hedge to cover their exposure. 'The single currency will remove exchange-rate volatility,' says Mr Lance Moir, finance director at First Choice, a UK-based tour operator. 'That will take some of the uncertainty out of tour operators' profits, which could lead to sharper pricing.'

Even though Britain will not join Emu in 1999, its travel industry will still be affected by monetary union. Ectaa puts changeover costs at between 1.8 per cent and 3 per cent of a travel company's turnover in a briefing memo on the impact of the euro on the travel industry. This is a significant cost for the low-margin industry which makes gross profit margins of 10 per cent in a good year. Travel agents with a large foreign-exchange business will also suffer loss of income, particularly if Spain joins Emu at the earliest stage in 1999. More than 40 per cent of UK package holidaymakers go to Spain which is also the most important destination outside Germany for German holidaymakers. Thomas Cook, the UK travel agent owned by the Dusseldorf-based Westdeutsche Landesbank, which claims to have more than 20 per cent of the British travel foreign-exchange market, acknowledges that Emu will have a significant impact on its business but says that it is exploring other ways of replacing the lost income.

These include new products such as Visa Travel Money, which is being piloted in the UK and Far East. This acts as an electronic travellers' cheque by allowing users to buy a card with a predetermined value to withdraw cash from cashpoint (automatic teller) machines. While some tour operators believe the costs of changeover will push up holiday prices, others think the euro will foster more competition through its greater transparency which could lead to a fall in prices.

By making price comparisons easy, straightforward products, such as air fares, could fall, believes Mr de Blust. 'If you combine monetary union with the development of on-line sales, such as the internet, the euro will probably encourage a decrease in prices in those markets which are expensive compared to others.'

Those living near a border will be particularly well placed to take advantage of pricing differences by comparing the euro price on each side of the border and then doing their travel shopping in the country with the cheaper price. Although this effect could spill over into package holiday prices, these are perhaps too culture-specific to lead to a fundamental shift in holiday habits. 'Do you really think British people would like to travel with a German tour operator and be welcomed in German at their destination?' asks Mr de Blust.

Mr Gerd Hesselmann, president of Deutscher Reisebüro Verband, one of Germany's largest travel agent companies, doubts that Emu will herald lower package holiday prices because of the industry's low profit margins. 'We already have a highly competitive market and there's no room for prices to fall, otherwise companies will produce losses.' Where competition is likely to be at its keenest is between the monetary union countries and those outside it. Destinations such as Spain and Italy, which had relatively weak currencies in the past, could find themselves at a competitive price disadvantage to Turkey, Greece and North Africa if they join a strong euro.

The German travel industry is particularly fearful of a potential downturn in the Spanish market, since many of its package holiday companies, including TUI, Europe's largest in turnover terms, own hotels in Spain. 'This is our main concern about Emu, particularly since we would like the euro to be strong,' said Mr Hesselmann. 'We do not want the euro to become a competitive tool for different companies, so we are working towards a common standard for the industry.' AVAC, the association of Catalan travel agents, sees no reason for Emu to push up Spanish holiday prices. But if it does, Spain will compete on quality of service and new products.

First appeared 24 June 1997

Agriculture: *the euro is likely to bring many benefits and end complex disputes*

MAGGIE URRY

The arrival of the single European currency means more to agriculture, perhaps, than to any other commercial sector. The Common Agricultural Policy is at the heart of the European Union. But it has had to operate for decades without a truly common currency. As one economist put it, 'trying to run a common policy, with a sizeable cross-border trade, in commodity products, has meant that exchange rates have become dominant in determining farmers' incomes'.

'The euro is the crown on the internal market,' says Albert Dierick, chief economist at Rabobank, the Dutch co-operative bank which has its roots in farming. Brian Gardner, of EPA Associates, a Brussels-based consultancy, says: 'In theory, the single currency should mean the completion of the agriculture internal market. The (current) system has prevented a common market in agricultural products.'

The first benefit to farmers from the move to a single currency will be the ending, at least for those joining Emu, of the complex and costly agrimonetary system. This system is necessary to convert the range of EU farm subsidies from Ecu into national currencies. It involves a matrix of so-called 'green exchange rates' which are used to translate Ecu amounts into each member state's currency. A mind-bogglingly complex set of rules is used to determine what happens when a member state's market exchange rate diverges from the green rate.

It has often been the source of fraught negotiations in Brussels. One official, who has been involved over years in negotiations over the agrimonetary system, says: 'Throughout its life it always gets sorted out late in the day. The December farm council is the normal place to agree details of the following year's arrangements.' It took three days of talking, finishing with an all-night session, when the last reform of the system was agreed in 1995. A previous system had cost the EU Ecu 30 billion over its ten-year life. So its removal will be a great relief to all involved.

Equally fraught, at times, have been the arguments between producers in countries with strong currencies and those with weak currencies, over the substantial amount of trade in agricultural products between member states. Those with strong currencies have seen the value of their subsidies in their own currencies decline as their green rates revalued, while producers in countries with a falling currency gained from devaluation, enabling them to export more readily.

Udo Folgart, who runs a large mixed farm near Berlin, a former East

German co-operative holding, says: 'The euro is good news, because we think in Germany that the conversions between the Ecu and the D-Mark were not good for German farmers. The subsidies farmers get from the EU through the conversion was better for the southern states of Europe.' Once all farmers receive their subsidy cheques in the same currency, competition between farmers in different states should become fairer, some say. One long-running dispute has been between French and Spanish horticulture growers. The French have often protested against floods of Spanish products which they claim undercut French prices.

Jean-Jacques Benezit, a French government agriculture official, says such disputes between France and Spain 'will vanish. The row has been caused by the devaluation of the peseta and also differences in production costs. One of the main reasons (for the argument) will not be there any more.' Rafael Cavestany, the Spanish agricultural counsellor in London, says that while in the short term Spanish farmers might have benefited from devaluations, it has not been good for them in the longer term. 'To have a devaluation is the worst thing you can have in a country,' he says. The euro will present Spanish farmers with 'a challenge to keep competitive, because we cannot devalue'. Mr Benezit agrees. 'Having a single currency will definitely reduce the distortion of competition. It will bring more transparency in trade.' Further, he says, there will be considerable savings for farmers as the foreign exchanges costs of exporting are removed. He estimates French farmers could see more than FFr3 billion of savings.

While prices to consumers will be clearer, farmers should also benefit from more transparency in pricing of their supplies and equipment, from fertilizers to tractors. Risto Volanen, secretary-general of Copa, the European farmers' union, says: 'The market for supplies and products will be transparent. Every farmer can compare his costs with those of every other farmer.' Fertilizer prices, for example, which are already similar across Europe through a process of 'price osmosis', are likely to converge further, says Sean Mackle, of the European Fertiliser Manufacturers' Association. 'It is going to be more transparent, simpler and therefore will enhance consumer power.' Price differences will still reflect variations in transport costs, qualities and so on, but the 'powerful psychological effect of the euro' will force manufacturers to find other attributes than price to sell their fertilizer.

With all these advantages expected from the euro, it is not surprising that farmers' unions in the 'pre-in' countries, such as the UK, are anxious for their countries to join. Siân Roberts, economist at the National Farmers' Union of England and Wales, says: 'The dangers of sitting outside the single currency are becoming blatantly clear.' A new agrimonetary system for the pre-ins is expected to be less generous than the old one, which allowed compensation for revaluing currencies and no penalties for devaluations.

As well as the removal of the exchange rate problems, farmers in countries which join Emu in the first wave will also enjoy, at least at first, lower interest rates than those in the UK, for instance. That puts British farmers at a competitive disadvantage in investment. However, farmers in the pre-in countries hope that under the new system they will have the option to take their EU subsidies in euros rather than in their local currencies.

First appeared 30 April 1998

B Case studies

BMW gears up for monetary union

PETER NORMAN

BMW has its headquarters in Munich, centre of German scepticism about the euro. Through its Rover subsidiary it also has a huge stake in Britain, which has an opt-out from the European single currency. But neither its location nor its investment has deterred the Bavarian luxury carmaker from enthusiastic support for economic and monetary union and from drawing up plans for the single currency in the growing belief that Britain will be linked to the euro by 2000.

For Wolfgang Stofer, the head of treasury, accounting and taxes who is responsible for BMW's adaptation to the euro, the single currency is a 'historic opportunity' which should serve as 'a booster' to the German and European economies. 'I can see no disadvantages from the euro,' he told the *FT*.

BMW began preparing for the euro in 1996 and would be in a position to switch its operations from the D-Mark in 1999, the target date for Emu. Adoption of the single currency will be a step-by-step affair, however, if only because the German public administration will not abandon the D-Mark for the euro until 2002.

The company expects to seek shareholder approval at its next annual meeting in spring for powers to put its capital on a euro basis, most probably by converting its DM50 nominal shares into securities with no par value. It has yet to decide whether to convert its balance sheet from

D-Marks to euros in 1999, although Mr Stofer says he 'could imagine' such a switch. BMW founded a project team of just three people to manage the switch to the euro, after first analysing the problems and then working out a timetable for Emu. Overall, up to 300 people will be involved in tackling the conversion. Because BMW's top management took a decision in favour of the euro, there is no scope for internal debate about whether or not to move ahead with preparations. The project trio can cut through hierarchies. 'We have a "to do" list and no one can stand in the way,' one manager explains.

BMW is combining its switch to the euro with the adoption of a new standard software and measures to tackle the year 2000 computer problem. This makes it hard to estimate the overall cost of conversion. Mr Stofer puts it around DM40 million (£14 million), a modest amount for a group with annual sales of DM60 billion. 'Europe is facing a historic choice between keeping up with global competition or falling back economically into small scale nationalism,' Mr Stofer says. 'For us the euro is so important, because 25 per cent of world trade will be invoiced in euros, with a good chance that it will grow to 35 or 40 per cent. It will be the number two behind the dollar.'

The euro will bring greater stability through its growing importance as a global currency and, unlike the D-Mark, is not expected to overshoot in value.

The single currency will have a direct impact in reducing the share of BMW's turnover, subject to currency risk. At present 64 per cent of worldwide sales are at risk from currency fluctuations. The share of sales at risk from European currency movements will shrink with the euro to 10 per cent from 26 per cent. Mr Stofer expects economies of scale and more security for investment. 'We have a lot of medium-sized multinationals with around 10,000 employees in Germany. One in two German medium-sized companies sells about 70 per cent of its products in Europe – in "euro land". They have a huge opportunity because they have already gone through the process of shedding labour and introducing lean management.'

But will the euro be such good news for Rover? Problems would arise if sterling were to become established at the equivalent of the August exchange rate of DM3 to the pound. This would necessitate structural changes at Rover to ensure its profitability and would create a big unemployment problem in Britain by 2000. Mr Stofer believes flight capital will flow back to Germany from Britain after the switch to the euro has been digested, and that this should push sterling down to a more sustainable level.

First appeared 7 October 1997

***ICI:** the chemicals group is making sure everyone is involved in preparations for monetary union*

STEFAN WAGSTYL

'The sight of 1 January 1999 in the desk diary really concentrates the mind,' says Peter Everett, spokesman for a multi-disciplinary Emu team at ICI, the UK chemicals company, preparing the group for European monetary union. Mr Everett says the 'diary effect' has suddenly made many more executives aware of monetary union. 'They can't ignore it any more.' ICI itself has been getting ready for monetary union for nearly eighteen months – a lot less time than some European companies, which began five years ago – but well ahead of most of British industry.

ICI decided from the outset against limiting Emu preparations to the information technology and financial departments for which it presents the most obvious challenges. Instead, the group has chosen to view Emu as a very broad issue affecting the whole range of its business activities. Pricing, branding, cross-border management, customer and supplier relations all come into the picture, says Mr Everett. 'It's a commercial issue of huge importance. It's not just a treasury or IT issue.'

ICI's preparations started in the autumn of 1996, with a paper to the board from Richard Freeman, its then chief economist, urging directors to put aside any thoughts that Emu might not happen and to make ready for a union that would almost certainly embrace a large number of European Union countries. Alan Small, the chief financial officer, took overall responsibility and created a steering committee under Richard Sykes, the group's head of information technology, with Mr Everett as his principal assistant. Mr Everett says the committee included representatives from all ICI's operating divisions as well as head office staff from departments such as IT, treasury and tax.

The committee spent the first few months researching Emu-related material from the European Commission, the UK government and other sources. Its work was briefly held up last year when executives were diverted to work on ICI's restructuring. However, by mid-year, the Emu committee was back on track and held a conference of about forty key executives to review progress and make detailed plans. The meeting was addressed by consultants from KPMG, the accountancy firm, who highlighted the potential effects of Emu on pricing and branding.

The executives left the conference with plans to make detailed commercial preparations at the divisional level. The company is now conducting an internal audit of these preparations in advance of a second conference in June this year.

At the heart of ICI's plans is a conviction that the commercial impact of Emu will be relatively small in wholesale markets, where products are already traded on a global or Europe-wide basis, and relatively great in consumer markets. But precise effects will vary from industry to industry and from country to country.

For example, the company expects Emu to make little difference in bulk chemicals, which have long been traded across western Europe in D-Mark prices on transparent terms. A single market priced in a single currency is already well established. However, in consumer markets, in which product prices vary between countries, ICI thinks Emu could cause a significant decline in prices, with consumer pressure forcing price cuts in higher-priced national markets. 'There is likely to be price erosion. Retailers won't accept those cuts themselves and will try to pass them on to manufacturers,' says Mr Everett. The problem is exacerbated by the issue of price points – that is, the prices which retailers find most psychologically tempting to consumers, such as £9.99 or FFr99. With Emu, companies will be obliged to change their prices in Emu-member countries into euros. But a French franc price of, say, FFr99 will not translate directly into a psychologically attractive euro price. Retailers will be under pressure to reduce prices to the nearest attractive price point.

And suppliers selling the same product in more than one country will be under pressure to adjust prices in two or more currencies into one euro price – at an attractive price point. Mr Everett says that some companies will be able to justify different prices in different countries by providing a greater choice or better after-sales service. Distance from the manufacturing site could also lead to price differentials.

Moreover, companies could try to maintain prices by marketing different brands in different countries. National characteristics will remain important after monetary union, he says. However, Mr Everett expects that in border areas, where consumers can shop freely in more than one country, the pressure for price uniformity will be intense. 'The issue for business will be to harmonize prices or justify differences.'

First appeared 10 March 1998

Siemens use Emu as a basis for expansion

JENS TARTLER

Siemens, the German electronics multinational, wants to be ready when the going gets tough. To that end it has been preparing comprehensively for the conversion to the euro. From the beginning of 1999 – when the euro is introduced for non-cash transactions – the company will be able to conduct all its external business in the new currency. On 1 October 1999, the start of its first fiscal year after the euro's introduction, it will also convert its accounts and records. Karl-Hermann Baumann, a member of its executive board, emphasizes: 'From that point on, the euro will be the company's official currency.'

Over the past two years, the Munich-based enterprise has been fine-tuning its activities in numerous specialized areas: business transactions, accounting, treasury, tax and legal arrangements, purchasing, human resources and data processing.

At a more fundamental level, the introduction of the single European currency will affect Siemens's corporate strategy. 'The euro is expected to accelerate the integration of European markets,' says Mr Baumann. 'This will strengthen our European business and provide the company with a solid foundation for further expansion in the fast-growing Asia–Pacific region, the Americas and Eastern Europe.'

Mr Baumann, who is responsible for finance, expects increased price transparency to intensify competition and erode the price differences that persist despite the convergence which has taken place since 1992. 'General price reductions in Siemens's business will continue,' he predicts. On the other hand, he expects some regional price differentials to remain because of transport costs, local variations in labour and component costs, and differences in the strength of competitive pressure. 'This should not be surprising considering that even in the US there are significant regional differences in the prices of consumer and industrial goods,' he says. Mr Baumann believes that European monetary convergence will, nevertheless, cause 'painful short-term adjustments in some cases'. Companies will have to adapt their pricing and payment policies accordingly. 'The introduction of European-wide price lists and discount schedules will vary from branch to branch, but price pressures can be expected to increase across the board,' he expects.

Competition will intensify among dealers and suppliers as well. Retailers have to join forces and increase their effectiveness – a structural change that large-scale distributors have had to go through already. For suppliers, demands for low prices, high quality and good service will rise. 'Every company will be measured against an increasingly high standard of performance and cost. Siemens must adapt to this just as its suppliers must,' Mr Baumann believes.

More than half Siemens's sales and expenses are generated in the currencies of the likely euro area so the company expects to make annual savings in the two digit million range of German marks. The company will no longer have to spend as much hedging against interest and exchange rate movements, and transaction costs for cross-border payments will be lower. In addition, smaller differences in interest rates within the euro zone will save significant amounts of money, says Mr Baumann. Siemens will need fewer bank accounts and improvements in cash pooling and management within the euro area will also be possible. It should be able to simplify business transactions and logistics. Mr Baumann predicts that there will be more co-operation between Siemens's regional units.

On the cost side, Siemens expects higher expenditures primarily in data processing. 'We want to use this challenge as an opportunity to streamline our software and prepare for a seamless transition to the year 2000,' Mr Baumann says. During the transition period from 1999 to 2002, before euro bills and coins are introduced, Siemens expects conversion costs to exceed DM100 million or roughly 3 to 3.5 per cent of total data processing costs. But 'our euro-investment will pay for itself through associated savings within three years,' Mr Baumann predicts.

When Siemens converts to the euro on 1 October 1999, the company's internal transfer prices – used to price goods and services traded between different parts of the group – will in most cases be quoted in euros.

First appeared 21 November 1997

Istituto San Paolo di Torino: *getting ahead of the game – the bank has set up a special task force to prepare for the advent of the euro*

JAMES BLITZ

The advent of the euro appears to have caught many Italian banks unawares. But Istituto San Paolo di Torino, one of Italy's leading banking institutions, likes to think it has done more than most to prepare for the new environment in the post-Emu world. It was back in 1995, when European Union heads of government set out their technical plans for Emu, that the bank decided it needed to develop a rounded strategy for a single currency. It set up a special task force for the advent of the euro, examining issues such as the need to adopt new trading systems and develop new products. It now has some 350 members of staff working on its teams, believing the euro could make a significant difference to competition in the banking sector in Italy.

'There have been many occasions in the past two years when certain politicians were suggesting that Italy would never make it into the first wave,' says Mrs Marina Tabacco, the bank's head of marketing strategy who is charged with the euro project. 'But throughout it all we took the view that the euro would go ahead and Italy would get in – and we never deviated from that.'

The work being done by Mrs Tabacco and her team focuses on three broad areas – overall strategy, technical reform and the need to educate staff and customers. 'Any bank that wants to prosper in forthcoming years needs to take a long hard look at developments in each of these areas,' she says. The work on developing strategy has partly focused on ways in which the bank must develop its trading and settlement systems in the post-Emu world. Mrs Tabacco says the advent of a single currency means banks must speed up transactions.

Like all other banks, it will be compulsory for San Paolo to use real-time gross trading – the so-called Target system – when it conducts wholesale money market transactions with the European Central Bank in Frankfurt. But the bank does not intend to stick to this system alone. It has, therefore, been an active participant in the development of EBA – the clearing system used until now for Ecu transactions – that will now be employed by some fifty banks across Europe for clearing cheques denominated in euros.

It is considerably cheaper to use than Target but will allow transactions to be cleared on the same day, though not in real time. The bank is also looking at new products and services. Like many Italian banks, it has traditionally relied on wide interest-rate spreads as one of the main means of making money through loans. But the reduction in Italian interest rates that will arise from Italy's Emu membership will make this activity less lucrative.

San Paolo is considering offering a wider range of specialized client services as a way of making money. It has just launched a new fixed-rate mortgage – with an option to switch to a floating rate from 1999 – believing that many Italians could otherwise be attracted to banks in other European countries which sell these instruments. It is also developing equity-based investment products in response to the growing wave of Italian investors who are moving out of Italian bonds in the run-up to Emu. The decline in interest rates is making bond investment less lucrative.

On the technical site, the main challenge is to ensure that all clients can open accounts in euros from 1 January 1999. This has been a highly complex operation, requiring the bank's transactions systems to be able to calculate in euros and convert from other currencies to the single currency from the moment that Emu starts. 'It is important to any bank's credibility that it can offer such a service from the moment that monetary union begins – and that there are no mishaps,' Mrs Tabacco says. The last area on the bank's mind has been the dissemination of information about the euro to clients and bank staff. San Paolo has therefore been busy publishing leaflets and booklets, setting out what the euro means and the changes that it will entail for customers.

First appeared 21 November 1997

Saint-Gobain: *quick to start preparing for Emu*

DAVID OWEN

Saint-Gobain, the French glass, ceramics and abrasives manufacturer, is a company with impeccable European credentials. Little surprise then that it was quick off the mark in starting detailed preparations for the expected arrival of the planned single European currency: the company created a project team charged with providing for and coping with the introduction of the euro as early as January 1996.

François Janny, treasury and financing director, recalls that many said the move was premature at the time of the six-member team's creation. But there has been plenty of ground to prepare in the intervening period. And the group's initial assumption – that the new currency would be introduced on time in 1999 – has proved remarkably prescient.

Mr Janny says the team's first task was to draw up an inventory of what needed to be done – a task accomplished in the first half of 1996. 'The conclusion was that there were many internal problems to resolve,' he says, 'and that a clarification of the regulatory framework was necessary. But we identified no major problems.

'We quickly realized that the biggest problem would be the updating of computer systems. We had to tackle the problem in a decentralized way since the group does not operate with a common software package.' It was at this point Mr Janny and his colleagues realized that Saint-Gobain's more than 200 European subsidiaries would need to be involved in the project from an early stage. As a result, additional four- or five-member teams were established in the main countries which would be directly affected by the new currency's introduction.

There is no team in the UK because, according to Mr Janny, the company's working hypothesis was that, while the euro would probably have a 'wide base' (meaning the currency would be introduced from day one in southern European countries such as Spain and Italy), the UK would probably not join from the outset. 'The British are kept informed but are not in the teams,' Mr Janny says.

In non-EU countries where the company operates, such as the US and Brazil, a so-called *note de doctrine*, designed for everybody in the group, has been circulated. This sets out the main principles underlying the group's handling of the currency's introduction. The next step was to draw up an analysis chart, with the help of the group's computer experts, setting out what each subsidiary should do to prepare for the euro's impact in this key area. This suggested that units list all programs incorporating monetary values (virtually all of them); contact suppliers of their software packages to ask them how they were tackling issues arising from the new currency; and try to form 'clubs' with other users to exchange information.

Mr Janny says the company is trying to make sure any potential problems linked to the so-called millennium bug are sorted out at the same time as it undertakes this operation. The central team has also asked subsidiaries to think about what changes they might need to make in their internal organizations as a result of the euro's introduction. Mr Janny says the team has not asked for lists of suggested changes, but it will take note of the dates subsidiaries have chosen to shift to the new currency. 'We think, at the holding company level, our responsibility is to follow how things are going and, if there is a problem with the date, to sound the alarm.'

The group has decided on a flexible approach to making the switch, moving to the euro from 1 January 1999 for its consolidated accounts, but allowing subsidiaries to decide at what point in the three-year transition period they will make the change. Mr Janny says he should know which units have opted to make the move at the first opportunity early in the new year, and those that have decided on 1 January 2000 by the end of June 1998. The most significant figures in the group's consolidated accounts will be given in euros as well as French francs in 1998 and in French francs and euros until the end of the transition period.

He thinks subsidiaries supplying glass to the automotive industry might well switch at the earliest opportunity. By contrast, building materials businesses, whose clients tend to be more locally based, will probably be among the last to move. The group will give itself a one-year 'safety margin' by insisting all subsidiaries start accounting in euros by 1 January 2001, unless there are reasons not to do so.

Commercial decisions relating to price lists, the rounding of national currency amounts into euros and whether to give prices in national currency and euro terms will also be decentralized. 'It is essential for people close to the business to take those decisions,' Mr Janny says. Perhaps surprisingly, the group has not imposed a cost ceiling on subsidiaries for making the changes. Mr Janny seems more concerned that they may not spend enough to ensure the transition goes well.

'They could be tempted to say "we won't do it now to save money",' he says. 'To prevent that we have fixed the rule that all costs linked to the euro are expensed as charged.' He thinks the overall cost to the group will 'probably be measured in tens of millions of francs'. Most of this expenditure is still to come.

First appeared 21 November 1997

***Chase Manhattan:** helping hand for single currency*

MICHAEL PREST

Almost as soon as it was clear that Emu was going ahead, Chase, the giant US bank, took two basic decisions. At the practical level, the bank would be fully prepared right across its global business for the arrival of the euro on 1 January 1999. At the strategic level, Chase would treat the new currency as an opportunity to try to steal a march over competitors.

For almost two years the bank has invested thousands of working hours in meeting those objectives. The eventual estimated cost is put at about $75 million. Chase set up a bankwide steering committee and an Emu project office which reported to Bruce Hannan, the head of the bank's Global Treasury Unit. Mr Hannan is a member of the bank's senior policy council, which reports to the board.

The man in day-to-day charge is Anthony Davies, the Emu project manager, based in London. Appointed in 1996, Mr Davies admitted that he approached the myriad complexities and uncertainties of the task with some trepidation: 'The start, to be honest, was a matter of getting to grips with the mountain of information and uncertainty that was out there.'

It quickly became apparent that there was only one way of reducing the job to a human scale. Each product had to be disassembled to analyse the possible changes Emu might bring through the product's life-cycle 'from price source to payments', in Mr Davies's words. The product – whether foreign exchange, a swap or a security – could then be reassembled to incorporate necessary changes across the bank's global business lines. Discipline would be maintained by drawing up a common schedule for the whole bank.

The timetable called for a definition of the business changes by mid-1997, followed by identification of the functional requirements in the autumn and development of the vital supporting systems by the end of last year. Coding was due to be completed by early 1998, and testing of the revised products and systems by their users within the bank will start soon. Integration testing – making sure all the components fit together – is scheduled for June and July. Full dress-rehearsals are planned for November, leading up to the moment of truth – the 'conversion weekend' of 1–3 January 1999.

Breaking down the products into their component parts was painstaking. Nigel Knight, product and project manager for the euro in Chase Treasury Solutions, a key part of the bank, said that in his area alone some forty different products had to be analysed. Moreover, few bank products these days are 'pure'. Many are hybrids which touch on more than one of the bank's global business lines.

So Chase formed product groups which brought together experts from different backgrounds around the bank. Mr Davies said: 'You had to take a product out of its traditional home and create a multidisciplinary body to analyse it.' The leaders of these groups also conferred with outside experts and customers. Indeed, consultation with clients has been a theme of Chase's policy, partly to make sure that changes work and partly to keep an eye on the competition. Mr Knight said: 'All our thinking throughout this process has been to see it as a strategic opportunity, not just a defensive need.'

The bank identified two different types of change: mechanical and strategic. Mechanical changes covered items such as holiday dates, number of trading days, and redenomination of currencies into euros. All systems had to cope with these adjustments. Strategic issues were more closely related to the bank's goals. How might the market change? What did customers want? Where was there scope for new products? Could current product prices be converted directly into euros, or would adjustments have to be made for different markets? One essential decision made on the vital Treasury Solutions side was to adopt a hub approach to clearing.

Instead of each of Chase's operations in Emu member countries dealing separately with local clearing systems, business would be funnelled through Frankfurt and processed at the bank's existing centre in Bournemouth. After a while, however, Mr Davies said, a number of overarching issues began to emerge. These included continuity of contract when a product was redenominated into euros, settlement instructions, price sources, and governing law. Such questions had to be addressed regardless of where a deal might arise in Chase's global network.

But substantial uncertainties remain. Mr Knight believes that customers might decide to change their settlement instructions after 4 January 1999, the first working day for the new currency. He said: 'The world changes very dramatically on 4 January 1999 because you can't implement settlement instructions ahead of that.'

The bank had no choice but to embrace the euro – and even, as a leading global institution, felt a duty to help the new currency into the world. But Chase will be sorely disappointed if its elaborate preparations do not also yield new business.

First appeared 23 March 1998

Citibank: emphasis on neutrality

WOLFGANG MÜNCHAU

No sector of the economy will be as profoundly affected by economic and monetary union as the banking industry. Emu is a monetary event in the first instance, and it is the responsibility of the banks to handle whatever complications arise during the transition to Emu. But there are also strategic issues involved. On average that applies to some markets, such as Germany, more acutely than it does to others.

Several European banks have sought to enhance their position through consolidation and mergers. But what are the US banks doing about Emu? At Citibank the strategy comes down to two broad strands – treat the Emu zone as a genuinely single market including the retail banking business, which for most other banks is a purely home market business activity with virtually no cross-border spill-overs, and play on the strength of the neutrality of an outsider. An American bank has less reason to favour one European region or financial centre over another.

At Citibank's office in the Docklands area of east London, Bill Grant, managing director of Citibank's global relationship banking and director of the Emu project, has spent two years with his team preparing the bank's systems and, in particular, putting an Emu strategy in place for the bank's clients.

Citibank's corporate bank has 250 to 300 large multinational clients, grouped into 14 business sectors. Emu preparations keep about 200 Citibank employees occupied for a large part of their time. Janet Ellen, who is in charge of marketing communications for the Emu project, says Emu will affect Citibank's customer groups in different ways. Financial sector and retail clients will be most affected, while in the pharmaceutical industry much of the strategic adjustment has already taken place.

As other banks would also agree, the preparation for Emu is not entirely an internal affair limited to a bank's systems and operations. What is equally important is the effect it will have on the bank's clients and the way those clients interact with their bank. Business experts predict that Emu will result in a large number of winners and losers across all regions and sectors. While there is no simple rule of thumb, most Emu consultants would agree that, the more global a company's operations are, the more it stands to benefit from Emu.

Citibank stresses strongly its US roots, its worldwide presence in almost 100 countries and, in particular, its emphasis on emerging markets. With European revenues of $3.4 billion, assets of $57 billion and more than 13,000 employees, Citibank is among the larger institutions operating in the European Union, although smaller than some of the top European banks in their home markets.

Mr Grant argues that Emu forces the bank to adopt a new strategy: 'I think we are seeing big shifts in the area of integrated capital markets, and a growth in those markets associated with a shift from bank lending to disintermediation – the raising of finance by way of securities. I see growth there. There will be euro-denominated funding and, as a result, a development of new products. With the trend from traditional forms of bank lending to capital market-based products, Europe will increasingly begin to resemble the US. Securitization – the conversion of an asset into a tradable security – will become more common.'

The emergence of the pan-European capital market at the expense of largely nationally based traditional lending operations is expected to be one of the driving forces behind cross-border banking. As a neutral operator with no vested national interests, Citibank sees an opportunity in this area. Ms Ellen says: 'The neutrality appeals to a lot of multinationals because it is currency is linked to a location. According to the size of the economy there are different liquidity pools. With the euro you can settle anywhere in the EU. Location is no longer that important. The question is, where will the liquidity be – in Germany, France or Britain? National banks have vested interests. We can operate in any of these countries, and that gives a lot more choice to our clients. Citibank divides its services into two broad groups – transactional products, such as cash management, security settlement and trade services, and trade products, for example foreign exchange and derivatives trading. It has the largest foreign exchange operation of any bank in the world. Superficially, the effect of Emu is to dispense with national currencies and their cross-border exchange rates.'

For the bank's currency business this means a shift of emphasis from intra-European trading, which has already happened in the past few years, to new markets, especially emerging markets. This is no bad thing in itself since intra-European trading has become a low-margin, commodity-style business.

Citicorp bankers emphasize that, despite all the work necessary for its preparation, Emu does not constitute a strategic break but a continuation of existing strategy. Ms Ellen says: 'Our whole product line was built on the principle of an integrated Europe anyway. One focus was to be a conduit into Europe from Japan or from Latin America. The same pan-European approach also applies to the bank's European consumer banking operations, which are based in Brussels. Citibank had a retail branch presence in 10 out of 15 EU countries, with a relatively small exposure to Britain but a formidable 300-branch network in Germany.'

Jeff Walsh, Emu programme director at Citibank's consumer operations, says: 'Consumers are looking for reassurance from their banks. Customers should also get better value from their banks, better prices. People will compare mortgage prices between Spanish and German institutions. Margins will come under pressure. We will have to become more efficient.'

First appeared 23 March 1998

Unilever's preparation for Emu: *the Anglo-Dutch group expects the euro to accelerate its expansion on a European scale*

JOHN WILLMAN

In January 1999, eleven European countries will enter into a monetary union, the most far-reaching development in Europe since the fall of the Berlin Wall. Few companies will be as well prepared for its arrival as Unilever, the Anglo-Dutch consumer group which operates in every country in the single currency zone and which makes products as diverse as ice cream, tea, margarine, Calvin Klein fragrances, Elizabeth Arden cosmetics and Persil soap powder.

For the past three years, this epitome of a European enterprise has had a high-level taskforce planning for the birth of the euro. And Niall FitzGerald, chairman of its UK wing, has warned constantly of the dangers to British industry of being outside the monetary union. Yet Hans Eggerstedt, Unilever's German finance director, takes a surprisingly relaxed view of the impact of the single currency. 'The world won't change because of the euro,' he says. 'Currency is a denominator – nothing more.'

There is no division between Mr Eggerstedt and the chairman, however. The significance of the euro lies not so much in the creation of a single currency as in the contribution it will make to a much bigger process – the completion of the European Union's single market. By removing one uncertainty in doing business across borders inside the single currency zone, the euro will allow groups such as Unilever to develop further on a European scale. But it will only accelerate a process that is already under way. 'As a European company, we are a great supporter of the single market,' says Mr Eggerstedt. 'Business and the European Union have grown together and captured efficiencies.'

He understands why the politicians make so much of the single currency: the notes and coins handled every day by the EU's consumers will powerfully symbolize the deeper process. 'Hype about the euro is an essential part of completing the single market,' he says. The savings from the single currency will be surprisingly modest for large companies such as Unilever. Jan Haars, group treasurer, estimates the reduction in transaction costs at no more than £20 million a year – on European turnover last year of £13.6 billion. 'The benefit will be much greater for smaller companies for whom the transaction costs form a higher proportion of sales,' he says. 'We already operate in more than 100 countries and will still have to deal with almost as many currencies.'

Mr Haars has chaired the steering group that has been planning for the transition at corporate level since 1995. It was charged with making preparations for functions controlled centrally such as treasury management, taxation and reporting. It has also kept an eye on the national subsidiaries to make sure they did not diverge in the decisions they made on the single currency. There will be no immediate move to managing cash balances centrally across the single currency area. 'The different countries will remain and it won't be possible to net off the individual balances in a single total,' he says. 'It takes a day to transfer balances between countries and cash management is all about today.'

But the group's foreign-exchange operations will be centralized as soon as possible after 1 January 1999. 'Once the euro arrives, all foreign currency positions in the members of the monetary union will be netted – a huge simplification.' Unilever will start pricing in euros for transactions between its European subsidiaries from 1 January. Those outside the euro zone will have to hedge if they want to close off the currency risk. Mr Haars expects the impact of the single currency on the EU's capital markets to be significant. 'Liquidity will improve, giving sharper margins and better prices,' he says. 'It will offer more opportunities for institutions such as pension funds by reducing the risk in cross-border investments.'

The group will use euros for internal reporting from 1 January 2000, one year after the launch of monetary union. However, it will start accounting in euros next year to supplement the existing sterling and guilder figures and help executives get a feel for the new currency. For a group that already operates in more than 100 currencies, this will be relatively simple.

Beginning to use the euro next year will also provide 1999 data for comparison purposes when the full switch is made in 2000. The absence of appropriate data for 1998 – when the exchange rates for entering Emu could still be changed – persuaded Unilever not to make the switch from 1 January 1999. The Dutch wing will report to its shareholders in euros from 2000 onwards, with the British wing following suit as soon as possible. 'The London Stock Exchange is very pro-Emu, so I expect euro reporting for big British companies will happen before the UK adopts the single currency,' says Mr Eggerstedt.

Unilever will not be making an early move towards EU-wide prices for consumers: it leaves such decisions to its operating companies in the various countries. Mr Eggerstedt expects the euro to increase the pressure for price harmonization – it will be much easier for consumers to spot the variations inside the monetary union. 'That pressure will be felt by manufacturers, retailers and the authorities responsible for taxes such as VAT,' he says. The single market is already forcing prices down all the time and will continue to do so. Value added tax rates, which varied between 5 per cent and 25 per cent two decades ago, are bunching in a much narrower range. 'Anyone who believes they can force prices up by the change to the euro is dreaming,' he says.

Large organizations like Unilever are already comparing prices and buying supplies on an EU-wide scale, however. And the single currency will affect the allocation of resources within the single market, since decisions must always involve a currency assumption. 'The UK will be an unpredictable currency area for the rest of Europe,' says Mr Eggerstedt, 'despite its advantages as a manufacturing centre. It's an unpredictability thing and we don't like that. We already have to deal with the consumer, the competition and the authorities – so we like to eliminate other uncertainties.'

First appeared 4 June 1998

6 The finance sector and other industries

Banks, insurance companies and other financial institutions will be the businesses most immediately affected by the arrival of the euro. Their raw material – money – is undergoing a complete transformation. The currency barriers which have kept their markets separate will be swept away, unleashing a new era of intense cross-border competition.

First, though, as George Graham's opening article explains, financial institutions must cope with the practical task of conversion. He goes on to explain how commercial banks face an era of converging prices for their services – a big change in an industry traditionally divided on national lines. In the short run, wholesale banking will be the first to feel the impact of the new currency. In the long term, retail banking will also be affected.

Once the euro is a part of everyday life, European equity markets will merge into a single large pool of securities. Jane Martinson explains how this affects pension funds and fund managers; Simon Davies how it is creating a battle to become the benchmark index for European shares.

Barry Riley explores the consequences for equity markets. Edward Luce and Simon Davies examine the implications for bond markets and derivatives exchanges. In all three cases, the impact will be sweeping and immediate. Even before the euro comes into existence, pan-European structures to exploit the new currency are being created. And the deeper, wider more liquid bond market that many people will expect will offer new opportunities for borrowers and new threats to the traditional lenders, the banks.

Their investment banking arms stand to profit from the wave of pan-European mergers that Emu is helping to bring about, as Clay Harris describes. The consolidation spells danger for big fish in any of the continent's small ponds, since mere local leadership will no longer matter.

The introduction of the euro will accelerate the pace of industrial restructuring across Europe. The financial services industry will be among the first to feel the effects of this trend. But others will soon undergo the same experiences.

PETER MARTIN

Flashes of subdued panic

GEORGE GRAHAM

With the imminent arrival of the euro, bankers are starting to experience flashes of subdued panic at the sheer volume of work which remains to be done. While almost every financial institution in Europe expresses public confidence that it will be ready in time to start doing business in the new currency by 4 January 1999, many worry about the number of details which have not yet been determined. Many, too, harbour lingering doubts about the preparedness of their counterparties and of the payment systems they use. 'We won't be ready. We'll cope, but we won't be really ready,' confessed the IT chief of one European investment bank.

The overarching issues, such as the principle that contracts should not be voided by the change from national currencies to the euro, have been resolved. But a welter of detailed issues still needs careful attention. What page on the Reuters or Bloomberg information networks will carry the new price references such as the Euribor and euro Libor interest rates? The issue is important because some derivative contracts stipulate the prices published on specific pages. What arrangements will be observed for holidays? The Target euro-payment system linking European central banks has already made it clear that it will close only on Christmas and New Year's Day, but the option remains open for national payment systems to close on other days, and there is still much uncertainty about trading holidays for national financial markets.

Perhaps most crucially, when exactly will the final announcement be made on the euro's exchange rates? Bilateral rates between the currencies that will join the single currency were announced in May 1998, but it is already laid down that one euro will equal one ecu, and the ecu basket includes currencies which will not be joining in the first wave. That means that exchange rates of national currencies against the euro cannot be fixed until trading has ended for the year. With several European markets shut on 31 December this year to provide more time for conversion, this could mean closing rates on 30 December. It could also mean closing rates at lunchtime on 31 December, when other markets will shut, or even the end of the trading day in New York, hours later.

The uncertainty adds to the pressure during the conversion weekend, which promises to be one of the longest many banks' back office and systems staff have ever lived through. 'It is clear that skiing is off next year,' says David Clementi, deputy governor of the Bank of England. Curiously, some of the more advanced IT systems may prove to be a handicap. Martin Wise, director of the Emu project at Merrill Lynch, the US investment bank, points out the already tight timetable for the conversion weekend is shortened still further for banks with global trading systems: they will not be able to start the conversion process until New York has closed on 31 December, and must be ready by the time Asian markets open on 4 January, whereas a purely European system would have precious extra hours at either end. 'Ironically, those fragmented systems which most of us dream of replacing may turn out to be a competitive advantage,' says Mr Wise.

Once the conversion is out of the way, the challenges posed to the financial sector by monetary union will have only begun. Bank treasury departments are still working with their clients to figure out how their demands for cash management and payment services will change in the euro zone. Alan Verschoyle-King, of Bank of America, says that companies' views on the impact of the euro vary considerably. 'There is no single message from clients about how they want their banks to react. Only in the last few months have we started seeing industry trends – for example, the transportation sector is more concerned with the underlying transactions where the energy sector is more concerned with cash balances, because they are dealing in such huge sums,' he says.

Although several central banks would like Target to become the principal high-value payments system for the euro, most banks are hedging their bets and signing up for a variety of different payment mechanisms. Options include the updated version of the Euro Banking Association (EBA) ecu clearing system, which is cleared through the Bank for International Settlements in Basle but will move to the European Central Bank, as well as national systems such as the euro branch of Chaps, the high-value payments system in the UK.

This is partly because of uncertainty about whether all the national systems which are to feed into Target will function effectively – tests with the French real-time gross settlement system have alarmed many payments specialists – but also because clients may have different requirements. Some may prefer a net end-of-day settlement system such as the EBA over Target, which offers the immediate certainty that a payment has arrived but is likely to cost more. Indeed, Martin Lebouitz of Chase Manhattan's treasury solutions division points out that a payment from one French account to another could in future be routed through the bank's Frankfurt payments hub, rather than staying in the French clearing system.

'It blurs considerably the distinction between what is a cross-border and what is a domestic payment,' Mr Lebouitz says. Although banks have another three years to get ready for the full-scale introduction of the euro at the retail level, some lines are already being drawn in this sector, too. Partly under pressure from the European Commission, which was worried consumers would revolt against the euro if they thought the conversion would cost them, banks have promised not to charge customers for changing their accounts into euros.

'We will certainly not take advantage of this changeover to the euro to rip off our customers,' said Nikolaus Bomcke, secretary-general of the European Banking Federation, which has promised only to use the official conversion rates and not to charge except in rare cases where a 'substantial service' is involved.

First appeared 23 March 1998

Banking: *cross-border sales will grow but most retail banks are nervous about marching abroad*

GEORGE GRAHAM

National banking markets in Europe have undergone dramatic deregulation since the mid-1980s, partly under the influence of EU legislation such as the second banking directive of 1988 or the 1993 investment services directive. But despite these changes, Europe is still a long way from boasting a single market in banking services. If anything, banks have retreated further within their national borders, as efforts to build pan-European banking networks, such as Crédit Lyonnais's ambitious expansion plan in the 1980s, have come to grief.

Will the introduction of the euro prove to be the last remaining stone needed for the construction of this single market? In corporate banking, the euro is bound to accelerate the integration of the European market. Companies will increasingly demand services such as the ability to pool euro cash balances held in several different countries. They are also unlikely to accept that charges for cross-border payments should remain at their current levels, roughly 100 times higher than for domestic payments.

For personal customers, however, few bankers believe the euro will be enough to create a single market on its own, though most believe it will give a boost to cross-border sales of financial products and to multinational alliances between banks. 'There isn't a single market, and there won't be on 1 January 1999,' says Jan Kalff, chairman of ABN Amro, the Dutch bank. 'The fact that you have one currency does not automatically create one market. It helps, it's one impediment less, but it's not enough.' Daniel Bouton, chairman of France's Société Genérale, agrees: 'I haven't changed my mind about retail banking activities. I still consider that differences in mentalities, savings regulations and fiscal laws will continue for several years to be very efficient barriers to multinational retail banking activity.'

A number of factors will help to level the playing field between domestic and overseas competitors after the introduction of the euro. In the first place, the elimination of currency risk will make financial products more accessible across borders. In addition, banks based in, say, Germany, will be able to use the low-cost retail deposits collected through their domestic branch networks to fund loans in another country which may offer more attractive lending margins. That should, in time, lead to an approximate equalization in pricing for retail financial products throughout the euro zone. Specific products such as credit cards, too, could advance because of their ease of use in cross-border purchases.

Mr Bouton, whose bank is looking to build up its market share within France before it turns abroad, also argues that it will not be more than five years before consumer pressure leads to tax harmonization and the creation of a much more unified savings market. Nevertheless, most banks remain nervous about their ability to march into new national markets and compete against strong local players with established customer bases. Some merger activity has taken place across national boundaries, with monetary union as an important driving factor, but this has mostly been confined to regions which already showed a significant degree of integration. In Scandinavia, for example, Merita of Finland and Nordbanken of Sweden have merged. In Belgium, Banque Bruxelles Lambert has been taken over by ING of the Netherlands, while Genérale de Banque is in discussions with Fortis, the Dutch–Belgian financial services group.

Several other national banking markets, while large, are insufficiently profitable to be very attractive to other European competitors. France, for example, has seen interest margins under intense pressure for five years, with private sector banks facing protected or subsidized competition from mutual and co-operative banks such as Crédit Mutuel and Crédit Agricole, as well as from the state-owned Crédit Lyonnais. Although UK banks have been much more profitable than their French counterparts over the last five years, many British bankers acknowledge that their cost structures would not stand up to French-style margins.

Germany, too, offers a competitive landscape shaped by the strength of the public-sector Sparkassen. In Spain, where several banks radically overhauled their structures in the 1980s and now boast very high levels of operating efficiency, foreign competitors will venture at their peril. 'In retail banking things won't change much. Other banks that have tried in Spain have gone away,' said Emilio de Ybarra y Churruca, chairman of Banco Bilbao Vizcaya.

Italy, on the other hand, still boasts interest margins which are opulent by the standards of other European markets, while most of its banks remain extremely inefficient and overmanned – which means the market is eyed hungrily by banks in several other countries.

For the time being, however, there remains ample room for consolidation within national banking systems, and that is where most banks are concentrating their attention. The creation of pan-European banks may have to wait.

First appeared 30 April 1998

The pensions industry: *the euro may change the ownership structure of companies*

JANE MARTINSON

Reports in the *FT* of a practical guide to the single currency for pension funds prompted more than 200 calls to the organization behind the guide in under two weeks. Rob Ten Wolde, secretary of Opf, the Dutch foundation of company pension funds which produces the guide jointly with VB, the association of industry-wide pension funds, said the demands for further information were 'enormous'. Inquiries for the English language version of the document came from all over Europe as well as from New York and Hong Kong. 'The response really gave the idea that the whole world is interested in this subject,' he said.

And well it might be. The introduction of a single currency is expected to lead to fundamental shifts in the way money is managed in Europe as well as providing logistical and administrative headaches for thousands of companies. The guide – the creation of a specially formed Dutch euro project group of pension funds – attracted keen interest at the biennial conference of international pension fund providers and managers in October 1996. More than 200 delegates attended three sessions devoted to the issue of what the consequences of European economic and monetary union could be. One pension fund manager at the meeting described the impact of a single currency as greater than that presented by the millennium problem of converting software systems.

While the administrative and legislative burdens on the pension funds are expected to be huge, however, more work appears to have been done on the upheaval in the way funds are managed. A single currency is expected to lead to a different ownership structure for European companies, to create a more diversified bond market and to accelerate consolidation in the industry. The possible extent of the changes has excited keen interest among investment bankers.

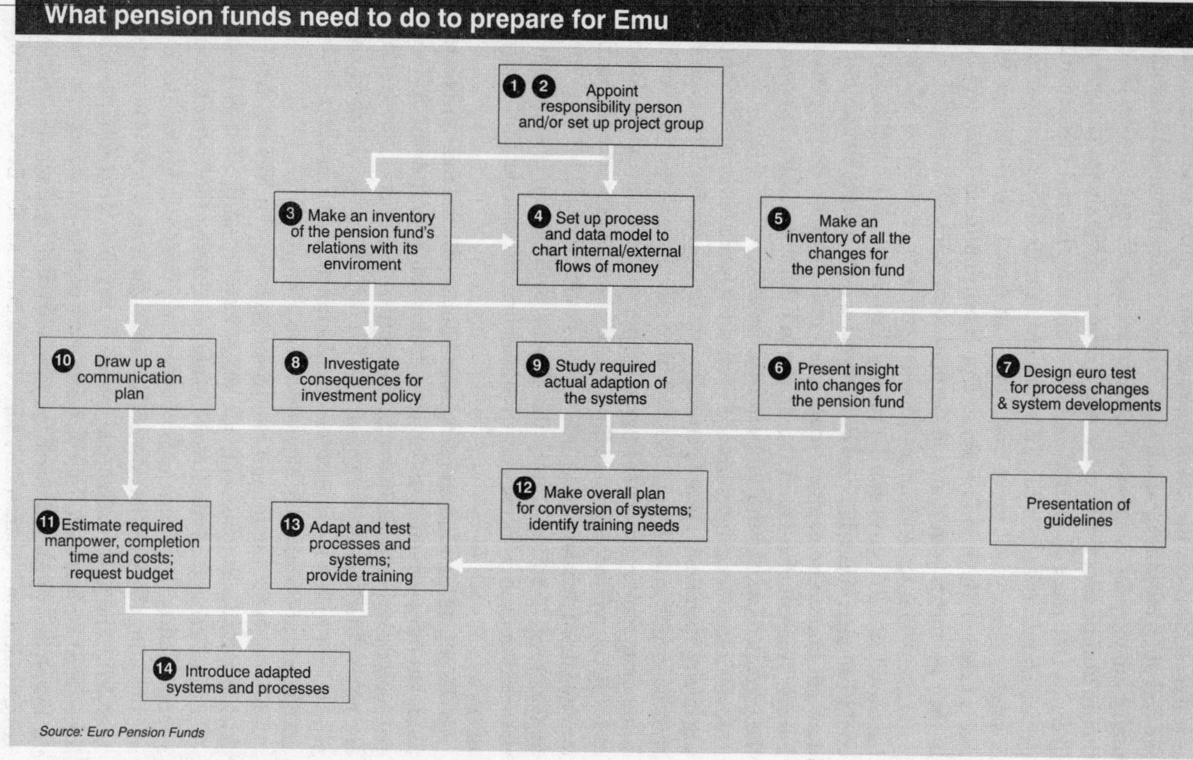

Source: Euro Pension Funds

NatWest Markets, the UK investment bank, wrote a research note at the end of October 1997 which said: 'The arrival of Emu and a looming under-funded pension crisis will drive convulsive changes in asset allocation in Europe over the next few years.' The most significant changes are likely to take place in asset allocation. Currency risk and pension rules demand funds cover their liabilities with investments in the same currency. A single currency will mean that funds can match their liabilities with assets held anywhere in Europe, so Dutch pension funds can cover part of their payments with shares in German companies, for example.

Edmond Warner and James Montier, analysts at NatWest Markets, have predicted that cross-border money flows resulting from this change could be huge. They have estimated that a 10 per cent switch out of domestic bonds into equities would result in $100 billion moving around Europe. Analysts also expect the change in liability matching to result in the increased use of pan-European benchmarks.

Many institutional investors and investment banks have already started organizing their research on a pan-European basis because of this expected shift in investments. It surprises few in the industry that much work is being done on the issue of a single currency in the Netherlands. As well as being committed to joining Emu in the first wave, the country has the second largest pension fund sector in Europe after the UK. Mr Ten Wolde at Opf says: 'I am optimistic that Dutch pension funds will be well prepared to change to the euro from the first relevant date (of January 1999).'

Its large pension fund industry contributes to the fact that the Netherlands has more capital than domestic investment opportunities and so is particularly interested in making cross-border investments. But developments in other countries suggest that the issue is being addressed elsewhere. The Irish government issued a document in the summer of 1997 called Ireland's National Changeover Plan.

The reason for the interest is obvious, says Jos van Niekerk, head of Stichting Unilever Pensioenfonds and a member of the Dutch group. 'The practical and administrative issues of adapting to the euro should prompt action. Directors and managers of pension funds will have to start tackling the introduction of the euro right now. There is not much time left.' The guide which has caused so much interest outlines what steps need to be taken for a fund to start paying pensioners in euros in five years' time. The need for new software, legal compliance and communication with members adds weight to Mr van Niekerk's warnings.

First appeared 21 November 1997

Fund managers gear up for big changes. *'Conservative Europeans' may invest more in equities after monetary union*

JANE MARTINSON

When UK fund managers talk about European equities they exclude UK stocks. Yet most believe that their industry faces profound changes in the run-up to European monetary union. A single currency is expected to lead to a different ownership structure for European companies, to create a more diversified bond market and to accelerate consolidation in the industry.

The most significant changes could take place in asset allocation. In his research paper 'Don't Worry. It is only a Revolution!', published in May 1997, Jan Mantel, a senior fund manager, argues that Emu will accelerate the move towards cross-border ownership. His research for Merrill Lynch, the US investment bank, found that European pension funds invest between 70 and 90 per cent of their assets in home markets. Currency risk and pension rules demand funds cover their liabilities with investments in the same currency. Emu will mean German pensions can be matched by French income and vice versa. Mr Mantel argues that this shift will not only lead to changes in ownership but in the way a fund measures its performance. He believes domestic benchmarks such as the UK's FTSE All-Share will make way for a pan-European index with managers asked to beat the average for the continent.

Such shifts will lead to fundamental portfolio changes as domestic investors include a broader range of industries. Tim Stevenson, head of European equity team at Henderson Investors, an independent UK fund manager, realized how significant this shift could be when he was asked to give a presentation to a large Dutch pension fund in the summer of 1997. The fund, which wanted to know how it could prepare for Emu, was told that 'the changes that are going to happen are enormous'.

A typical Dutch investor has about 32 per cent of his domestic equity invested in oil stocks, mainly because of the dominance of Royal Dutch/Shell in the Dutch index. In Henderson's definition of a 'broad Emu' band of ten member states the oil sector accounts for just 11 per cent (of equity holdings). A shift away from a domestic to a pan-European benchmark would also push the Dutch into the pharmaceuticals market, which accounts for 11 per cent of European shares but nothing in the Netherlands. Georg Inderst, Italian head of fixed-interest investment at Foreign & Colonial, believes there will also be a gradual convergence in investment practices across European countries.

The situation where UK fund managers typically hold 70 to 80 per cent of their portfolios in equities while their German counterparts own just 10 per cent will not outlive monetary union. 'Over the next ten years you can see European institutions, particularly from the more conservative countries, move up to 25 to 30 per cent in equities,' he says. This shift of ownership is a potential gold mine for investment banks who aim to control this cross-border ebb and flow. Such growth prospects will also accelerate the takeover wave in the industry, according to Mr Mantel. Some changes have already taken place. Fund managers and investment bank research analysts have started to measure individual company performance on a pan-European or global scale. ICI, the UK chemicals group, is typically compared with Germany's Hoechst, for example, rather than its UK peer group.

Gartmore, the fund manager owned by National Westminster Bank, has reorganized its research team and appointed a global head of research. Andrew Fleming, the recently appointed head of equities, argues that the new structure with a single equity department will make it 'easier to address the issue of a single currency' when it arises. Equities are not expected to be the only asset type to be profoundly changed by Emu. Convergence will bring to an end the ability to bet on the differences between bond prices. This will prompt fund managers to look for other kinds of bonds to diversify their portfolios, Mr Inderst at Foreign & Colonial says. He forecasts 'the development of a quasi junk-bond market' with more companies issuing bonds to raise finance. This shift will bring Europe into line with the US, where a highly developed high-yield corporate, or junk, bond market already exists.

Mr Inderst also predicts a surge in emerging market bonds, particularly in eastern Europe. A single currency will end the currency risk of the participating countries. One fund manager who specializes in stock rather than currency selection said this meant he had a 'lot less to worry about'.

First appeared 23 September 1997

Stock market: *indices line up for benchmark battle*

SIMON DAVIES

The eleven-member Emu-bloc will have a combined stock-market capitalization of about $3,300 billion, making it the second largest stock market in the world. But it will still be a long way from being a genuine regional stock market. One impediment may have been removed with the creation of a single currency, but plenty more will remain, from tax and regulation to cultural sensitivities. But a substantial barrier will have been breached, and it is only a matter of time before investors move beyond their traditional domestic benchmarks towards a pan-European approach.

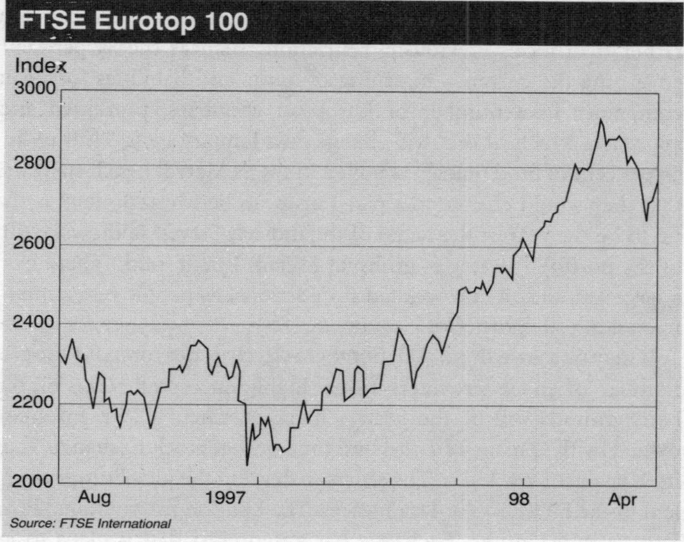

The birth of the euro has also increased the potential rewards for success in pan-European equity investment. Tight fiscal policies and the convergence of bond yields around those of German government bonds have meant a collapse in yields in Italy and Spain, and declining yields throughout the Continent. This is driving a switch of investment from government bonds into equities. In March 1998 alone, $6.8 billion went into Italian equity mutual funds. Morgan Stanley estimates that annualized equity mutual fund inflows in the year to date are $94 billion in the seven countries it tracked: France, Germany, Italy, Spain, Sweden, Switzerland and the UK. Three of these are not going to be part of the first wave of Emu, but the growth rate in the four countries that will be has been far higher.

Mark Howdle, European equity strategist at Salomon Smith Barney, argues that the euro-zone stock market could grow from $3,300 billion to $7,500 billion in current money terms in the next decade, even without any increase in valuations. He assumes just a 5 per cent annual increase in share issuance – the current growth rate – and a 0.4 per cent annual increase in return on equity. And since the euro will improve comparability between European companies, it should increase pressure on them to improve returns.

The increasing size of the single currency market is going to create considerable pressures for change. Institutional investors will demand lower dealing costs for switching between exchanges, and investors will increasingly require fund managers to beat pan-European benchmarks, rather than local. Previously, restrictions such as the 85 per cent rule governing the currency matching of assets and liabilities for insurance companies in a number of European countries, prevented such an approach. Much of that will change on 1 January 1999. With more than 50 per cent of fund managers polled in 1997's Merrill Lynch survey saying that they would change to a pan-European benchmark, 1998 is shaping up to be the year of the battle of the indices. Steve Malinowski, director of the portfolio strategies group at Merrill Lynch, said: 'There has been a large amount of euro-related transactions, as people restructure away from domestic portfolios.'

It may be a growth market, but there clearly is not room for the growing number of index providers to be highly successful. One of the key battlegrounds will be the futures markets, where FTSE International, owned by the *Financial Times* and the London Stock Exchange, is pitting itself against Dow Jones. The aim is to develop the pan-European equivalent of the FTSE 100 or Dax indices. The London International Financial Futures and Options Exchange has announced that it plans to launch contracts based on the Eurotop 100 index, formed by FTSE and the Amsterdam Exchanges, on 12 May. Eurotop has created 100 and 300 stock indices for both the euro bloc and Europe. Meanwhile, Liffe's European arch-rival Deutsche Terminbörse is to start trading in Dow's Stoxx indices on 22 June, along with the French and Swiss futures exchanges. Stoxx is offering euro and European 50 stock indices. It also has a broader euro index with more than 300 companies, and a pan-European index with about 600.

Mr Malinowski said: 'In order for either set of futures contracts to be successful, one would have to see the development of a liquid index arbitrage market.' FTSE International will be competing, via its *FT/S&P* Actuaries indices, with MSCI and the broader Stoxx indices for dominance among institutional fund managers for more complex portfolio bench marking. Here, benchmarks need to offer broader representation of the underlying markets than a retail index, which is more concerned with the ability of investors to arbitrage between the future and the underlying stocks in the index. Given the cost to fund managers of switching benchmarks, and the ongoing barriers to genuine pan-European investment, the victors in this battle may take a long time to emerge. Mr Howdle said: 'I think that by the year 2005 we will have one fantastically deep and liquid euro bourse with most European companies, and it will have one mighty main index.' That leaves room for an awful lot of disappointment.

First appeared 5 May 1998

Bond markets: *powerful forces for change*

SIMON DAVIES

It did not take the European bond markets long to adjust to the implications of European economic and monetary union. By the start of 1998, the convergence process had virtually come to an end in the government bond markets, with yields on Italian bonds a whisker away from Germany's, having been 6 percentage points – or 600 basis points – higher just three years ago.

However, Emu will have much more wide-reaching implications for European bond markets – implications which have investment bankers salivating, but which could also bring substantial economic benefits to member nations. At present, the European bond markets are fragmented for a number of reasons, from domestic regulation and taxation to currency. Joe Cook, global head of capital markets at J. P. Morgan, says: 'If you boil it down, the drivers for change in the European capital markets are the pressures on governments to meet the Maastricht criteria, shareholder value, the desire for personal choice in investment, and improvements in technology. But Emu will be a catalyst to speed up the process.'

The European bond markets have a long way to go. It is not so much the size, which is similar to that in the US, but the fact that the European markets have always been dominated by government bonds and AAA-rated bonds from supranationals such as the World Bank.

The corporate bond market remains little developed, primarily because historical relationships with domestic banks have held back issuance. In Germany, bank loans amount to 100 per cent of gross domestic product, compared with only 45 per cent in the US. In addition, European fund managers have concentrated on taking bets on currency movements rather than analysing corporate credit quality. With yields of more than 10 per cent on Italian BTPs, or government bonds, investors could get a high yield without taking on the complexities of corporate credit. As a result, it is estimated that, within the eleven euro-zone countries, capital market securities have accounted for about one-third of corporate debt. In the US, it is about 80 per cent.

Emu will undoubtedly help narrow the gap, and a number of investment

Before Emu: fragmented capital market

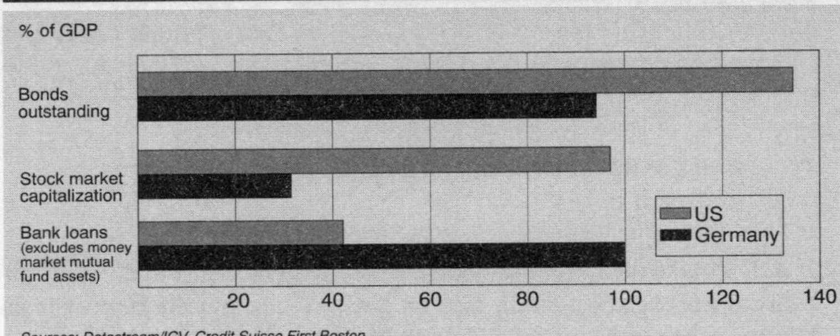

Sources: Datastream/ICV, Credit Suisse First Boston

10-year bond yields (%)

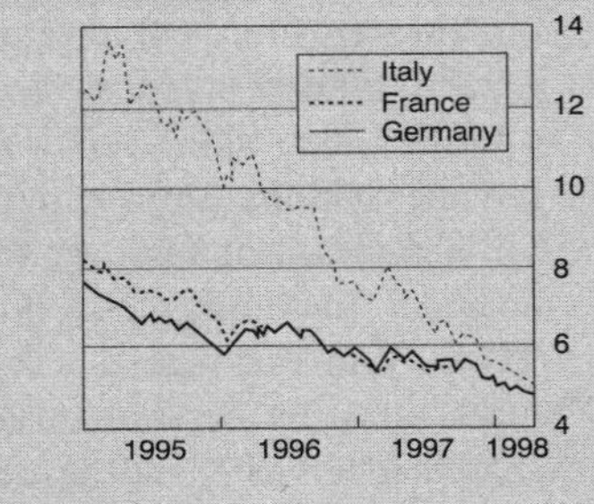

Paul Danial (left): a pan-European capital market will evolve in less than five years
Joe Cook: Emu will speed up the process of change in European capital markets

banks are forecasting that the corporate bond market in Europe will reach $3,000 billion by the year 2003. Paul Daniel, head of fixed income for Morgan Stanley Dean Witter in Europe, said: 'I initially thought that it would take five years for a pan-European capital market to evolve. Now I think that it will be much quicker.' One factor, which is already apparent, is the rapid decline in the issuance of government debt, as a result of austerity measures by countries struggling to meet the criteria for joining monetary union that were set out in the European Union's Maastricht treaty.

Net debt issuance by European governments is expected to fall by $50 billion in 1998, representing a decline of one-third, according to J. P. Morgan. This has been one of the forces driving down government bond yields, but it will also create a vacuum to be filled by increased issuance from corporate borrowers. But there are many other factors supporting this process. At present, most insurance and pension funds have to match a large proportion of their liabilities with assets in the same currency. For the majority of European insurance companies, 80 per cent of assets and liabilities have to be matched in the same currency. From the start of 1999, this will open up an enormous array of new investment opportunities. Furthermore, as fund managers start to take on pan-European benchmarks for investment performance, instead of their traditional domestic indices, they will be forced into a radical alteration of their investment approach.

Then there is the development of fully-funded pension schemes throughout Europe. The Maastricht criteria made potential Emu members focus on the extent of their growing pension liabilities, and this will encourage a shift towards privately funded pension schemes for all but the very poor. This in turn will create a larger pool of funds for investment in the equity and bond markets, and create demand for longer-term bonds, to match longer-term pension liabilities.

Mr Cook believes that forcing pension liabilities off corporate balance sheets and fully funding them will be inevitable, and that Europe needs legislation such as the US's Employee Retirement Income Security Act to force that change on a pan-European basis. The impact of this would be to create a huge pool of funds for investment in the European equity market. But it would also create substantial demand for capital market funding from those corporations concerned. The costs of funding these liabilities, particularly at current low bond yields, should in theory be compensated for by the impact of this vast new pool of capital on share prices, creating a virtuous circle – one that is particularly virtuous for European pensioners, many of whom are unhealthily exposed to the share performance of their employers.

Indeed, the development of this broad and liquid regional bond market, which will exceed that of the US, should help to bring down the cost of debt capital in the euro zone, which in turn should fuel economic benefits throughout the region. However, there is bound to be considerable resistance to these changes. Banks, for example, will be concerned about increasing competition for corporate loans, while politicians and regulators may be concerned by a decline in their influence. This could slow the development of the new capital market, but the end result looks inevitable.

First appeared 30 April 1998

Derivatives exchanges jostle for position

EDWARD LUCE

Most agree that the market will shrink quite dramatically after Emu. One trading day last month, German derivatives officials found the perfect excuse to pop the proverbial champagne cork. After months of intense competition, Deutsche Terminbörse – Germany's main derivatives exchange – had finally overtaken its London counterpart in trading on the key futures contract on the ten-year German government bond.

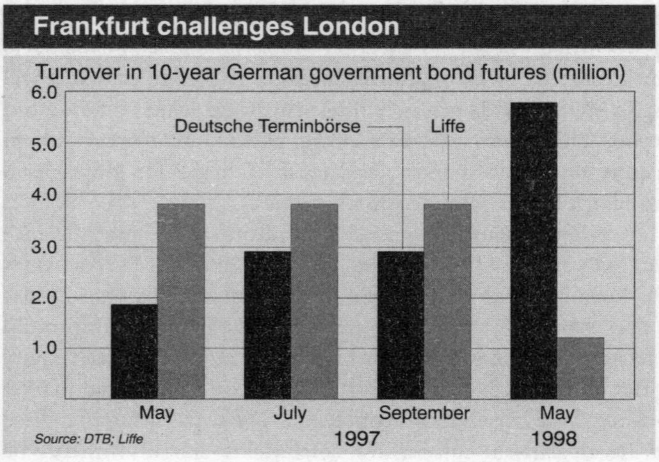

The DTB's market share in that contract has since settled at about an average of 48 per cent per day. Liffe – the London International Financial Futures and Options Exchange – accounts for the rest. But the event was undoubtedly a cause for celebration in Frankfurt. 'We have proved that we can overtake London in the most traded bond future in Europe', said a DTB official. 'This means that we can win dominant market share in the euro after 1999.'

Europe's leading derivatives exchanges are jostling frantically for market position in advance of European monetary union in January 1999. The abolition of up to thirteen currencies and thirteen separate interest rates will drastically reduce the cross-border volatility on which derivatives thrive. Derivatives – futures and options contracts which are based on underlying instruments such as shares, bonds or interest rates – will be one of the principal casualties of Emu.

Officials at Liffe and DTB are, therefore, focusing on how to win dominant market share in the contracts which will be based upon the future euro. At the beginning of 1997, the DTB, which trades about half the volume of contracts traded on Liffe, announced a tie-up with Matif, its Paris-based counterpart, and Soffex, Switzerland's leading derivatives exchange. The alliance, which will enable clients to trade in the contracts offered by all three exchanges on just one electronic system, was seen as the first blow in a war to undermine Liffe's dominance.

Overtaking – albeit briefly – Liffe's volumes in the long-bund future was viewed as the second blow. 'Liffe cannot afford to be complacent,' said an official at a brokerage company which trades on Liffe. 'DTB and its partners are starting to catch up with it.' The continental alliance, which will also involve a common settlement system and a formula for revenue-sharing, has not yet got off the ground. But officials are confident it can undercut the cost of trading on Liffe.

Unlike Liffe, which retains an 'open outcry' pit trading system for most of its contracts, the DTB is entirely electronic. Matif, which operates a hybrid open outcry and electronic system, will introduce all new contracts solely on its screen-based trading facilities. This will effectively isolate Liffe as the only pit-trading system of any note left in Europe. Is this an advantage or a problem? Executives at Liffe argue that open outcry provides the sort of liquidity which is still unavailable on screen-based trading. This means that traders can buy and sell billions of dollars worth of underlying contracts within seconds without overloading the system.

Proponents of electronic trading say this is no longer the case for trading in futures contracts on government bonds – the German long-bund, for example. In addition – and most importantly – they claim it is several times cheaper to trade on a screen than it is to maintain an army of salaried brokers on a trading floor. Jorg Franke, director of DTB, says clients are increasingly moving towards electronic trading in a move to squeeze cost-margins. Mr Franke concedes that open outcry remains the more liquid system for trading in short-term interest rate contracts or on options – where Liffe still commands more than 90 per cent of volumes – but says the gap is narrowing as software becomes more sophisticated. Officials at Liffe say they are keeping their options open. But the fact that the exchange is planning to shift to a much larger floor in Spitalfields (on the edge of the City of London) has persuaded many that Liffe is irrevocably committed to open outcry. 'Why pour all these overheads into floor space if you are going to find out that all you need is one small room with a computer in it?' asked one brokerage official.

Analysts also point out that Liffe ironically owns probably the most sophisticated electronic system in Europe – the Automated Pit Trading system which has recently been upgraded. APT, however, is only used for after-hours trading, although it will form the basis of strategic links with other exchanges after a pit-trading link-up proved disappointingly illiquid. 'The question everybody is asking is why Liffe does not allow trading on APT and on the floor at the same time?' asks one broker. 'That way it could give its clients a choice.' Liffe, however, says it would be too expensive to operate both systems simultaneously.

The argument between traditionalists and technologists is unlikely to abate. In the meantime, both Liffe and its continental rivals are attempting to woo customers with new products and gimmicks such as waiving fees altogether on some contracts including the long-bund future. 'The nearer Emu gets, the more intense the competition will be,' says one official in London. Few are confident enough to predict who will predominate. But most agree that the market will shrink quite dramatically after January 1999.

First appeared 21 November 1997

Aim for bourse without borders: *Europe is upstaging Wall Street, and the euro offers investors hope for even more vigour*

BARRY RILEY

Shares on Wall Street may have been gliding ever upwards, but recently European ones have been doing even better. By mid-May 1998, the index for Europe excluding the UK is up 28 per cent in dollar terms – nearly twice Wall Street's gain. This sparkling performance has focused renewed attention on the potential of the historically unexciting Continental European bourses.

Hopes are high that the euro will provide the trigger for a revitalization of the Continent's fragmented capital markets. At the very least, the single currency will lead to a profound shake-up in the operations of stock exchanges and financial institutions. 'A broker's life will change more over the next two years than at any time in the past,' says Mark Brown, strategist at ABN Amro. And Jan Mantel, chief investment officer for Europe at Dresdner RCM Global Investors, says funds across Europe will be forced to re-balance and reorientate their portfolios.

'It will be the mother of all programme trades,' he promises. Potentially, there is more. At best, the European corporate sector could be modernized and liberated from the shackles of nationalism and political interference. The biggest prizes could go to Europe's corporate giants, which have already seen their share prices multiply under the impact of global investment flows – much of it from the US. This sector of leviathans is also being expanded through the wave of Continental European privatizations. Consider the example of Germany's Daimler-Benz. Until only a few years ago, it was a near-basket case of muddled flag-carrying and industrial conglomeration. But now it has been re-invented as a shareholder-friendly multinational sufficiently self-confident to launch, as the dominant partner, a merger with America's Chrysler.

But what about the medium-sized and smaller company sectors? Germany's Mittelstand of privately-held companies, for instance, has traditionally been a vital part of the country's economic strength. More German companies are going public than in the past, but across Europe the smaller companies are of comparatively little interest to international investors. Thus, a two-tier European corporate economy seems to be developing. Some 200 to 300 big corporations are likely to make up the pan-European market. For the foreseeable future the smaller company sectors are likely to remain primarily local and domestic – although exchanges such as the Brussels-based Easdaq are attempting to develop a Europe-wide new company market in the more glamorous and international sectors, notably technology.

The separation between international and domestic was on display in the UK during 1997 when the FTSE 100 Index, packed with multinational blue chips, returned a growth rate of 29 per cent while the corresponding 250 Index of middle-ranking stocks rose only 10 per cent. The shift wrong-footed many of the big UK investment institutions.

As the big companies grow more international, stock exchanges are becoming aware that the need to carve out a role in the cross-border markets of the future is more pressing than their traditional focus on their domestic empires. For example, co-operation between the Paris and Frankfurt bourses, and their derivatives equivalents, is putting pressure on London, which has dominated international business.

Flagship national equity market indices composed of market leaders, such as the DAX, the CAC 40 and the FTSE 100, face a limited future: some say ten years, others five. The race is on to design and promote the Europe-wide index to replace them: contenders so far include FTSE's Eurotop series and Dow Jones's Stoxx indices, while Standard & Poor's has a product almost ready for launch.

Which index will flash up on 21st-century TV screens across Europe, as a snapshot of the day's stock market progress? We should get an early indication of the winner from the performance of the various new futures and options contracts to which these pan-European indices are being linked. Meanwhile, the euro poses a direct challenge to Europe's labyrinth of nationalistic controls on investment institutions. Insurance companies and pension funds in many countries have been constrained to invest in domestic assets, rather than foreign ones, and restricted in their ability to hold equities rather than bonds.

But from 1 January 1999 a much wider choice of assets will become domestic for institutions in the eleven countries that will form Euroland. This will immediately open up the bond markets. And it is expected that cross-border demand for equities will increase too, as institutions become more international and governments respond to the demographic pressure for the increased funding of future pensions. There are worries in Europe that the big winners will be the Americans, who are used to seeing Europe in the round, rather than the Europeans themselves who will continue to be limited by their lack of perspective. Arguments are going on, for instance, about whether Europe should be carved up for investment purposes into euro and non-euro segments, and European Union and non-EU territories.

Does Euroland represent a coherent economic entity? Not necessarily from the global investor's point of view. Dutch pension funds don't want to exclude Switzerland, with its big pharmaceutical companies, says Mr Mantel of Dresdner RCM. So investors are inventing their own economic geography: they talk about Pan Europe (the whole EU, including non-European economic and monetary union members, plus Switzerland and Norway) or even Extended Pan Europe (which includes some countries to the east).

Borders are becoming fuzzy. Stock market analysts are currently fascinated by the decline of country and the rise of industrial sector as influences on share prices. A pointed example of this shift came last month when the London-based fund management group Foreign & Colonial decided to wind up its German Investment Trust and merge it into a sister Pan Europe fund.

A Brussels firm, European Benchmarks, says four European stock market sectors can be identified: pharmaceuticals, financials, oils and consumer brands. Others are emerging as national influences fade. But investment banks conducting similar studies have come up with conflicting results: ABN Amro thinks chemicals is the most coherent sector, but Goldman Sachs cannot make the correlations work at all well.

The big investment banks are themselves well ahead with restructuring, even if their strategies vary. ABN Amro executives have just embarked on a global roadshow, emphasizing the Dutch-owned institution's resources in nineteen European countries. The big US investment banks tend to be more concentrated in London, from where their analysts cover the developing European megastock sector. Investors, though, are lagging behind. Only a handful of London's big fund management houses have attempted to integrate their UK and European teams.

Jeremy Tigue, manager of the giant Foreign & Colonial Investment Trust, a global fund, puts forward the typical wait-and-see argument. 'It would be premature to merge the UK and Europe until it is evident whether the UK is going into Emu,' he says. According to Adrian Paine, senior portfolio manager for Europe at American Express Asset Management, US-owned managers have therefore been able to steal a lead in the Pan Europe stakes while rivals squabble about domestic versus the rest of Europe. 'It's a fantastic opportunity for us,' he says, claiming recent strong performance. 'We just focus on the larger stocks where the change is going on. Amex's 320-stock European universe cuts off at a minimum market capitalization of $2.5 billion (£1.5 billion).'

For European corporates, the surge in share prices promises a reduction in the cost of capital, and the opening up of a euro-denominated bond market will bring important benefits too. But there will also be costs of adaptation to this effective Americanization of the capital markets. Much depends on the acceptance by European politicians and company executives of concepts of shareholder value. US investors have substantial aggregate stakes in the leading Continental markets, and UK institutions have some $250 billion invested across the Channel. They are inclined to flex their muscles and insist that companies are run to benefit shareholders – which is still a controversial subject in several European countries where banks and trade unions have been much more important stakeholders.

Attitudes to equity buybacks, for instance, still vary, although obstructive German legislation is shortly to be changed. The acceptance of mergers remains patchy: they have become important in Switzerland, but Europe-wide cross-border rationalization in sectors such as banking or motors, though badly needed, remains noticeable for its near absence. And defence industry restructuring, plagued by flag carrier considerations, has proceeded at a snail's pace in Europe compared with the US.

But there is scope for progress. American investors, having given up on east Asia, are pinning their hopes on Europe to accept the baton from a tired Wall Street. Changes in government, corporate and investor behaviour are likely to combine to raise the average valuations in equity markets in Euroland, says Mike Young of Goldman Sachs.

For the time being, though, Europe remains characteristically divided. Half of its stock market capitalization is outside Euroland. Currency exposure will remain a problem in the UK, Switzerland and elsewhere. French socialism is a significant and obstructive force.

Battles remain to be fought. But when they are engaged, companies and investors are likely to emerge as clear winners with a little help from the euro.

First appeared 18 May 1998

Mergers and acquisitions: *a crop of deals is already beginning to sprout from Emu*

CLAY HARRIS

Until recently, European mergers and acquisitions activity sparked by the imminence of economic and monetary union had resembled *Waiting for Godot*: a great deal of expectation with little to show for it. That is now beginning to change, with a stream of deals directly related to the coming of the euro and changes that Emu will bring to Europe. M&A specialists at investment banks believe it heralds years of activity. 'I don't think we have any reason to think that 1998 will be a peak year in Europe,' says Rod Peacock, a managing director at J. P. Morgan, while Bertil Rydevik, co-head of M&A at Lehman Brothers, expects deal flow to be strong enough to keep activity buoyant through any economic downturn.

According to Paul Achleitner, co-head of Goldman Sachs' Frankfurt office: 'The euro is accelerating and accentuating changes that would be inevitable over a longer period anyway.' Gary Weiss, co-head of financial institutions for Merrill Lynch in Europe, agrees that Emu is speeding up trends such as globalization, a greater emphasis on shareholder value, and disintermediation – the greater use of securities at the expense of bank lending. The mutually reinforcing nature of these trends was manifest in the European reaction to Citicorp's globally ambitious link-up with Travelers Group. 'Citigroup was a wake-up call,' says Alistair Walton, head of the European financial institutions group at Credit Suisse First Boston.

The deal has galvanized thinking within Europe's financial services industry, one of the favourite sectors for consolidation. Most mergers so far have been regional in nature even when they cross borders, as in the case of the Dutch ING Group's take-over of Banque Bruxelles Lambert. The creation of the Finnish–Swedish bank holding company Merita Nordbanken after consolidation within each country is not that different from domestic combinations elsewhere.

Whether in Bavaria or Spain or Italy, they mark a desire to create sufficient size to participate more equally in the inevitable next stages of consolidation, moving towards what Mr Walton of CSFB calls the 'global endgame'. Only the take-over of France's AGF by the German insurer Allianz, in a complex deal involving Generali of Italy, approaches the second stage of this process. But it also demonstrated the political limits of cross-border take-overs, since the French authorities signalled that the next such deal would have to be French-led in the interest of reciprocity.

When deciding the fate of CIC, France's fifth largest banking network, the government opted for Crédit Mutuel over offers from Société Genérale and ABN Amro that would have meant, respectively, job cuts and foreign ownership. The euro's most explicit effect will be to make companies within the zone more transparently comparable to investors. Fund managers will no longer have to allow for currency differences, meaning that on whatever bourse a company is listed, it will be assessed against its European peers. Within Euroland, country weightings should disappear as a tool for fund managers. Inside the zone, the definition of a 'domestic' security is transformed. For investors outside the zone as well, much of Europe effectively will be without borders.

This spells danger for big fish in any of the continent's small ponds, since mere local leadership will no longer matter. 'It only matters if you are in the top three in Europe,' says Julian Callow, European economist at Dresdner Kleinwort Benson. Banks have anticipated this evolution by organizing their corporate finance, research and distribution by sector on a pan-European basis.

Simon Robey, co-head of European M&A at Morgan Stanley, believes Emu will 'drive a fundamental reappraisal of strong versus weak investment opportunities within sectors' since managers will no longer focus on domestic stock market indices. As this becomes established, stronger companies will be rewarded by the market, while share prices of the weaker will suffer. This will open them to take-over bids from the dominant companies or prompt them to take drastic restructuring measures.

'Companies will be struggling to develop a competitive equity story that distinguishes them from others,' argues Mr Achleitner of Goldman Sachs. One way, following the US pattern, will be to become an aggressive predator. 'Big deals will give you profile,' he says, and thus boost share prices. The euro should also make mergers easier because investors will be more willing to take shares, rather than demand a premium in cash, according to Hugh Scott-Barrett, chief executive of European corporate finance for ABN Amro. Complex structures driven by the demand for shares denominated in local currencies will no longer be needed.

Mark Florman, managing director of Swedish corporate advisory boutique Maizels, Westerberg, notes that, for companies themselves, the euro removes the equity risk of investing or buying assets in countries prone to having weak currencies. Even more important, says Mr Callow, it will focus attention on labour cost differentials within the euro zone, increasing the attraction of companies in southern Europe. He believes M&A activity may take time to develop as competition increases. 'It's two to three years down the road when you'll see a real quantum leap.' So Emu is less likely to take its inspiration from *Waiting for Godot*, than from *Field of Dreams*. If you build it, they will come.

First appeared 30 April 1998

7 Britain and Emu – on the outside looking in

The British have always been in two minds about economic and monetary union. Doubters question whether the diverse economies of the future euro zone can sustain the discipline of a single currency. Emu advocates argue that it is the essential building block for completion of the single market, the catalyst for deeper integration ahead of EU enlargement to central and eastern Europe.

This chapter offers an in-depth exposition of the pros and cons of Emu from a British perspective. We see how the City of London has become jittery about losing business to the continental bourses, notably Frankfurt; and how industrialists such as Adair Turner, director general of the Confederation of British Industry, are worried about the impact on business of the government's decision to remain initially outside monetary union. Wolfgang Münchau ponders whether the UK's enviable record in attracting inward investment could be hurt by remaining an outsider looking into euro-land.

Yet Martin Wolf, the *FT*'s chief economic commentator, offers powerful reasons why Britain in 1997–8 was in no shape to join the founder members of the single currency. In his commentary 'No, Prime Minister', he shows that these reasons are primarily economic: the British economy was simply out of synch with its continental counterparts, having started its recovery much earlier in the cycle. To force Britain prematurely into Emu on political grounds would be irresponsible.

The *FT*'s articles offer an insight into the tortured political debate in Britain over the timing of a future entry into monetary union. We read an analysis of Chancellor Gordon Brown's statement to the House of Commons, setting out five economic criteria which must be met before Britain can join Emu. As Philip Stephens notes, these look largely like a cover for what is ultimately a political decision to delay entry after the next general election and after a referendum. The importance of coaxing British public opinion round to the idea of abolishing the pound in favour of the euro is a leitmotiv.

The chapter also includes the *FT* front-page story which reported that the Labour government was preparing for early entry into monetary union – a story which convulsed the markets and led to dramatic selling of the pound. As a snapshot of the debate at the highest levels of the government, the story had a far bigger impact than many could have imagined. Historians will argue how far the story affected the final government policy on the timing of future British entry into Emu.

LIONEL BARBER

Best policy for Britain: *the UK should help set up a successful Emu as a precursor to joining*

ADAIR TURNER

After four months of consultation, and many more before that sitting on a very crowded fence, the Confederation of British Industry decided its policy on economic and monetary union. It supports UK membership of a successful Emu, but says Britain should join only if and when the conditions for success are in place. Not all our members argued for this specific line – some prefer a more sceptical approach, some an unreserved commitment to early entry. But a large majority can support this conditional commitment to membership of Emu. I believe it is the best policy for Britain. For some, Emu is primarily a political question. Some believe it a necessary precursor to a desirable political union: others a threat to national sovereignty. And it would be absurd to deny that Emu has a political dimension. But I think some of these arguments are overplayed.

National economic sovereignty is severely constrained by the facts of economic life. The issue is how to maximize economic success, not the illusion of national control. It is on the economic arguments for and against that we need to focus, and on these that an organization like the CBI has a remit to comment. Emu could bring big economic advantages, but only if it goes ahead under the right conditions: if those conditions are not in place, it could do harm.

The aim of policy should be to bring about a successful, not a damaging, Emu. The potential benefits of Emu are transparency, certainty, and stability. Emu would help complete the single market; with everything priced in euros, competition would be more open and intense, bringing lower prices for the consumer and stronger companies better able to compete across the world. And Emu would create a single European capital market for debt and equity – a more efficient mechanism for allocating savings to the highest-return investments.

Monetary union would also eliminate intra-European exchange rate risk from future trade and investment decisions, focusing companies on the fundamentals of business – productivity and quality – rather than on managing financial risk. And the benefits of that risk elimination could put the UK at a disadvantage if a successful Emu developed and Britain stood permanently aside.

Equally important, Emu would protect the 58 per cent of British trade with other EU countries from the damaging impact of large irrational exchange-rate overshoots. Sterling's 30 per cent appreciation against the D-Mark over the past year – in spite of almost identical inflation rates – is severely disrupting long-term planning among UK exporters to Europe. A similar roller-coaster in the lira/D-Mark rate induced first unsustainable boom and then recession in Italian manufacturing in 1995–6. Eliminating those swings will remove unnecessary volatility from the real economy, a volatility the US – which has a much smaller percentage of gross domestic product traded across currency boundaries – does not have to face.

But while Emu has significant potential advantages, and while there are risks for Britain if we stay permanently outside, there are also risks in monetary union – particularly if it goes ahead under the wrong conditions. For the single currency to succeed, inflation rates must have converged, exchange rates must be sustainable, and the public finances of members must be sound. More vitally still, if we abolish exchange rate flexibility, which can help bring real wages in line with productivity levels, we need the alternative of labour market flexibility. For Emu to work, wages in different regions must be set by the competitive circumstances of the companies based there: the wage rates at a car company's plants in Germany and in Spain must be set by local conditions and productivity, not by pan-European collective bargaining. If they are not, if European labour markets evolve in a less flexible direction, Emu could create big problems.

In an ideal world, those conditions for success would argue for great caution about the speed at which Emu is implemented. Inflation rates across Europe have converged to a surprising extent, but the fiscal positions of many potential participants fall short of obvious sustainability and the direction of EU labour market policy remains unclear. In theory there are good arguments, either for a small core group proceeding in 1999 or for the whole project being delayed for several years.

Equally, however, we have to live with the reality that the ideal path to Emu may not be available. The political momentum behind the 1999 timetable is huge, and delay itself could bring major economic costs through exchange rate volatility and higher interest rates on government borrowing. The likelihood that Emu will go ahead in 1999, but in less than ideal circumstances, forms the context against which the UK must decide its policy. That policy should be focused on ensuring the emergence of a successful Emu, which Britain should then join. That means arguing for the conditions required for Emu's success – conditions that ideally would be in place before Emu proceeds, but which could also develop in the years following Emu's start. Britain's ability to argue for that development will be enhanced if it is clear that our desired end point entails both Emu's success and Britain's membership.

The author is director-general of the CBI

First published 23 July 1997

No, Prime Minister: *the level of sterling and the UK's cyclical position mean it would be suicidal for Tony Blair to take Britain into Emu in the first wave*

MARTIN WOLF

Whether and when to join European economic and monetary union are by far the most important questions facing the British government. It is not just whether it would be wise to risk joining this irrevocable monetary marriage. The question has as much to do with when it would be wise to do so.

Everything suggests Emu will begin, on time, at the start of 1999. Moreover, it will include eleven countries. That is every EU member except Greece, which will not qualify, and Denmark, Sweden and the UK, which have chosen not to join then. In its World Economic Outlook, the International Monetary Fund forecasts the 1997 general government fiscal deficits of all EU member states – except Germany, France, Italy and Greece – at or below the Maastricht treaty target of 3 per cent of gross domestic product. But Germany's will only be 3.1 per cent and those of France and Italy 3.2 per cent.

Effectively, all members, Greece apart, meet the deficit criterion. The IMF also calculates that all members, except Greece, have cyclically adjusted fiscal deficits of well under 3 per cent of GDP, most of them below 2 per cent. The UK's actual deficit is forecast at 2 per cent. As growth proceeds, deficits elsewhere should converge on cyclically adjusted deficits, making even the 1 per cent deficit target in the growth and stability pact attainable.

Against this background, the two big obstacles to a single currency – French unwillingness to undertake further fiscal austerity and German reluctance to embrace a broad Emu – are almost irrelevant. The government of Mr Lionel Jospin does not need to impose much austerity.

German politicians may huff and puff over Italian membership. But the technocrats in the European Commission and the European Monetary Institute have now concluded that all members – again with the exception of Greece – have met the criteria. A German refusal to join would be tantamount to an act of war on European integration. It is not going to happen.

As this reality dawns, the British government is rightly debating how to respond. Tony Blair must be asking whether to exercise his option of trying to join in the first wave, at the beginning of 1999. The answer he should be given is: 'No, Prime Minister.'

Business opinion is moving in favour of joining as soon as possible. The fiercest opponents are the tattered remnants of the Tory party. Never is the political background likely to be more favourable, Mr Blair may reasonably conclude. Unfortunately for his ambitions, the economic background is just the opposite.

If Mr Blair tries to put sterling into Emu in 1999, things will almost certainly go seriously wrong. There are two linked reasons: the currency's level and the UK's cyclical position. Together, they make entry in 1999 suicidal.

All measures of the real exchange rate suggest sterling is overvalued. The International Monetary Fund, for example, offers a measure of relative unit labour costs adjusted for the state of the economic cycle. At the end of July 1997, UK relative labour costs were higher than at any time since late 1983. Between July and the third week of September, sterling's trade-weighted nominal exchange rate depreciated 2 per cent. But this is not enough to change the picture. Merely to bring relative costs to the middle of the range in which they have moved since the end of the extraordinary appreciation of 1979–82, sterling's nominal effective exchange rate needs to fall about 10 per cent. Given long-standing weaknesses in the production of tradable goods and services, such a depreciation is the least one should hope for. A depreciation of 15 per cent would be safer. If the exchange rates of the UK's trading partners were to remain stable, this would imply a rate against the D-Mark of DM2.40. To lock sterling in at a rate very much higher than this would be quite mad.

There is more. At present, UK short-term interest rates are 4 percentage points higher than in Germany. This reflects the very different position in the economic cycle. In the UK, broad money is growing at an annual rate of close to 12 per cent, against 6 per cent in Germany. National estimates of unemployment in August 1997 are 5.3 per cent for the UK and 11.6 per cent for Germany. The UK's economy is expected to have expanded at a rate of 2.9 per cent a year between 1992 and 1997 and Germany's at only about 1.5 per cent. UK consumer price inflation is above Germany's, in spite of the 20 per cent effective appreciation of sterling since early 1996. Against this background, stabilization of UK inflation will demand short-term interest rates well above those in most of Europe's core for a substantial period.

Suppose then that rates started to fall in anticipation of entry into Emu. This might bring sterling down. But it would also stimulate a credit-driven surge in domestic demand. The combination of an initial sterling depreciation with lower interest rates and faster growth in domestic demand is likely to push underlying inflation well above its 2½ per cent target for some years. Suppose, for example, that inflation were to be a little over 3 percentage points higher than in the European core for three years, or 2 percentage points higher for five. Either would mean a real appreciation of roughly 10 per cent. Even an entry rate of DM2.50 would, within a few years, leave the UK as uncompetitive as it is today.

The classic way to claw back such a real appreciation is a squeeze on the profitability of industries producing tradable goods and services. This would lead to a fall in their output and distort the structure of the economy. But it would also ultimately produce lower inflation. An extremely tough fiscal policy would help. But remember that annual inflation in the euro area is likely to be around 2 per cent. The UK would need five years of zero inflation to recover a real overvaluation of 10 per cent if its productivity growth were the same as in other member countries.

Elsewhere, perhaps, political commitment to European integration might allow a government to survive such a long period of decline in manufacturing and semi-stagnation in the economy. In the UK, it would be a recipe for a nationalist upsurge against the EU. A government that put the country in such a mess would be doomed.

Whatever Mr Blair might prefer, entry in 1999 is out of the question. But tight monetary and fiscal policy could perhaps make it possible by 2002. This date would have the advantage of coinciding with introduction of the new notes and coins. Should the early period of Emu be as turbulent and unstable as some fear, the UK could avoid it. The option of joining cannot safely be exercised next year. But that of later entry must be kept open. Whether it makes sense to risk a referendum on an option that will not be exercised for some years is a tactical matter. The timing of entry, however, is not tactical, but fundamental. Some wonder whether the time will ever be ripe to join Emu: what is certain is that it is not ripe now.

First published 30 September 1997

***Eerie Tory echoes:** even in opposition, the issue of Europe continues to divide the Conservative party like no other*

PHILIP STEPHENS

In opposition as in government, Europe courses like a virus through the veins of the Conservative party. It is the issue that brought the party to ruinous defeat. But, defying all remedies, the fever will not abate. At another moment, this would hardly matter. The Tories are out of office for five years. More likely, it will be a decade. But Europe, and most potently the single currency, now presents its agonizing choices to Tony Blair's government. The prime minister is a cautious politician. The state of health of his opponents will weigh heavily in his calculations.

Any thoughts that the Conservatives might rid themselves of the European malaise were banished at the party's 1997 conference in Blackpool. The patient's temperature, it is true, is lower than in some past years. After eighteen years in office, defeat has been the coldest of showers. Michael Portillo, now reinventing himself as a standard-bearer of tolerant politics, no longer rails against federalist plots to put British soldiers in European uniforms.

This is no cure. William Hague's victory over the pugnaciously pro-European Kenneth Clarke in the post-election Tory leadership contest shifted the party's centre of gravity. Only four in the current shadow cabinet of eighteen are avowed pro-Europeans. They have been placed in the least consequential positions. Mr Hague shares the sceptics' instincts if not their prejudices. He is in tune with the activists. The odd pro-European voice was heard from the podium in Blackpool. Touring the fringe, Sir Leon Brittan, the party's representative on the Brussels Commission, offered an energetic exposition of the case for pragmatism over ideology.

The foot-stamping cheers, though, were reserved for those who spoke the language of Europhobia. I am no anti-European, said one zealot, but the French 'eat their horses'. Norman Lamont demands that Mr Hague makes rejection of the euro the *raison d'être* of his leadership. As for his future, well, Mr Lamont is seeking a bolthole in the European parliament. There was an elision too with the ugly English nationalism that still claims a place on the right of the Tory party. Thus Norman Tebbit, softly but venomously spoken, juxtaposed the threat from without (Europe) with an imaginary danger within (Britain's multicultural society). The applause was thunderous.

For all this, Mr Hague is unproven. Cecil Parkinson, the party chairman, wonders aloud at his choice of close political aides. Shadow cabinet colleagues struggle to sound supportive. Mr Clarke, a lion among cubs, admits that he still hopes that one day the party will call him to the leadership. Others conceal their ambition behind the thinnest veils of loyalty.

Mr Hague must know, too, that, while the pro-Europeans are in the minority, they are numerous enough to wreck any prospect of a Tory revival. Mr Clarke and his allies must be accommodated. So the leader has promised a free vote in parliament should Mr Blair seek to scrap the pound. He hardly had a choice. It would be silly to expect as big a politician as Mr Clarke to do anything but make up his own mind.

For a sane opposition, that would solve the problem. But on this issue, Conservatives long ago lost sight of reason. To defeat Mr Clarke, Mr Hague promised the sceptics he would oppose economic and monetary union for a decade at least. This was a bargain always without logic. Sterling, it says, is safe in Tory hands but only until 2007. The formula has the merit neither of principled opposition to the euro nor of practical politics. As such, it is rejected both by those who say never, and by those who pay heed to the real world.

Mr Hague responded with a fudge: the Tory policy would be to oppose Emu for 'the foreseeable future'. There is an eerie echo here of the wait-and-see policy that so vexed John Major. Old hands noted a certain poignancy in the fact that Mr Major was among the first in Blackpool to utter the latest formulation.

It will not last. Already Mr Hague is signalling he wants to revert to the ten-year ban on participation. Margaret Thatcher, ever a brooding presence at the annual conference, demanded it of the new leader from the moment of her arrival in Blackpool. Following her advice will cost Mr Hague at least one and possibly four members of the shadow cabinet. And Mr Clarke will have none of it. He is happy to reject participation in the first wave of Emu. Mr Blair, after all, has made it clear that prospect will not arise. Beyond that, though, Mr Clarke is unwilling to be bound.

The whole argument, of course, is futile, as senseless as Labour's self-destruction over unilateral nuclear disarmament during the early 1980s. It surrenders the capacity to harry Mr Blair over the most difficult decision of his premiership. The interesting question is how he will respond. Here, there are two theories.

The first has it that Mr Blair will prolong the agony. A referendum on the single currency before the next election would be a hazardous venture. Defeat would jeopardize his premiership. Far better to torture the Tories for a few years, deferring a decision until the general election. The issue could then be put to the people in Labour's manifesto, side-stepping the promise of a referendum.

The contrary case has it that Mr Blair should strike sooner while the Conservative divisions are at their sharpest. A referendum predicated on joining Emu in, say, 2001 would tear open the Tory wounds. Mr Clarke and his supporters would find it hard not to support the government. Mr Hague would find it impossible to reunite his party. A change in the electoral system for the House of Commons would deliver the *coup de grâce.*

Of these two possibilities, I think the second more likely to appeal to Mr Blair. There are formidable economic obstacles to early participation in Emu. But the political costs of staying out weigh heavily on a prime minister for whom the domestic stage already seems claustrophobic. Mr Blair will want to hold his options open until the euro is a certainty rather than a high probability. My guess is that his promised statement of intent later this year will be more mood music than substance. The harder choices will come next summer. But the prime minister cannot complain. Never has an opposition been so accommodating.

First published 10 October 1997

Cabinet shifts towards Emu: *declaration expected shortly on UK entry soon after launch*

ROBERT PESTON

The government is on the point of adopting a much more positive approach to European economic and monetary union, with a statement shortly that sterling is likely to join at an early opportunity after the 1999 launch.

'It is now clear that we must indicate our willingness to be in there,' said a minister, adding there was 'still work to do on how we would word such a declaration of intent'. Senior members of the cabinet are openly canvassing the prospect of sterling participation around the turn of the century, possibly before the next general election. This represents a big shift from the negative tone of most government statements only four months ago. 'It is no longer ridiculous to suggest we could win a referendum (which is a pre-condition of UK membership),' said a minister. 'The climate has changed.' A statement outlining the conditions for sterling's membership would be made after parliament resumes at the end of October, he said. 'Because of the constitutional significance, you have to wait for MPs to return.'

The changed approach to Emu stems in part from a growing convergence of views between Robin Cook, the foreign secretary, and Gordon

Brown, the chancellor, who had previously been seen at loggerheads. Mr Brown has long been persuaded that sterling should participate in Emu, while the foreign secretary is more sceptical about the principle of monetary union. 'Robin still believes it is the wrong project for Europe at the wrong time,' said a colleague. However, Mr Cook now feels that if Emu is launched on robust foundations, the UK would be damaged if it remained on the sidelines.

Under the terms of the UK's opt-out from the project, which was negotiated by the previous government, there is a deadline of 1 January 1998 for deciding to participate in the first wave at the start of 1999. The prime minister has for the past year made clear that joining at the outset is extremely unlikely, but has been careful not to close off any options. Even so, there is a growing realization among ministers that their ambition to play a leading role in the EU would be fatally undermined if the UK remained outside the single currency at the launch and made no commitment to join at a later date. 'We have to be in the thick of the debate,' said a minister. 'But that will be impossible if they (other governments) think that we have no plans to join.' The UK is expected to meet the Maastricht criteria for membership, so it needs to outline a series of other conditions for sterling to join.

First published 26 September 1997

Taking the Emu plunge: *the UK's dilemma over the European single currency*

ROBERT PESTON

Europe's single currency has suddenly become the most urgent of issues for the UK government. As the stock market soared and the pound slumped yesterday, ministers and officials were in a quandary over how to respond to a report in the *Financial Times* that the government was becoming more favourably disposed towards joining economic and monetary union. They did not want to deny that they were changing their minds. But they were not yet ready to elaborate, still less to spell out the terms and conditions for sterling's eventual participation in Emu. So they stuck to the tried and tested formula of describing the report as 'speculation'.

Ministers hope to make a formal statement on Emu after parliament resumes at the end of October. This is necessary because – under the terms of the UK's single currency opt-out – there is a deadline of the turn of the year for the UK to decide whether to be part of monetary union when it is launched on 1 January 1999. The option to join at the outset remains theoretically open. But a senior minister confirmed that 'there is no chance of us going in then'.

The reasons are threefold: being in the first wave would be seen as breaking a manifesto pledge; the Treasury is concerned that British companies, especially banks and retailers, are not ready to join; ministers fear that the UK and continental economies are, as one puts it, 'dangerously out of synch.'

But a bald statement ruling out entry in the first wave would do damage to Tony Blair's hopes of playing a leading role in shaping the European Union's future. 'We want to use our presidency of the EU (in the first half of next year) to establish our influence in Europe,' said a government member. 'That would be impossible if we are perceived as hostile to the only European project of any importance.'

So ministers intend to use a *de facto* 'declaration of intent' in the autumn to signal that sterling will join soon after 1999 – and will spell out the underlying factors that will determine the date of entry. The government is likely to say business cycles in the UK and on the continent need to be more closely aligned and continental labour markets need to be more flexible. But 'we have to make it clear that we are on our way in, not setting up insuperable obstacles,' says a cabinet member. In the language of Maastricht, the UK wants to be treated as a 'pre-in', a country making preparations to join.

This represents a significant shift since the general election on 1 May 1997. Before then, the Labour party's Emu rhetoric was broadly sceptical and its policy was to establish a series of hurdles in the way of joining. So what has changed in those four months? First and foremost, the prime minister has acquired a confidence that stems from his huge parliamentary majority. He has also been advised by his officials that he should no longer act on the assumption that the single currency is likely to be delayed. There has been no formal cabinet decision on a new Emu approach. But that is not relevant, since there are only three people whose views count – the prime minister, the foreign secretary and the chancellor.

Of the three, Gordon Brown, the chancellor, has long been most in favour of Emu, while the foreign secretary, Robin Cook, has been sceptical. Mr Blair's approach has been pragmatic. The important development is that the views of Mr Brown and Mr Cook have gradually converged over the past few months. The foreign secretary is now convinced that sterling cannot remain outside a single currency for long after a successful launch.

There is therefore a consensus that sterling must be inside by 2002, when notes and coins are to be converted into euros. What remains unclear is whether sterling should join earlier.

Mr Blair has promised a referendum before any entry during the five-year lifetime of this parliament. The logical time for such a plebiscite would be at the same time as the 1999 elections for the European parliament. A minister said that the most likely option at the moment is that the next general election would be fought on the Emu issue. This would have the advantage of not requiring a separate plebiscite.

However, there is growing confidence that the vote would be won by the government, whenever it happens. On the Yes side would be Labour, the Liberal Democrats, the Confederation of British Industry and the trade unions. On the No side the Tories may be feeling exposed in opposition to Emu. Suddenly, the prospect of British membership no longer seems so remote.

First appeared 27 September 1997

Preparing to fire starting gun on run-up to Emu

WOLFGANG MÜNCHAU

Forecasts that logistical hurdles could prevent UK membership of economic and monetary union for up to ten years appear improbable. The Treasury's internal timetable suggests it would take only about a year from when the government declares its intent to join Emu until the necessary legislation is in place. This means that the UK could join as early as July 2002. The European Union will also need to sanction UK entry, but much of the two approval processes could occur in parallel, according to both UK and EU officials.

The Emu clock will not start ticking until after the election, as Gordon Brown, the chancellor, made clear on 6 October 1997 when he told the Commons: 'There is no realistic prospect of our having demonstrated before the end of this parliament that the UK will be ready for Emu.' If the election is held in the spring of 2001, as observers think likely, UK membership could start by July 2002. If the election were held in May 2002, the latest possible date, the earliest time of joining Emu would be the summer of 2002.

This will be the UK timetable for Emu:

- The prime minister and chancellor make up their minds on whether it is time to join Emu. A decision will need to be endorsed by the cabinet.
- A formal Act of Parliament – to be approved by both Houses – has to be passed, according to the 1993 European Communities Amendment Act, before the UK can formally notify its European partners it wants to join.
- Legislation is needed for a referendum, which must be won. After this,

the process splits. In the UK, parliament will have to approve further legislation.

The most important changes are:

- An Act strengthening the independence of the Bank of England. With Emu, the Bank of England will become an operating branch of the European Central Bank. The Bank's legal framework must be made compatible with the European Central Bank. The most important requirement would be to allow the Bank of England to set the inflation target, which is now set by the government.
- Legislation to reform the Bank's ways and means facility – the government's own account with the Bank of England – to ensure the Bank no longer provides short-term finance to the government.
- Legislation to change the exchange-equalization account, the legal framework governing the central bank's reserves.
- Legislation on notes and coins that says the European Central Bank will be the sole issuing authority.

After a 'yes' vote in a referendum, a second branch of preparatory process will begin at EU level:

- The UK formally notifies the council. The European Commission and the European Central Bank make recommendations on whether the UK has met the convergence criteria of the Maastricht treaty.
- The council votes on UK membership in a qualified majority vote.

At present, the UK fulfils most of the convergence criteria, especially the three key economic requirements on deficits, debts and inflation. Convergence of long-term interest rates tends to be a self-fulfilling prophecy for any country with a realistic chance of joining. The remaining criterion – on exchange-rate stability – is subject to a dispute between UK and EU officials. The Maastricht treaty stipulates observance of 'normal' fluctuation margins of the ERM for two years as a precondition for joining Emu. The government argues that this criterion is void after the 1993 widening of the normal ERM bands from 2.25 per cent to 15 per cent. But this issue is not settled.

After Emu entry the pound will not immediately disappear. Like the first-wave members, the UK will go through a transition phase during which pound notes and coins will remain in circulation. During that period people and companies can use either euros or pounds. For first-wave member states, this transition period will last from 1999 to the end of 2001. For the UK, its duration is likely to be shorter, constrained mainly by the time it takes to print the new banknotes. If the UK were to enter Emu by July 2002, this would mean that the pound would vanish in about 2004 or 2005.

First appeared 31 October 1997

Stability without weapons: *the UK statement puts back a decision on Emu membership, but market developments are reducing the scope for independent monetary policy*

SAMUEL BRITTAN

After the turmoil, the familiarity: the UK will join economic and monetary union when the time is ripe. If anything Gordon Brown's statement to the House of Commons on 27 October put back any decision even further. Not merely will the government not join in this parliament. It will not even put the issue to a referendum before the next election or make it an issue then if it can help it. The decision will be made in the next parliament.

Not all the pro-European rhetoric in the world can disguise the fact that the UK is doing what it has done in all other European ventures. The government will wait to see if Emu works; if it does, it will join subsequently, as a latecomer. Understandably, the likely founding members have already decided to set up an informal economic council which will gather before the full meetings of the European Union's finance ministers and will inevitably become the main influence upon the euro.

Meanwhile, the financial markets have to make the best guesses they can. On the morning before the chancellor's statement Michael Saunders of Salomon Brothers noted that they already assume that the difference between German and British three-month interest rates will fall from over 3½ per cent to 1 per cent by September 2000. Earlier on, the National Institute for Economic and Social Research estimated that the gap would fall to ¼ per cent by the end of 2002 and disappear altogether by 2005. 'A possible conclusion is markets are expecting sterling to join the monetary union in about five years at a rate of around DM2.63.'

An incidental effect of the mismanagement of the last few weeks is that the Treasury is back in the driving seat of policy management. Had euro enthusiasts ignored the spin doctors and the statements of middle-ranking ministers committed to Emu they would have taken more notice of the high degree of scepticism running all the way from the governor of the Bank of England to the official Treasury and even the prime minister's own economic advisers. This scepticism is different from Tory scepticism because it dismisses all questions of national sovereignty and political objectives as so much hot air and focuses on the supposedly hard-headed economic obstacles.

The Treasury paper makes a brave attempt to render operational the chancellor's five conditions: cyclical convergence; flexibility; investment; secure financial services and help to employment and growth. But the first has both the longest and most rigorous analysis. The judgement on the others will be mainly a matter of political hunch.

On the cyclical aspects the Treasury can happily underline the large differences between the shape of the business cycle in the UK and on the continent. These make short-term interest rates of little over 3 per cent appropriate in France and Germany compared with 7 per cent in Britain. A point may arrive when the short-term interest rates are similar on both sides of the Channel. But as, the official paper admits, even this may be nothing but a cross-over point, when British rates are on their way down and continental rates are on their way up.

That is not the only reason to be cautious when interest rates are similar. Even if business conditions were roughly similar, short-term interest rates have a more potent effect in Britain due to the prevalence of short-term housing finance. On the continent their indirect impact on long-term rates matters a good deal more. The most disappointing aspect of the chancellor's statement is that there are no policy measures taken or even hinted at to bring about either cyclical or structural convergence. Gordon Brown was not even allowed to bite the bullet and foreshadow the final phasing out of mortgage interest relief. He did not even exhort banks and building societies to move towards medium-term finance. His reference to considering the possible lowering of the inflation target was only a reiteration of what he had already said at the Mansion House outside the Emu context.

The most glaring omission was any reference to the Exchange Rate Mechanism to which countries preparing for Emu ('pre-ins') are expected to adhere. It was just possible for the previous chancellor, Kenneth Clarke, to wave this aside on the basis that sterling had enjoyed a period of *de facto* stability and that rejoining a wide band of 15 per cent around the central rate would make no practical difference. But sterling's upward movement in the last fifteen months makes this no longer plausible. Emu members would be entirely justified in insisting that Britain rejoined the ERM if it wants to be considered seriously for membership even in the next parliament. There is a risk that members will want to narrow the band, but Britain will be quite powerless to prevent this from outside.

There are no certainties. One cannot even rule out a last minute revolt by anti-Emu forces in Germany. And while the return of a Eurosceptic Tory government in Britain at the next election looks unlikely, Tony Blair himself is sufficiently worried to prepare a fallback strategy in which he would depend on an alliance with the Liberal Democrats. The most probable outcome, however, is that interest rates will continue to converge on the assumption of eventual UK membership. This means that the ability of the Bank of England to use interest rates either to stimulate or to slow down the economy will decline.

I used to advocate Emu membership as a European Central Bank modelled on the Bundesbank was a better bet for UK price stability than leaving matters to British policy-makers. But this seems much less plausible since the Bank of England was granted operational independence and since the German finance minister's abortive plan to use the Bundesbank's gold reserves to fudge its budgetary numbers. Fiscal policy may not matter as much as the German authorities claim; but the retreat on the gold plan did show a weakening of the stability-oriented psychology that has governed Germany for nearly fifty years.

Indeed, the NIESR is right to say that inflation is likely to be less stable under the ECB than under Bank of England management. A real case for Emu must put the emphasis on avoiding exchange rate overshooting and under-shooting and unpredictability, which remains a menace for much of the business world. It is not possible to expect a single monetary policy to be appropriate from Lapland to Sicily. But neither is such a policy precisely appropriate from Alaska to Florida and all points between – and the US federal budget does not make it so.

A large currency area involves accepting large temporary and local discrepancies from the long-term inflation goal, as occurred frequently under the Gold Standard which was the most successful monetary union the world has seen. There is a positive merit in temporary price fluctuation in response to pressures and shocks. What matters is that in the long run prices are as likely to fall as to rise and that contracts can be made for future generations without building in inflation clauses. But that is a piece of wisdom still waiting to be rediscovered.

First published 28 October 1997

Government awaits a swing in public opinion: *whether or not the UK joins, the euro may well arrive via the back door*

WOLFGANG MÜNCHAU

Clarity is what business leaders wanted from Britain's new Labour government. But the clarity provided by Gordon Brown, the UK chancellor, when he explained the government's position on the single currency on 27 October was not necessarily what they had sought.

Mr Brown confirmed that the UK would not be a founding member of economic and monetary union in 1999. He also said it was inconceivable that the UK would join during the current parliamentary term, which must end by the spring of 2002. A more likely election date, according to political observers, is the spring of 2001. From then onwards it would be at least one year before the UK could be a member of Emu – essentially the time it would take to hold a referendum and pass the necessary legislation. That leaves the summer of 2002 as the earliest possible membership date.

While there is no clarity about the UK's eventual entry date, Mr Brown's statement at least gave the pro-Emu lobby one reason for optimism. What has changed is that the government is now in principle committed to Emu membership. The chancellor says the delay is due purely to economic reasons. More likely, the delay is due to hostile public opinion – with around two-thirds of the population firmly opposed to giving up the pound – aggravated by the promise to hold a referendum before entry.

The government's official line is that the UK is not yet ready for Emu because of various economic obstacles. Mr Brown has put up five 'tests' – in addition to the Maastricht treaty's convergence criteria – which the UK will have to fulfil before entering Emu. They are:

- Business cycles must converge
- Labour markets in the UK and in the other EU countries must become more flexible
- Emu must benefit investment in the UK
- It must benefit the UK financial sector and
- It must have a positive impact on the real economy – on growth and employment.

These are largely qualitative criteria, subject to some elastic interpretation. The five Maastricht criteria – on budget deficits, public debt, inflation, long-term interest rates and exchange rates – have all numeric targets.

The first of Mr Brown's 'tests' – convergence of business cycles – is widely considered to be the most important. Business cycles currently diverge significantly. On the current cycle the UK has just gone past the peak, with the economy heading for lower output in the next few years. This position in the cycle usually suggests an interest rate at, or close to, the cyclical peak and falling once deflationary pressures emerge. UK short-term interest rates are currently 7.25 per cent.

By contrast, the core-Emu group is on an economic upswing, a period during which interest rates are low and rising. Emu-core group interest rates are 3.3 per cent. The consensus among forecasters is that these rates will have to rise to between 4 and 4.5 per cent by the time Emu starts. By then, UK rates may have fallen, although probably not to anywhere near Emu-core levels.

The trouble is that the business cycle does not end in 1999. Emu rates are likely to rise during the first two or three years after 1999, largely for cyclical reasons, but also because the new European Central Bank – more so than any established central bank – will err on the side of caution in its monetary policy. It is the consensus among EU central bankers that the ECB will take no risks with inflation.

For the UK, this could prove a dilemma. While the interest-rate cycles may cross over at some point, they could easily diverge again soon afterwards, as the core-Emu group and the UK trade places on their respective business cycles. It is conceivable that UK entry may be just as difficult to justify on cyclical grounds in 2002 – or indeed in any other year – with the only difference being that the UK might be at the bottom of its cycle while the core-Emu might be at the top of its cycle.

Mr Brown also insists the other four criteria are important but most Emu observers are less convinced. There is one potential structural problem in the UK, the housing market. Almost 90 per cent of UK mortgages are variable rate, while most mortgages in the core-Emu group are fixed rate. The UK economy is, therefore, much more susceptible to fluctuations in short-term interest rates, especially the fluctuations that some forecasters are predicting will emerge in the initial, and potentially turbulent stages, of Emu. But some economists have pointed out that UK housing finance will adjust quickly once low-rate fixed-term mortgages become available upon Emu entry.

What are the implications of this considerable uncertainty for business? First of all, UK companies are among the worst prepared for Emu in the EU, according to opinion polls and business consultants. Whether the UK joins or not, there is a strong chance that the euro will arrive through the back door. Some continental companies, notably Siemens and Daimler-Benz of Germany, are planning to force their UK suppliers into accepting the euro as the sole means of payment. UK bankers expect that the euro would be pushed through the supply chain, as the affected suppliers might hedge against the resulting currency risk by forcing their own suppliers to accept euros. Marks & Spencer, the UK retailer, will even accept the euro at its cash desks, which means that they will accept cheques denominated in euros – there are no banknotes and coins during the interim period.

These examples demonstrate that non-participation will not shield the UK from the effects of Emu. Some companies will prepare irrespective of the government's strategy – in terms of their technical systems, financial systems, and even corporate strategy. UK companies will be affected by the way in which their European competitors change their strategy. If Ford Europe or BMW change their pricing strategy so that cars carry a single pre-tax price tag in euros, that will no doubt have profound effects on the UK car market. One way or the other, Emu will become a reality for UK businesses.

In terms of politics, what matters are not the five criteria. Rather, it seems to be the government's strategy to wait until the benefits of joining Emu become so obvious that public opinion will swing in favour of it. Once the opinion polls have shifted, the UK, it seems, will have miraculously met all of the criteria.

First published 21 November 1997

In Brown who trusts?: the UK seems to think it can insulate itself from the consequences of economic and monetary union. It cannot.

LIONEL BARBER

New Labour, old Britain. Europe will take scant comfort from UK Chancellor Gordon Brown's statement on the single currency. Once again, a British government is sitting on the fence, unsure about whether to join the most far-reaching political and economic project since the 1957 Treaty of Rome.

Not even the most raving euro-enthusiast expected the British to be present at the creation of economic and monetary union on 1 January 1999. But any number of optimists hoped that Labour would offer a declaration of intent to join monetary union by mid-2002, when euro notes and coins come into circulation. Barring an act of God or 'some fundamental change in economic circumstances', the British government intends to take a decision on Emu early in the next parliament. Even assuming the public at large gives a favourable verdict at a referendum (promised by both parties) this would still leave Britain scrambling to reach the mid-2002 when the euro will become reality for the ordinary citizens of at least eleven and possibly more of the fifteen member states of the European Union.

There were some consolations. EU governments will welcome the statement that there are no constitutional hurdles to joining Emu. The economic tests for joining monetary union, especially on the need for 'convergence' between Britain and the rest of Europe, are well understood. But what was glaringly absent in Mr Brown's speech was any notion that British participation could actually help to make Emu a success. The timidity of approach was also summed up by the decision to close off the option of an early referendum, which would form the basis for joining in the next parliament.

Of course, Tony Blair, the prime minister, could accelerate the timetable by copying President Jacques Chirac of France and calling an early general election. But he will not want to do so. Mr Chirac's spring gamble saw his Gaullist majority go up in smoke. Mr Blair wants a second term. He has no intention of going for broke on Emu.

Whatever made Continental Europeans think that he might? The harder-headed members of the diplomatic elite always had their doubts. They looked at British public opinion, a hostile British press, and a British economy that has thrived since the UK abandoned the Exchange Rate Mechanism in September 1992 – all formidable obstacles to early entry.

Yet Mr Blair was supposed to be different: a politician of the younger generation with an open mind, a huge parliamentary majority, and a self-proclaimed mission to assume a leadership role in Europe. He used phrases like 'constructive engagement', and he promised a break with the non-co-operative policy of his Conservative predecessors. Mr Blair's stock rose higher after a confident performance at last June's Amsterdam summit. He mastered his briefs better than most other leaders. He was refreshingly undogmatic, and helped to broker a new constitutional treaty that secured British interests on borders, defence and employment without offending others.

Now that the Labour government has come clean on Emu, Europe is bound to take a second look at Mr Blair. As one senior adviser to Chancellor Helmut Kohl asked aloud: is Labour pursuing a tactical approach to Europe rather than a strategy? Does it appreciate the degree to which Emu will occupy centre-stage once it has happened?

In October 1997 Mr Kohl had a private session with Mr Blair at Chequers. The two men spent one-and-a-half hours talking about Europe and Emu. The chancellor assured Mr Blair that he would 'keep the door open' for Britain, adding mischievously 'just like I did for John Major'. Whether Mr Blair squirmed is not known, but Mr Kohl's message is unambiguous: Mr Blair's failure to offer a clear-cut commitment to joining Emu risks painting Labour into the same corner as the Conservatives, boxed in by the British press and constantly appealing for sympathy from the rest of Europe.

There is a second risk. Mr Brown's statement suggests that Britain can insulate itself from the impact of Emu. This is highly questionable. For the past five years, Britain has enjoyed the best of both worlds on Emu. Ministers have taken part in the negotiations on the terms of the single currency, but have kept their options on joining open. But now that EU leaders have decided which countries qualify for Emu, Britain no longer has a seat of real influence at the table. The UK had no vote on the appointment of Wim Duisenberg, the Dutchman who will run the new

European Central Bank. Nor will the British have a say on the monetary policy that the ECB will pursue in the euro zone. Inside the council of EU finance ministers (Ecofin), the UK position will also erode. The British will have no seat on the new informal grouping of Emu-bloc countries, which will gather ahead of the monthly Ecofin meetings and discuss matters such as tax, euro exchange-rate policy and other macroeconomic issues.

The British government has underestimated the speed with which events will move now that eleven countries are committed to joining the single currency in January 1999. From an economic point of view, there could be an accelerated convergence among the Emu group, making it harder for the British to catch up. Mr Brown's desire for a 'period of stability' may turn out to be just wishful thinking if investors put their faith in the euro rather than sterling.

The chancellor's pledges to observe the principles of the budget stability pact governing fiscal discipline in the euro zone is more reassuring. So is his offer to monitor Britain's inflation target in the light of the ECB's monetary policy. These are welcome signs that Labour is not pursuing a 'go-it-alone' policy towards the single currency.

On the other hand, Mr Brown has offered no sign that he is ready to commit sterling to the new Exchange Rate Mechanism – which has been set up to govern relations between the euro and non-participating currencies. Like his Tory predecessors, Mr Brown disputes the view held by the French, the Germans and European Commission that participation in the ERM is a pre-condition for entry into Emu. They view ERM membership as a statement of good faith towards exchange rate stability.

Mr Brown says: trust us. This was the thrust of his statement to the House of Commons. Europe may be inclined to give Labour the benefit of the doubt. But we can no longer be sure.

First published 28 October 1997

A parallel pound: *the use of the euro alongside sterling could help reconcile the needs of the domestic economy with those of exporters*

SAMUEL BRITTAN

Generals are not the only ones who fight the last war; members of the economic establishment often try to avoid the mistakes of the last business cycle, only to repeat those of the cycle before. Many British economists are so determined to avoid what they regard (usually with hindsight) as the mistakes of the late 1980s – when interest rates were kept down too long so that sterling could shadow the D-Mark – that they seem determined to repeat instead the errors of the early 1980s. Then, the preoccupation with domestic monetary discipline led to an overshooting of sterling and a severe recession, initially in manufacturing, but finally in the whole economy.

The decision of the Bank of England Monetary Policy Committee at its June 1998 meeting to keep interest rates on hold is a merciful relief. But it will not resolve the conflict between the needs of the domestic economy and the sectors exposed to overseas trade.

Gavyn Davies of Goldman Sachs has been trying to act as chief whip to the MPC by proclaiming that its duty is only to keep down the forecast for one particular measure of inflation two years ahead. He puts quite excessive emphasis on a variation in the small print of the 1998 Budget Red Book which omits earlier references to 'supporting the government's economic policy' without prejudice to the inflation goal. Yet this wider objective remains part of the Bank's remit. It is curious that an economist who supports the government should reproach the MPC for being too concerned to support that government's growth and employment goals.

More important: the MPC consists of people, not automata. National currency managers have no option but to engage in an uneasy compromise between domestic objectives and exchange-rate stability. The more they insist on the primacy of one, the more sure we can be that events will force them into a U-turn, all the more shattering for being delayed. Even in the days of Bretton Woods, Germany had at times to revalue the D-Mark or let it float upwards to contain domestic inflation. Governments that have tried to ignore the exchange rate have also had to eat their words. After years of 'benign neglect', the Reagan administration initiated in 1985 an international attempt to reduce the value of the dollar. Even the Thatcher government started to redefine monetary policy in the early 1980s when the strength of sterling became too much of a good thing and unemployment started to shoot upwards.

Membership of Emu would of course end the pound's violent swings by getting rid of sterling as a separate currency – some 90 per cent of UK gross domestic product would then be traded within the euro zone. But the problem of currency fluctuation would be replaced by a different one: an interest rate designed to meet average conditions in more than eleven countries – but in practice heavily influenced by the needs of German and French industry – would often not be suitable for the UK. Ireland, which is experiencing an even greater boom and which expects to join Emu at the outset, should provide a trial run.

Meanwhile, several UK-based international companies have said they intend to present their accounts in euros as well as sterling. They may also in time invoice exports in euros. These actions remind us that Latin American countries have long used the dollar as a parallel currency for external and large domestic transactions while retaining domestic currencies for other internal business. A similar dual system applies in Russia and other former Communist countries. Dual currency systems already exist in border areas of Europe. Austrian ski lifts will often post up prices in D-Marks as well as schillings.

Simply using the euro as an alternative unit of account will not be enough. If wages are paid in sterling, and domestic components and services are also priced in domestic currency, profit margins will still come under heavy pressure when the pound rises. Companies will still have to lay off workers whom it no longer pays to employ. To relieve the problem, a dual currency system will have to go further. Workers who want security of employment will have to accept the option of being paid in euros, and the same option will have to be offered to suppliers of intermediate products.

The competing currency approach has quite a long, if chequered, history in British policy. It was first proposed by Nigel Lawson as an alternative to a single European currency. This was after Lady Thatcher had taken her ministers and officials by surprise at the 1988 Madrid summit by offering to prepare an alternative route to monetary union. Sir Peter Middleton, then Treasury permanent secretary, was so astonished to hear the news on the radio that he nearly drove his car into a tree.

A second version of the plan, known as the 'hard Ecu', was put forward by John Major when he was chancellor. It was a scheme to transform the Ecu from a simple basket of currencies into a real currency that could be held by European nationals if they so chose. It also imposed complicated convertibility obligations on national authorities (*see* Nigel Lawson's *The View from Number 11*, New York: Doubleday, 1993, pp. 938–44, and Philip Stephens's *Politics and the Pound*, London: Papermac, 1998, pp. 160–65).

Both plans fell on stony ground because they were offered as alternatives to the single currency that the main EU players had already decided to adopt. Lord Lawson had got the idea of competitive currencies from the free-market economist Friedrich Hayek. He had arrived at currency competition out of despair that governments would adopt sound money policies without the threat of their own currencies being abandoned. Treasury officials strove to shift the emphasis from competition between actual currencies to competition between monetary policies.

Conditions have now revived for currency competition in the earlier Lawson form. The fact that it does not require a new international institution or treaty, which was seen as a disadvantage compared with the hard Ecu, is now an advantage. Moreover, the idea can now be simplified. Instead of competition between an indeterminate number of currencies, the choice is likely to be between pounds and euros.

There is still work to be done. The original British plan did not go into detail on matters such as legal tender. Moreover, if the euro is to stand a chance of competing against sterling in domestic transactions, it will be important to allow taxes to be paid in it. Some spin doctors suggest that Gordon Brown is toying with just such a reform. The merit of currency competition is that it can be market led. The difficulty will be to persuade workers and suppliers to agree to be paid in euros, the sterling value of which will fluctuate.

This is but a special case of what I call Brittan's Law. This says that it is possible for workers to have security of employment, or security of pay, but not both. The more you have of one the less you have of the other. This principle has wide implications outside the present UK monetary debate. It supplies the clue to what workers and managers can do to reduce the job insecurity which some observers see arising from globalization and new technology.

First published 16 April 1998

Life on the outside: *plans to form a 'euro-club' of founding Emu members have taught Britain it cannot have its cake and eat it*

LIONEL BARBER

Since the Labour government entered office in May 1997, it has pretended that delayed entry into economic and monetary union would be virtually cost-free for Britain. A single Gallic thrust has exposed the policy as threadbare.

In the words of Dominique Strauss-Kahn, France's finance minister, monetary union is a marriage. And as he observed with undisguised relish at a December 1997 meeting of EU finance ministers in Brussels: 'People who are married do not want others in the bedroom.'

So now we know. No special favours for Britain. No more illusions that the City of London, the size of the UK economy, or the 'Blair-effect' will alter the fact that life outside the single currency zone will be a lot colder.

For more than twelve hours, Gordon Brown, the chancellor, pleaded with his fellow finance ministers for equal treatment from the future Emu members. But he returned empty-handed. The issue looks innocuous enough: a Franco-German plan to create an informal 'euro-club' for the founder members of Emu. Indeed, not so long ago, Mr Brown dismissed inquiries on this subject as trivial. But at the Brussels meeting, he upped the ante, exposing the emptiness of Labour's rhetoric about 'leadership in Europe' and its fears about second-class European Union membership.

The euro-club was dangerous and divisive, declared Mr Brown. It would undercut the Ecofin council of EU finance ministers, the chief decision-making forum on macroeconomic policy. Emu was a work-in-progress, not a one-off event. Countries aspiring to join Emu should be taken at their word. The new euro-forum should be open to all. The chancellor drew support from the Danes, Swedes and Greeks, all of whom have declared they will not be ready to join the first wave of Emu. The Irish also offered good neighbourly noises. But the reaction of the other ten countries, particularly the French and Germans, was uncompromising.

No one could prevent the euro-bloc holding meetings, they said. Issues such as enforcing fiscal discipline on Emu members and discussing euro exchange-rate policy against the dollar were a matter for Emu members alone. The only question was this: would the UK-led opponents agree to a common understanding on the operation of the euro-club or risk the 'ins' meeting outside the safeguards of the EU treaties?

Here is the line in the sand. For six months, Tony Blair, the prime minister, and his colleagues have persuaded themselves that there was no such division. Theirs was a policy of flirtation towards Emu. Britain will join, but not yet. Labour will hold a referendum, but not until after the general election. Perhaps in early 2002.

As a domestic political strategy, the Emu policy has worked a treat. Labour's statement that there were no constitutional objections to joining the single currency triggered turmoil in the Conservative party. The plan to win over the business constituency, massage public opinion, and consign the Tories to permanent opposition looks like a winner. High-flying Labour takes a second term for granted. Ministers talk about Mr Blair dominating the European stage long after the likes of Helmet Kohl, Germany's chancellor, and Jacques Chirac, France's president, have shuffled off into retirement. Sure, the Emu policy is about buying time; but the goal is its co-leadership with the French and Germans.

Labour, like its Conservative predecessors, appears to have misunderstood the political nature of the Emu exercise. As Mr Strauss-Kahn says, sharing a single currency is something intimate. It is not like sharing fish quotas.

In recent months, the Emu debate has undergone a subtle change. No one is talking any more about whether France, Germany or Italy will meet the public deficit criterion for entry into monetary union. In Brussels,

Paris and even in the Federal Reserve in Washington, the code is 'E-11', meaning all but four countries are likely to be present at the creation of the single currency on 1 January 1999. Now that finance ministers have stopped squabbling over decimal points, they are turning to the serious issue of how to co-ordinate macroeconomic policy in the post-Emu world. The agreement on a code of conduct regulating tax competition is just one straw in the wind. So was the agreement on guidelines for employment and job creation thrashed out at the November 1997 jobs summit in Luxembourg.

Of course, there are risks in the Emu enterprise. The French pay lip service to the independence of the future European Central Bank but want a Frenchman in charge. Paris sees the euro-club as a political counterweight to the ECB. The Germans are fixated by price stability. The Bundesbank is nervous about forming a single currency zone with inflation-prone Mediterranean countries. But the political will to make it work is as strong as ever.

British participation in the euro zone would increase the credibility of the new currency. All EU member states agree on this point. But for the moment, Labour has failed to exploit its position as a desirable future member. Instead, Mr Brown has staked his government's reputation on a lost cause: membership of the euro-club.

All is not lost. Jean-Claude Juncker, the Luxembourg prime minister, says he wants a compromise involving all fifteen member states. Mr Blair could make clear that he accepts that the 'ins' have a right to meet and to establish clear limits to their discussion. Britain could also receive a summit declaration that Ecofin remains the prime decision-making forum.

Without a deal, the risk is that the Emu group moves ahead without any safeguards for the outsiders. Bad blood could spill into other issues such as enlargement where Britain has a vital interest. An all-or-nothing approach would spell a rerun of the busted Conservative policy towards Europe. For Labour, this was the week in which the reality of life in Europe is beginning to sink in.

First published 3 December 1997

Life on the outside: *while politically attractive, the opt-out clause may be costly to the UK's exporters in a euro/dollar-dominated world*

WOLFGANG MÜNCHAU

The decision to launch the single currency with eleven members from January 1999 has not only made European economic and monetary union a reality but also the UK's opt-out. It is now unlikely that the UK will join Emu until 2002. This leaves UK companies outside Emu for at least three years.

The dangers of life outside Emu are compounded by economic uncertainties in the UK. Despite a boom in the service sector, the manufacturing sector has been trading at close to recession levels. Exporters have been suffering from the strength of the pound, especially against the D-Mark, but continued strong domestic demand has fenced off the worst consequences of sterling's rise.

While the independent Bank of England may succeed in its monetary policy strategy and engineer a soft landing, the economy could also fall into stagflation – that is, with inflation, interest rates and the exchange rate relatively high while the economy is contracting. Stagflation would be far more damaging for UK exporters, if the rest of Europe were to surge ahead under Emu.

Emu-related risks for UK-based exporters exist on different levels – technical, strategic and commercial. On the technical level, it is clear that UK companies will not be as well prepared as their euro zone competitors. Companies can pursue two strategies: a Big Bang involving the replacement of national denominations, such as the D-Mark and the French franc, in all internal and external systems from next year. Such companies would still be able to accept payments in national denominations, but these would be immediately converted into, and accounted for in, euros. The alternative is a dual system. Both have cost advantages and disadvantages, but allow companies to conduct business in the new currency.

However, the euro is not just another currency. A transition period means that the euro and the existing national denominations must co-exist for three years. Furthermore, the relationship between the euro and the national denominations, and national denominations themselves, will be governed by a complicated set of rules. UK exporters, for example, could find customers or suppliers insisting on transacting in euros from 1 January 1999. Others may use existing national denominations, or even both.

Companies may not always be able to let their banks handle the payments in the new currency since the accounting follows rules which software is not equipped to handle. System experts refer to it as the euro-bomb, which could have consequences equally serious as the millennium bomb.

For example, conversion between national denominations and the euro follows six significant figures, which could involve the use of four digits after the decimal point – a task some accounting software and spreadsheets are incapable of handling, without upgrades. Another problem arises when translating one national denomination into another. It will not be possible to translate directly from francs into D-Marks. Companies will need to use triangulation, that converts francs into euros first, then euros into D-Marks. Most software cannot handle this.

None of this matters for a small UK-based exporter who sells products into the euro zone, invoices in sterling or dollars, and whose internal and external accounting system does not rely on currencies other than sterling. Such a company can simply ask his bank to handle the euro payments.

But in addition to immediate technical problems, Emu has longer-term strategic implications. Acquisitions and mergers are taking place in many European industries and Emu is partly the catalyst for this. Experts expect this process to continue beyond 1999. It is likely to involve companies whose home countries participate in Emu to a greater extent than those who do not. UK companies are therefore more likely to be affected in this context by what happens to their competitors.

More direct, however, will be the commercial effects. The combination of Emu and the maturing of new technologies, such as internet shopping, is likely to accelerate the process of euro-wide price convergence. Companies will find it harder to maintain the price discrimination for tradable goods. This will affect all exporters, whether or not their countries are part of Emu.

The most important commercial factor for UK companies in the short-term is the uncertainty over the exchange rate. There is much speculation about whether the euro will be a strong or a weak currency. Emu's institutional set-up, including the focus on price stability, is likely to imply a strong or at least stable currency in the long term, but uncertainty persists in the short run.

This could trap the UK in cross-currents of a volatile relationship between the world's two dominant currencies – the euro and the dollar. Volatility between these two will translate into volatility of the sterling rate and the Bank of England's already reduced ability to influence sterling's exchange rate will diminish further. The UK may find life outside Emu extremely uncomfortable. As attractive as the opt-out seems politically, the costs are often ignored. UK exporters may have to pay a larger share of these costs than they had reckoned.

First published 11 June 1998

Battle of the bourses: *the birth of the euro could add to growing pressure on London as a financial centre. But the City could turn the single currency to its advantage*

SIMON DAVIES

For more than a century, London has been at the heart of the financial markets of Europe. But the City's position is looking vulnerable, particularly with the arrival of the single currency of which sterling is not a part. From London's point of view, the birth of the euro comes at an awkward time. Britain no longer has any powerful investment banks following the recent sale of the equities businesses of both Barclays and National Westminster to foreign banks.

As if this were not enough, the London International Financial Futures and Options Exchange (Liffe), Europe's largest futures market, has lost its pre-eminent position in German bund futures, Europe's most important government bond contract. London's open-outcry market has been elbowed aside by an upstart electronic system at the Deutsche Terminbörse in Frankfurt. Although Liffe plans to respond by going at least partially electronic, Jorg Franke, the DTB's boss, has described it as 'a psychological victory for Frankfurt'.

Electronic trading makes it easier to shift location, potentially loosening London's grip. 'The DTB has shown Liffe and everyone else that, when there is something better, the financial markets will move,' says Howard Lutnick, president of Cantor Fitzgerald, the US securities firm. Frankfurt has scored other victories too. Deutsche Bank, which had alarmed the German establishment by relocating most of its investment banking business to London, has recently put its focus back on Frankfurt. A new trading floor there will run its euro-denominated debt business, which could soon dwarf the volumes of its London team.

Meanwhile, the London Stock Exchange's new order-driven trading system has had teething problems beyond its worst fears. In the long run, the new system is vital for attracting trading in euro-zone shares. But so far it has looked more like a deterrent. All this is happening at a time when London's 'franchise' as the centre for Europe's largest markets is under threat. From January 1999, the largest single currency, stock and bond markets will be denominated in euros rather than sterling. That is bound to stir a vast euro-oriented institutional investor base.

There is an intense European effort to prise business from London. One of the aims of economic and monetary union is the creation of a unified single currency capital market to match that of the US. Many European politicians think control of these markets should be a privilege of Emu membership. London could, for instance, be squeezed by a push to build up a new Europe-wide benchmark for bank lending: Euribor. The aim would be to challenge the current benchmark, the London Interbank Offered Rate, or Libor, which is set in London.

Euribor takes prices from a far wider range of European banks, and is considered by many to be unwieldy and less representative of genuine market rates. But there have been signs of political pressures on European banks to adopt Euribor. And the DTB is expected to launch Euribor futures contracts. The winner in this struggle between Libor and Euribor will provide the benchmark for all short-term lending in euros. If that is set outside London, it could have a big psychological impact on the City's position as a banking centre.

Another potential battleground will be the longer-term benchmark yield curve; this provides bond yields for a series of maturities, from one year to more than thirty, against which new bond issues can be priced. In the US, the benchmark is US Treasury bonds. In Europe it is expected to be a variety of government bonds, depending on their relative liquidity. 'If the bund becomes the benchmark for Europe, then Frankfurt has an excellent opportunity to become the European capital markets capital,' argues Mr Lutnick. 'But without actions on transparency and regulation in Europe, London will probably be the financial centre by default.'

There are other initiatives to take business away from London. The Euro Alliance, formed between the Swiss, German and French exchanges, is aimed at forming a common base for trading first derivatives, and eventually shares. The aim is to build a one-stop pan-European securities market which could, in theory, more than match London for speed of execution and price. The Euro Alliance has agreed to launch futures contracts based on the Dow Jones Stoxx family of indices, in the hope of building up a leading benchmark for European investment. This will again pit them against Liffe, which has backed the Eurotop indices, launched by FTSE International and the Amsterdam Exchanges. The battle here could mirror that in the futures markets between Liffe's Euro Libor interest rate contracts, and the DTB's Euribor products.

Yet even if more futures contracts were traded outside London, this would not necessarily be disastrous for the City. 'In the US, you have the reference points (for Treasury bonds) in Washington, the futures exchanges are physically located in Chicago, but the capital markets are in New York,' says Thomas Juterbock, head of US and European government bond trading at Morgan Stanley Dean Witter. 'In an electronic environment, people will be physically located wherever they want to be.'

This suggests that the success or failure of Liffe may have limited repercussions for London. 'London has enough of a head start in fixed income and derivatives to dominate the scene,' says Joe Cook, global head of capital markets at J. P. Morgan. 'Its major threat comes from structural and regulatory changes, rather than market forces.'

Indeed, there are plenty of restrictive practices entrenched in the domestic European markets which, if enshrined on a pan-European basis, could cause London problems. Mr Cook is particularly concerned about moves to introduce a European withholding tax on savings, which would tax at source European buyers of European-issued bonds. 'It could create a significant impediment to the free flow of capital in a sector that purports not just to be a pan-European market, but a market of global importance,' he says. Amendments to the initial proposals are likely. But in the worst-case scenario, if the UK refused to accept the proposals because of the potential damage to the euro-bond markets, it could lead to the creation of a two-tier European bond market.

In all of this, it should not be forgotten that London has a number of in-built advantages. English remains the undisputed lingua franca of finance, while London has an established pool of skilled labour. It also has a cost advantage, helped by lower taxes and more flexible labour laws. London's strengths have been underlined in the run-up to the euro. Instead of moving to the continent, many US banks, which previously had offices scattered all over Europe to reflect the diverse currencies, have if anything tended to concentrate their operations in London. In other words, Deutsche Bank has been swimming against the tide.

'The greatest advantage financial markets can have is the flexibility to adapt,' says Gavin Casey, chief executive of the London Stock Exchange. 'That is something London has always had, and you cannot get it by diktat.' London has flourished in the face of restrictive practices in the past. The euro bond, which developed into one of the most profitable markets for London, was born of tax and regulatory restrictions in the US. It converged on London in spite of the fact that it was linking non-UK issuers with primarily non-UK investors.

Hans-Joerg Rudloff, one of the architects of the euro-bond market and now chairman of the executive committee of Barclays Capital, thinks that London, far from suffering, could turn out to be the greatest beneficiary of the development of the single currency. But Mr Rudloff warns against complacency. He argues that London had the opportunity to become the trading centre for all European equities in the late 1980s, but it gave continental exchanges the chance to catch up. 'It is not only the complacency of the British institutions that has to change, but that of the British (commercial) banks. You don't want to have the same thing happen as with the investment banks, which are now all owned by foreign institutions.'

Another senior City figure agrees that London has the potential to gain, at least in the medium term. 'In the next five years, I think there will be very great benefits to London from continuing to be the leading financial centre in Europe. But in the long run, if we are not part of Emu, there is the risk that activity will gravitate towards one or other of the alternative European centres.'

First appeared 14 May 1998

Probability game: *a plausible gameplan for Britain's euro entry has been elevated to a preordained fact with unpredictabilities brushed aside*

PHILIP STEPHENS

Never forget the ifs and buts. The present debate about whether Britain should join the euro is fast piling presumption on prediction, speculation on supposition. It assumes that politics and economics travel along perfectly straight lines. It presumes that Tony Blair's government has been inoculated against unforeseen circumstance. Real life isn't like that.

For all the insults hurled to and fro, Emu-enthusiasts and eurosceptics are in curious agreement on the starting point for the argument. Mr Blair, this convenient consensus says, will call a general election in spring 2001. He will win. A bill will be rushed through parliament that same summer and a referendum held in September. The prime minister wants sterling replaced by the euro within striking distance of the 2002 launch date for notes and coins.

This is a perfectly respectable scenario. I have heard it from cabinet ministers and senior policy advisers alike. Whitehall's mandarins believe it represents Gordon Brown's firm intention. Mr Blair is more circumspect, but I doubt that he would laugh at the possibility. After all, the prime minister has told us that the retention of national sovereignty is insufficient cause to guarantee the Queen's head on the currency. And hasn't he acknowledged that as long as Britain is outside, the less will be its influence in shaping Europe's future?

What's happened, though, is that a plausible gameplan has been elevated into a preordained fact. The government would quite like it to happen, so it will. The unpredictabilities of politics – Harold Macmillan's 'events' – are brushed aside. So too is the possibility that the founder members of the euro club just might want to set the terms for late entrants.

Yet it is striking that, save for some modest technical preparations and quiet backing for the European Movement's pro-Emu fundraising campaign, the government has thus far done precious little to advance its presumed cause. Ask the Treasury to spell out its strategy to achieve the necessary convergence between the British and European economies and the response comprises a few anodyne slogans about sound economics. The suggestion that other European governments might require rather more definitive evidence of intent elicits that familiar British complacency. Europe needs us more than we need it. Or so some in Whitehall still persuade themselves.

Yet simultaneously the government demands that the economic case for joining Emu must be watertight. As Mr Blair said at the Cardiff summit, 'the economic benefits must be clear and unambiguous.' He is frustrated at the refusal of commentators to take such statements at their word. The caution is commendable, but economics rarely delivers such clarity. The Treasury committee of MPs makes the point well in its excellent recent report on the single currency. Assessing the costs and benefits of joining requires a balance sheet of the pluses and minuses of standing aside. Both sets of calculations demand heroic assumptions.

Take sterling's brief flirtation with the exchange-rate mechanism. The heavy cost of membership during the early 1990s is now assumed to be self-evident. But we could also weigh the high price Britain paid for not joining five years earlier. And now, as then, there is nothing that says economic convergence is pre-ordained. It has to be worked at. Germany and France are moving into an upswing just as Britain heads in the opposite direction. If Mr Blair is taken at his word, it will not be enough for British and euro interest rates to meet for a month or two in 2001 as passing ships in the night. Here we come to the biggest 'if' of all: sterling. It is taken as read that the pound has to fall before it can be fixed permanently against the euro. A rate of DM2.50 to DM2.60 is mentioned in the corridors of power. We are not to ask, though, how and when it will arrive at that level.

With the honourable exception of the Treasury committee, no one seems interested either in how the government will deliver the two years of stability against the euro demanded by the Maastricht treaty. Mr Brown says Britain will not rejoin the ERM. Fair enough. But he also insists that the Bank of England targets the inflation, rather than the exchange, rate. It is left, it seems, to the hand of fate to stabilize sterling. Nigel Wicks, the Treasury mandarin in charge of these matters, said as much to the Treasury committee. His precise words bear repetition. 'If we secure our objectives for inflation, if we secure our objectives for fiscal policy, this will over time bring our exchange rate into some sort of convergence.'

A glance at any graph of the pound's gyrations in recent years well explains Sir Nigel's caution. For good measure Eddie George, the Bank governor, told the MPs that his monetary policy committee is not about to play fast and loose with the inflation target by shadowing the euro. 'Absolutely not,' is how the Emu-sceptic governor put it.

I have heard it said that once the government's eagerness is more apparent, the financial markets will do the job for it. If traders know that Britain wants to join at, say, DM2.60, they will deliver that exchange rate. Maybe. But that demands a far more explicit timescale than Mr Blair has hitherto offered. And it rather cuts across the idea of the government waiting patiently until it is confident the economic conditions are just so.

Understandably, the committee has asked the chancellor to clarify such points. The Treasury's position appears to be that it will be sufficient to demonstrate *ex post* that sterling has been well behaved for a year or so. Its continental counterparts retort that the treaty requires an *ex ante* commitment to stability – and, incidentally, an equal say for the euro countries in deciding the pound's putative entry rate.

We could go on in this vein. Even if you think (as I do) that Mr Brown's five economic tests for Emu entry are infinitely malleable, there are decisions to be taken, commitments to be made well before Britain applies for entry. These extend beyond setting up committees to change the slots in vending machines. And whatever Mr Blair's present intentions, the economics cannot be divorced from the politics. The one shapes the other. At the end of the day the balance he has to strike is that between the political costs of staying out and the risks (political and economic) of joining. There are no certainties in such calculations – for Mr Blair or for anyone else.

First published 29 June 1998

8 The international implications of Emu

It is our currency, but your problem. Hyperbole maybe, but that is what the Americans used to say about the dollar. It may hold true for the euro as well. The launch of the single currency is bound to have important ramifications for the international economy. This chapter presents different scenarios and opinions from both sides of the Atlantic.

Leading international economists have argued that the euro could develop into a strong currency against the dollar and the yen, and become a rival for the dollar as the currency of choice in international financial transactions. Vicki Bakhshi, economic leader writer at the *FT*, argues that a rapid rise in demand for the euro and large portfolio shifts could exert a powerful upward influence on the euro exchange rate. The exchange rate between the dollar and the euro could become the most important in the world.

Martin Wolf, the *FT*'s chief economic commentator, considers three questions: Could the euro become a global currency? What will determine whether it does? And what impact might its emergence have on the world economy? Turning to a similar theme in 'Euro versus the dollar', Richard Portes and Hélène Rey, two London-based academic economists, provide some of the answers. They argue that the Europeans and Americans must enhance their macroeconomic policy co-ordination to ease the probable tensions that will result if the euro comes to equal the dollar as an international reserve currency. But the absence of a euro zone treasury secretary will make this difficult.

Domestic factors will also influence the euro's exchange rate. Robert Chote, the *FT*'s economics editor, says the euro's long-term strength will depend in large part on the interest-rate policy of the European Central Bank and the budgetary policies of the member states. He warns that, if national governments maintain lax fiscal policies, this will undoubtedly trigger tight monetary policy, and the euro is destined to be overvalued.

Larry Summers, US deputy secretary of the Treasury, strikes a confident note about the euro and its effect on the US and the world economy. His argument is that 'if Emu works for Europe, it will work for us'. But most

American commentators are far more sceptical about Emu and the prospects for the European economy in general. Lionel Barber, the *FT*'s Brussels correspondent, laments the fact that many US policy-makers and opinion-formers are still ill-informed about the single currency. American 'snootiness' towards Emu may be understandable given the economic boom in the US. But the Europeans' capacity for improvisation and the confidence of the financial markets in the Emu project are too often ignored.

WOLFGANG MÜNCHAU

Watch out, dollar: *the euro could become an international currency with real clout more quickly than many people are expecting*

VICKI BAKHSHI

The introduction of the euro will transform Europe. But the creation of the world's second largest currency area will also have a huge impact on the global financial system. What is still unclear is whether the euro's influence will be primarily regional or whether it will come to rival the dollar as an international currency. The answer has important implications

The mighty dollar

	Share in world output (%)	Share in global reserve holdings (%)	*Share in two-way foreign exchange transactions (%)	Share in world export invoicing (%, 1992 figures)
US	27	56	84	48
EU	31	20	70	33
Japan	21	7	24	5

*As two currencies are involved in each transaction, the sum of transactions in individual currencies comes to twice total reported turnover

Sources: Bergsten, Foreign Affairs 1997; OECD; Portes and Rey

1995 figures unless stated

for both Europe and the US. The US dollar has dominated the international finance system for nearly a century. Because of its extensive use by third parties, its importance in global financial transactions far exceeds the US's 27 per cent share of world output (*see* chart). The dollar accounts for 56 per cent of the world's foreign exchange reserves, 48 per cent of export invoicing and participates in more than four-fifths of all foreign exchange transactions.

It is no accident that just one currency has gained pre-eminence. As the use of a currency rises, the market becomes more liquid and transaction costs fall, inducing even more people to use it. Once a currency becomes widely used, it is hard to dislodge. Neither the yen nor the D-Mark has made significant inroads into the dollar's dominance. So why should the euro be any different?

A big factor will be the sheer size of the euro area. The eleven prospective members have a combined gross domestic product of $6,300 billion, against the US's $8,100 billion. The euro area will be the world's largest importer and exporter, excluding intra-EU trade. And if, as planned, Emu is extended to all fifteen EU countries, the euro area will become the world's largest economy.

A huge economy means a huge new capital market, with much lower transaction costs. And, unlike Japan, Europe's capital markets are fully open to foreign investors. The effect on liquidity will be dramatic. Avinash Persaud, head of currency research at J. P. Morgan, predicts that transaction costs will collapse overnight. This will immediately make the euro more attractive as a vehicle currency for trade and foreign exchange.

The unification of the European currencies will also lead to economies of scale, making it more likely that foreign companies exporting to Europe will use the new currency to denominate their trade. Say, for example, a Japanese company exports 10 per cent of its output to Germany, 5 per cent to France and 5 per cent to Italy. Before Emu, the trade would probably be transacted in dollars because of the expense of dealing in several different currencies. But after Emu, with a fifth of its exports going to the euro area, it might well switch.

All this means the euro's use as a vehicle currency could quickly expand. In particular:

- Effects could be felt first in those countries expected to join the next wave of Emu – the UK, Sweden, Denmark and Greece. Hillary Thompson, head of European strategy at NatWest, says many European companies will ask their UK suppliers to invoice them in euros. Several of NatWest's larger UK clients, which have European-oriented businesses, have been discussing plans to switch their operations entirely into euros. Many suppliers in non-Emu countries could end up operating in euros to keep their customers happy – what Ms Thompson calls the euro supply-chain effect. She believes the euro could become a quasi-domestic currency in the UK within two to three years. This process is already beginning. In April 1998, British Steel became the second large UK company – ICI was the first – to announce that it would ask its suppliers to accept payment in euros.
- The euro is also likely to be widely used in eastern Europe and, to a lesser extent, north Africa, where many local currencies are already pegged to European currencies.

- It may start to be used in transactions between the euro area and countries outside Europe. Currency transactions between Japan and Europe, for example, are almost always intermediated through the dollar, while most exports from Asia to Europe are also invoiced in the US currency. As the euro gains momentum, this could change.
- Many of the world's central banks may also reduce their high concentration of dollar holdings by switching to euros. Central banks want greater diversification in their currency portfolios, particularly after many made big losses when the exchange rate of the dollar plunged in the late 1980s.

The euro's greater liquidity and lower transaction costs (compared with individual European currencies) will be a big attraction: a prime consideration in choosing a reserve currency is its effectiveness for intervening in foreign exchange markets. The denomination of a country's trade is also an important influence in the choice of currency. This means that any shift towards using the euro in trade will have a knock-on effect for the desirability of euro services. Given these expected changes, most economists agree that, sooner or later, the euro will achieve international status. The question is when. The most common view is it will take some time. Martin Brookes, international economist at Goldman Sachs, thinks that, although a bipolar financial system is economically logical, it will take a very long time before there is a big shift to the euro. And the International Monetary Fund, in its October 1997 World Economic Outlook, said the new currency would only achieve international status in the medium to longer-term.

The reasons most often cited for such caution are that the economic stability of the euro area has yet to be proven, while European capital markets are considerably smaller than their US counterparts. But neither factor should have a decisive impact. On the first point, it is true that an international currency needs the support of a stable economy.

True also that the euro area could suffer significant economic turbulence in the transition period. But these will be primarily structural problems concentrated in pockets of overheating or regions of persistently high unemployment. Such problems will not matter to international holders of euros so long as the overall macroeconomic performance of the euro area is stable and inflation remains reasonably low. And, with the European Central Bank likely to play it very safe as it establishes its reputation, continuing low inflation seems probable.

The second argument against the euro's rapid rise – that European capital markets are too small – is more relevant. The European domestic securities market is only two-thirds the size of its US equivalent. And without a central government bond issuer, European fixed income markets will remain more fragmented than in the US. In this, the early entry into Emu of the UK, with its deep financial markets, will be crucial.

There is a counter view to the idea that the euro will take a long time to mature. Some economists suggest the sudden fall in transaction costs will lead to the rapid adoption of the euro worldwide. The euro will become an international currency within a matter of months, not years, says Mr Persaud of J. P. Morgan.

Academics Richard Portes and Hélène Rey, in a paper recently published by London's Centre for Economic Policy Research ('The Emergence of the Euro as an International Currency', in *Emu: Prospects and Challenges for the Euro*, April 1998), share this view. They suggest that the shock Emu will bring to the international financial system is likely to be substantial and relatively sudden.

The internationalization of a currency is not just a status symbol. It has significant economic and political implications. First, the issuer of such a currency gains a direct economic benefit in the form of seigniorage: in exchange for almost costless notes, the issuer receives real resources – net imports. A second benefit is the greater liquidity in the bond markets that results from internationalization: this lowers yields, cutting the costs of borrowing for both governments and companies.

A rapid rise in demand for the euro would also affect the euro exchange rate. Unless it were offset by an equally rapid rise in the amount of euro assets issued, it would exert a powerful upward influence. The exchange rate between the dollar and the euro will become the most important in the world. But the US and the EU, being relatively closed economies, are unlikely actively to manage their exchange rates. This combination of factors has led Fred Bergsten, director of the Institute for International Economics, to warn that a quantum leap in transatlantic co-operation will be needed to avoid a damaging increase in exchange-rate volatility ('The Dollar and the Euro', *Foreign Affairs*, Volume 76, no. 4).

So far, American policymakers seem unconcerned at the potential challenger to their currency's dominance. The dollar will remain the primary reserve currency for the foreseeable future, Larry Summers, the deputy Treasury secretary, said in a speech last year: 'We expect the impact of the euro on the monetary system to be quite limited initially and to occur only gradually.'

Mr Summers and the rest of the US establishment, it seems, may be in for a surprise.

First appeared 23 April 1998

***Euro's world test:** if the euro is to be a reserve currency, Europe will have to provide assets to the world, as the US does. Is Europe ready?*

MARTIN WOLF

Is the euro going to be a serious rival to the dollar? French policymakers hope it will, most Americans assume it will not. Larry Summers, deputy secretary to the US Treasury, is not alone in arguing that the dollar will remain the primary reserve currency for the foreseeable future.

The EU as a sleeping monetary giant

%	US	Japan	EU15
Relative economic size			
Shares of world GDP, 1996	20.7	8.0	20.4
Shares of world exports (ex-intra-EU), 1996	35.2	6.1	14.7
Relative use of currencies*			
World trade, 1992	48.0	5.0	31.0
World debt securities, Sep 1996	37.2	17.0	34.5
Developing country debt, end-1996	50.2	18.1	15.8
Global foreign exchange reserves, end 1995	50.4	7.1	25.8
Foreign exchange transactions, Apr 1995**	41.5	12.0	35.0

*Shares denominated in currency (or currencies) of country (or EU)
**Shares adjusted for double-counting that arises from the fact that each transaction involves two currencies

Source: IMF

Robert Mundell of Columbia University, father of the theory of optimal currency areas, thinks US complacency is mistaken. For him, the introduction of the euro is at least the most significant international monetary development since the dollar replaced the pound as the dominant international currency during the first world war. Arguably, it is the most important event since the rise of the gold standard in the 1870s (Robert A. Mundell, 'The International Impact of the Euro and Its Implications for the Transition Countries', mimeo, paper presented at the Fourth Dubrovnik Conference on Transitional Economies, 22–4 June 1998).

Consider three questions: Could the euro become a global currency? What will determine whether it does? What impact might its emergence have on the world economy?

For a currency to achieve widespread use as an international means of exchange and store of value it must be liquid and safe. Liquidity is created by the breadth and depth of markets in which it is used. Safety depends on its monetary soundness and underlying political stability. The latter is particularly important for paper money, which tends to lose all value if the issuing state collapses.

The gross domestic product of the initial eleven-member euro zone is only 80 per cent of US GDP. But the addition of the UK and the other three outsiders (Denmark, Greece and Sweden) would make the area as big as the US (*see* table, p. 258). As for monetary stability, that is certainly what the European Central Bank will try to deliver.

The big doubt is political. The authority issuing the euro is far more likely to disappear than the US government. Outsiders might well need time or evidence of further integration before putting their faith in the euro – though the fact that Italian bond yields are already lower than those of the US suggests they may not need that much time.

The euro, in short, has the potential to become a world currency. What would it take for that to happen? An answer is provided by Richard Portes, director of the Centre for Economic Policy Research, and Hélène Rey of the London School of Economics (Richard Portes and Hélène Rey, 'The Emergence of the Euro as an International Currency', in David Begg *et al* (eds), *Emu: Prospects and Challenges for the Euro*, Oxford: Basil Blackwell, 1998). They start from the assumption that the euro will be deemed a sound currency. It will then be used as a store of value if it is widely used and it will be widely used if it is cheap enough to do so. But volume begets low cost, which begets increased volume, which begets yet lower costs.

Because US financial markets are so liquid it is cheaper to use the dollar as a vehicle currency than trade other currencies directly. This, argue Professor Portes and Ms Rey, could change if transaction volumes were big enough in euro-denominated markets. The emergence of the euro is bound to make all European markets more liquid. The question is how much more.

At present, the bid–ask spreads in the German and French bond markets are 4 basis points, while those in the US are only 1.6. The analysis shows that the mere fusion of the European markets will be insufficient to reduce transaction costs below US levels. For that to happen there must be further would-be institutional changes within European financial markets.

Professor Portes and Ms Rey demonstrate that the emergence of the euro could reduce the dollar's role, which is out of proportion to the size of the US economy and trade. But the shift depends on the credibility of the new currency and the efficiency of euro financial markets. My own guess is that Mr Summers is right: the euro is not a sufficiently good competitor to rival the incumbent in the near future. But the odds against its doing so are not overwhelming.

So it makes sense to ask what impact the euro would have if it became an international currency. It is likely to have a big impact. Hitherto, the US has financed its current account deficit in assets denominated in its own currency. The former French president Charles de Gaulle described this as the ability to be indebted to foreign countries free of charge. The implications are explained by Professor Mundell: over the past fifteen years the cumulative US current account deficit has been some $1,700 billion. This has been financed by around $1,000 billion in net capital inflows, plus foreign accumulation of dollar reserves of $700 billion.

Suppose the euro were to rival the dollar. Professor Mundell assumes that, between now and 2006, global reserves of foreign exchange would increase from $1,500 billion to $3,000 billion in line with the growth of world trade and the increased desire to hold reserves in a world of exchange-rate instability. He assumes also that the dollar share will have fallen from two-thirds of total reserves to 40 per cent, while the European share will have risen from a fifth to 40 per cent. On those assumptions, the total increase in official holdings of the dollar will be a mere $200 billion over the next eight years. The increase in holdings of euros will be $900 billion.

If anything like this were to happen, the outcome could be devastating, particularly in light of the Asian crisis. This, according to forecasts from the Organization for Economic Co-operation and Development, will raise the US current account deficit to $249 billion by 1999, while the EU-11 surplus is forecast at $152 billion.

If the rest of the world wanted to shift from the dollar to the euro when the US was running a big external deficit and the EU an almost equally big surplus, there would be a gigantic euro appreciation. Professor Portes and Ms Rey consider a shift of $600 billion in private and official holdings from dollar-denominated to euro-denominated assets and suggest the euro could appreciate 40 per cent.

The underlying reality is the EU would have to shift from a big current account surplus to a big deficit in order to accommodate the world's desire to hold euro-denominated assets. This would create big difficulties for management of monetary policy in Europe, which will be problematic enough as it is. Meanwhile, the US would be faced with a choice between a dollar plunge or higher interest rates.

Whether or not the birth of the euro is the most important change in the world monetary system for 129 years is an open question. But the impact could be particularly dramatic at a time of global financial and economic turmoil.

At the moment, the US is the global importer of last resort in dealing with the Asian crisis. If there were a widespread desire to shift into the euro, the US would find it more difficult to finance its expanding current account deficit. To offset this, the EU would have to accept a big swing into deficit. If it failed to do so, the world could move into slump. The euro would then be an unmanageable monetary shock, at a time when the world is grappling with the one emanating from Asia.

First appeared 7 July 1998

Euro versus the dollar: *Europe and the US may need to enhance their co-ordination to smooth tensions*

RICHARD PORTES AND HÉLÈNE REY

The European commission recently discussed the euro's role *vis-à-vis* the dollar with the US Treasury. The commissioner for monetary affairs, Yves-Thibault de Silguy, said the euro would 'progressively' challenge the dollar. The US Treasury secretary, Robert Rubin, countered that he did not 'think it's going to adversely affect the position of the dollar either as a reserve currency or in international finance'. One of them must be wrong – and in this case, one must lose.

This is, indeed, an example of the sort of dangerous 'zero-sum' conflict that economists try to avoid. The last transfer of currency hegemony was the displacement of sterling by the dollar between the two world wars – a period of deeply damaging instability. The emergence of the euro as an international currency will require careful, co-operative management. To manage the process, we need to understand it. There has been much talk of the potential international role of the euro, often contradictory because it has not been based on any analytical framework. It has been informed guesswork, using aggregate data.

In the April 1998 issue of *Economic Policy* we proposed an analytical basis for the discussion and calculated the consequences, using a new model and new data, some from the underlying microstructure of the key markets. Reserve currency status is not just an international virility symbol. It brings international seigniorage, benefits for 'home' financial institutions, relaxation of the 'external constraint' on macroeconomic policy, a greater role for the issuer in international institutions, and the wider geopolitical consequences of exercising currency hegemony. Our framework enables us to assess how far the euro will take on this role; to measure the effects of alternative scenarios on welfare in the main world regions; and to consider carefully the transition period as the international monetary system adjusts to the euro.

Previous work, our own included, focused on private invoicing behaviour, official reserve holding behaviour, and the use of an anchor currency (pegging exchange rates, e.g. to the dollar). According to a new analysis, all these will be secondary to the interactions between financial asset markets and foreign exchange markets.

The usefulness of a currency for financial transactions and for the denomination of financial assets increases with the number of people using it: there is a 'network externality' in currency use (as with fax machines, for example). The development of euro financial asset markets and network externalities among euro users in forex markets will support the euro's role as an international currency.

As euro securities markets become deeper and more liquid, transaction costs will fall, and euro assets will become more attractive, so the use of the euro as a vehicle currency in forex markets will grow. The two effects interact, and that synergy will bring the euro to challenge the dollar. Initially, we expect no more than a 'quasi-status quo' – the euro as a 'big D-Mark'. But taken together, euro-area government bond markets are of a size comparable to the US Treasury market.

As financial market integration in Europe progresses – with an expected speed that market participants continuously revise upwards – operating in the euro-denominated bond markets will become just as attractive as parking funds in New York or hedging with US government securities. Then the 'fundamentals' of international trade and investment could support either a 'medium euro' or a 'big euro' scenario. In both, the euro would replace the dollar as the main international currency for financial asset transactions (except between the US and Asia), but only in the 'big euro' scenario would the euro also take on the forex market vehicle currency role. The consequence could be a welfare gain of as much as 0.4 per cent of GDP (annually) for Europe (including seignorage), with a smaller loss for the US – as well as the other economic and geopolitical attributes of the 'hegemonic' world currency.

The transition period will see substantial portfolio shifts from dollar-denominated into euro-denominated assets, possibly creating excess demand for the latter. That would favour a 'strong' euro. To promote the internationalization of the euro, European policy-makers should focus on integrating European capital markets. Deregulation and policy harmonization (for example, in government bond issuing), as well as private market initiatives, could enhance the liquidity, breadth and depth of these markets.

So, improving the financial environment for savers and investors in the euro zone would also support the euro's challenge to the dollar. With the increasing integration of international capital markets and the size and speed of capital flows, changes in the international monetary system will happen faster than the historical displacement of sterling by the dollar.

Moreover, the early period could see considerable instability associated with the emergence of the euro, especially if the United States were to resist any decline in the international status of the dollar. On the European side, the authorities will have to take account of these instabilities and exchange-rate pressures in setting their monetary policy. Simple policy rules will be inadequate. But both sides may have to enhance their macroeconomic policy co-ordination to ease the tensions – something which is likely to be especially difficult in the absence of a euro-zone Treasury secretary.

First appeared 30 April 1998

Euro may unseat dollar

ROBERT CHOTE

The US dollar has been the world's top currency for more than sixty years, having supplanted sterling as linchpin of the international monetary system between the wars. Europe's putative single currency poses the first serious threat to its hegemony.

The euro's status as an international currency will depend on the willingness of public and private sectors around the world to use it as a store of value, medium of exchange and unit of account. That in turn will depend on several factors, of which the size and strength of its domestic economy will be among the most important.

In this respect, the euro clearly poses a threat to the dollar. Europe's economy is bigger than America's, with output of goods and services in 1996 totalling $8.4 trillion in the EU compared with $7.2 trillion in the US. At $1.9 trillion Europe's external trade (exports plus imports) also outstripped the US total of $1.7 trillion. Even a modest monetary union comprising only Germany, France, Austria and the Benelux nations would create an economy two-thirds the size of the US and carrying out more global trade.

As well as drawing attention to Europe's size advantage, Fred Bergsten, director of the Institute for International Economics, argued at an IMF symposium in March 1998 that 'the structural features of united Europe are likely to produce a euro that will ultimately challenge the dollar as the world's key currency'.

Bergsten noted that Europe had run modest current account surpluses in recent years, while the US had built up a $1 trillion external debt following fifteen successive years of current account deficits. He also predicted that the independent European Central Bank was likely to deliver the economic stability which financial markets crave. Both factors should make the euro attractive. In the dollar's favour remain the breadth, depth and liquidity of US capital markets. The dollar will also benefit from incumbency and inertia, which allowed sterling to maintain its international role long after Britain's economy had suffered relative decline.

Bergsten saw no clear winner in the short term: 'A bipolar currency regime, with Japan as an important, but less significant, player, will replace the dollar-denominated system that has prevailed for over half a century.' That prospect raises an important question: will the euro perform strongly or weakly on the foreign exchanges relative to its main international rivals? In the short term, this will depend in part on the degree to which private sector investors and central banks opt to switch assets denominated in other currencies into euros. Bergsten estimates that this portfolio shift, largely out of dollars, will total between $500 billion and $1 trillion, with private reallocations accounting for by far the larger share.

By way of comparison, Japanese investors shifted $230 billion from domestic into foreign assets between 1980 and 1985, during which time the dollar rose 25 per cent against the yen and 75 per cent against all G10 currencies. An increased demand for assets denominated in euros will certainly put upward pressure on its exchange rate, but by how much is not clear. Michael Mussa, chief economist at the IMF, told the symposium that shifts in interest-bearing assets were more likely to reduce the euro interest rate rather than push up its exchange rate. And William White, of the Bank for International Settlements, argued that the increased desire for euro-denominated assets would be met by a greater supply as more institutions chose to borrow in euros. The net effect on the exchange rate would therefore be ambiguous.

The euro area, like the US, will be a relatively closed economy with external trade accounting for a much smaller proportion of national output than it does for most individual European economies. Nonetheless changes in the euro exchange rate will still have important economic effects. Professor George Alogoskoufis, of the Athens School of Economics, told the symposium that portfolio shifts might well push the euro higher against the dollar, overshooting the level justified by economic fundamentals. Initially this would improve the EU's current account position (by making imports cheaper) and push up real interest rates. But the euro would then weaken as the trade position worsened and real interest rates fell.

In the longer term, the euro's performance on the foreign exchanges will depend in large part on the interest rate policy pursued by the European Central Bank and the budgetary policies pursued by the governments within the euro zone.

Paul Masson, of the IMF, predicted that monetary union would eventually help stabilize key economic variables within the euro area, but he added that the European Central Bank would at first have great difficulty using these indicators as a guide to policy. The ECB will need practice before it can interpret euro-area statistics and judge how the economy will respond to policy changes.

Masson concluded that the central bank's proposed inflation and money supply targets might therefore be difficult to apply. 'A more discretionary policy, in which the exchange value of the euro, among other indicators, is given a certain amount of attention, may instead emerge,' he said. Paul Jenkins, of the Bank of Canada, predicted that a 5–6 per cent change in the euro's exchange rate would have the same impact on a small single currency area as a one point change in interest rates.

But many economists dispute the usefulness of such rules. Several participants in the symposium also warned that the euro would be more volatile relative to the dollar than existing European currencies. That would make exchange rate movements even more difficult to interpret. The ECB will begin its life making policy in the dark. With no track record and everything to prove, the greatest danger is that it will err too much on the side of caution and keep interest rates too high. If governments respond by relaxing budgetary policy, then the euro may indeed begin its life as a strong currency – but to the detriment of the health of Europe's economy.

First appeared 24 March 1997

Nobody in charge: *if it had been up to Europe to prop up the yen, it probably wouldn't have done so*

WOLFGANG MÜNCHAU

Many people think the euro will soon rival the dollar as the world's leading currency, but how near is it to achieving that status? Would the recent currency intervention in support of the yen have happened if the euro had been the dominant currency instead of the dollar?

The answer is probably not, because no one in Europe would have been in charge. Such intervention could go well beyond the mandate of the European Central Bank to keep the euro stable. And, of course, the European Union runs on committee and consensus. In principle, finance ministers could have met in an emergency session, but they would hardly have sprung the kind of decisive and surprising intervention undertaken by Robert Rubin, US Treasury secretary. Recent interventions came about after intensive discussions between the Treasury and White House. But the ECB will have no political counterpart.

This raises two questions: what are the constraints for the euro as a leading international currency? And are the ECB's institutional arrangements equipped to deal with emergencies, including financial crises? The euro is unlikely to be just another currency. Research increasingly suggests it could challenge the dollar, both as an international reserve currency and in international private transactions. As the economic and monetary union area expands in the next five to ten years, the euro zone could outgrow the US in terms of gross domestic product and share of world trade. The euro could conceivably displace the dollar as the world's most important currency.

What then? The sudden emergence of a new world currency would open up a policy vacuum. Monetary policy in Europe under the ECB will take place in isolation. Fiscal policy and banking supervision remain national priorities. Exchange-rate policy and currency intervention will legally be a matter for EU finance ministers, provided such intervention does not impinge upon the ECB's constitutional goal of the preservation of price stability.

It is not yet clear how the division of responsibilities between the ECB and finance ministers would work. Would it involve all fifteen finance ministers of the European Union? Or just three, representing the current, past and future holders of the EU presidency, which rotates every six months? Maybe the task would fall to euro-X, the informal gathering of finance ministers of countries participating in the euro. Might it fall to the ECB itself? Whoever it is, there clearly is a large number of possible candidates, and the probable upshot is that no one would be in charge, and no one would be accountable.

For the ECB, the stability of the international financial system is no doubt important, but its primary goal will be domestic price stability. That means the ECB would be likely to act rather as the Bundesbank did during the currency crises.

The Bundesbank was never enthusiastic about large-scale intervention in foreign exchange markets. It initially opposed the creation of the European exchange-rate mechanism in the late 1970s. Otmar Emminger, a former Bundesbank president, secured the right to refuse intervention if it jeopardized the goal of price stability. The ECB does not even need to negotiate such a deal: the same principle is already contained in the Maastricht treaty. So it seems unlikely that the ECB can be relied upon to prop up the yen or the dollar. At least, it would not be able to if there were a risk of higher European inflation – which there always is during periods of sustained intervention, which pushes up the domestic money supply, threatening to reignite inflation.

On top of this comes the argument that currency market intervention does not address the underlying causes for misalignments – unless it is designed to counteract purely speculative money flows. The Bundesbank does not believe the Asian crisis was caused by events in the foreign exchange markets. Nor does it believe currency intervention can cure the problem. How would the ECB respond if such an Asian-style financial crisis were to occur inside Europe? Again, it could do little. The 1997 annual report of the European Monetary Institute, the ECB's precursor, stated: 'At this stage it is felt that it would be premature to envisage any transfer of supervisory powers from national authorities to the ECB.'

The ECB itself will have little more than a consulting role when it comes to new legislation about banking supervision. Furthermore, it will have no mandate to bail out banks in trouble. It will not act as a lender of last resort, unlike some national central banks. Likewise, there will be no bail-out for defaulting banks, except if the default has obvious implications for the entire financial system. And as if that were not reason enough for thinking the ECB will want to eschew currency interventions, there remains the innate conservatism of European central bankers, who dislike arrangements that are open to moral hazard.

Edgar Meister, a board member of the Bundesbank's directorate in charge of banking supervision, last week highlighted such problems in a speech in Frankfurt. He was critical of investors in Asia who acted 'in the expectation that the International Monetary Fund would come to the rescue in the event of sudden crisis situations'.

All this suggests Europe will be reluctant to intervene in international markets, first because it would be too difficult to orchestrate and second because central bankers do not believe in it. If the euro were to displace the dollar as the world's leading currency, Emu could turn out to be a culture shock not only for Europe, but the international financial system.

First appeared 22 June 1998

The euro will be good for the US if it helps strengthen and modernize Europe's economy

LAWRENCE SUMMERS

The US relationship with Europe has long been the cornerstone of our economic and foreign policy. We have supported European efforts towards closer integration since the very start, from the creation of the European Coal and Steel Community to the common market, the single market and now plans for further enlargement. Today, another ambitious project, the creation of a single European currency, seems close to becoming a reality and is attracting serious attention in the US.

The administration has never thought it fitting to enter the debate over whether economic and monetary union is right for Europe, nor over the details of how it should be structured. But we can hardly be said to be indifferent to how the project turns out. The US is well served when Europe is vibrant economically and working to open its markets and strengthen its ties with the global economy. Europe will prosper from an economic and monetary union that supports these ends. And if Europe prospers, this will help prosperity in the US.

There are two sets of issues that interest us particularly. First, how will Emu affect the EU as a major economy and international partner of the US? And second, what will be its impact on the international financial system as a whole?

Recent efforts towards increased European integration – including some of the changes that have been associated with preparations for Emu – have already brought significant gains. Yet no one doubts that Europe still faces serious economic challenges that will need to be overcome if Emu is to succeed.

First among these is Europe's high rates of unemployment and, partly as a result of those labour market failures, its serious fiscal imbalances. In recent years, many countries have made significant progress on the fiscal side. But as governments have themselves recognized, Emu will make it even more vital to proceed with structural reforms to give their economies the flexibility and dynamism needed to spur rapid job creation and investment growth.

If there is a shock to demand, individual members of Emu will no longer have the freedom to respond by devaluing their currency, or cutting or raising interest rates. Nor, given the terms of the stability and growth pact, will they be able to use fiscal stimuli to support growth. Policymakers cannot afford to allow Emu to distract them from pursuing fundamental reforms. As we have seen in the recent flood of cross-country mergers and acquisitions, the European private sector is already responding to the new situation. Governments need to build on the growing consensus in favour of reform and put it to work achieving genuine changes on the ground.

It is equally vital that Emu does not distract from the important international challenges that Europe faces, particularly the expansion of the EU to incorporate several countries of the former Soviet bloc. This offers an historic chance to cement these countries' transition to a market democracy.

Turning to the second set of issues, clearly the US has a strong interest in euro's potential impact on the international financial landscape. Two questions have been raised in this context: the effects on the international role of the dollar; and the implications for short-term and exchange-rate fluctuations.

We generally do not speculate about the future values of existing currencies, be they our own or others. This extends to future trends in the values of currencies that do not yet exist. With these qualifications, however, I would like to make a few general observations. The first point we in the US must remember is that the buck stops – and starts – with us. In the end, the dollar's relative standing in the international financial system will always depend more on developments here than on events overseas. If we stick to strong and credible policies, the dollar will remain a sound currency.

It is difficult to predict with any certainty what the role of the newly created euro will be. Those who foresee it growing very rapidly in importance point to the fact that it will be the common currency of countries representing a significant share of global output. Those who are more sceptical argue that the euro will be without a proven track record. Investors, they say, will want to observe progress towards price stability before making a commitment.

Where there is little disagreement is that, barring major policy errors, international currency holdings do not change at great speed. In particular, European financial markets are unlikely to transform themselves overnight. It will take time before the range of euro-denominated assets come close to matching the variety available in the US; or, given differing perceptions of the creditworthiness of government securities, the homogeneity of the US market for public debt.

On the matter of future trade and exchange rate fluctuations, we should remember that the main continental European currencies have been fixed among themselves for some time now, with little tendency to fluctuate. Equally, each country has tended to recognize the importance of strong monetary policies for achieving robust growth, and the need for these to be underpinned by a sturdy financial system, sound fiscal policies and independent central banks. In that sense, Emu will be a force for continuity. Indeed, the fiscal controls envisaged within Emu could well be a force for lower interest rates in the US.

Clearly, the US government has no direct role in most of the preparations for Emu. It is a different story for American private sector companies actively involved in international trade or finance, or those with European operations. They have a lot of work to do in such domains as accounting, finance, and information management – work which, given the close proximity of Emu, probably needs to speed up in the months ahead. Although I cannot guarantee US business that Emu will occur as promised, I would advise them to be ready.

The advent of the single currency will also raise issues for the future evolution of the G7 and for Europe's future participation in international organizations such as the International Monetary Fund. We look forward to engaging with the EU in these matters next year after the selection of the first members. The aim must be to ensure that Europe emerges out of Emu with the capacity to play an active, constructive role on the world stage on political, monetary and other matters. The corollary is that European policymakers will have to avoid being overly preoccupied with building and refining the architecture of monetary union.

But let me end by repeating the bottom line. The more the single currency helps Europe develop a robust and healthy economy open to world markets, the more welcome the project will be on this side of the Atlantic. Put it another way: if Emu works for Europe, it will work for us.

First appeared 22 October 1997

The Emu has landed: *Gerard Baker on how US support has turned to mild concern as Europe's single currency has become reality*

GERARD BAKER

For forty years, as Europe moved step by step towards ever closer union, the rest of the world, led by the US, has applauded enthusiastically. It has been an article of faith that economic and political integration is good – not only for Europe, but also for the rest of the world. That may be changing. As eleven members of the European Union took the biggest stride yet towards closer union (notwithstanding the usual family squabble over who should head the central bank), they did so against a background of international nervousness.

Much concern focuses on how the US will react. The critical question is how the euro will affect economic and political relationships across the Atlantic. No country has had a bigger strategic interest in the European project than the US. But the arrival of economic and monetary union poses a greater challenge to American economic and diplomatic orthodoxy than any previous stage of Euro-integration. Highly influential Americans are having second thoughts.

The official US position, since the Maastricht treaty was signed in 1991, has been to offer polite support for Emu. Bill Clinton, the US president, has said: 'An integrated Europe is America's natural best partner for the 21st century.' But behind the diplomatic niceties has been a quiet scepticism, a caution that stems from a complex mix of doubts that threatens to shatter the longstanding US orthodoxy about Europe.

Until not much more than a year ago, even those members of the policy establishment most engaged in international affairs privately doubted whether monetary union would ever take place. As the project has moved from probability to reality, the official US view has become more supportive. But even as the member countries have been hatching Emu in the past few months, the words of welcome from US officials have been larded with conditionals. If Emu is good for Europe it will be good for us is the mantra repeated by Larry Summers, the deputy US Treasury secretary, and the administration's most important thinker on Emu. But bland efforts to say nothing leave an impression that the US is uneasy. The Republican speaker of the House Newt Gingrich broke the silence in May 1998 when he made the blunt assessment that Britain should leave the EU and join the North American Free Trade area. Such an idea reveals the depth of US doubts.

Even the most ardent proponents of the project do not dispute that it is by far the most risky step taken towards European integration. Hence it is hardly surprising that there is a difference between the current ambiguity and cordial US support for previous steps – especially the expansion of the original six members to fifteen and the creation of a single market.

For European enthusiasts, however, the changed US attitude reflects two deeper concerns, both raised by the threat to the US of a successful Emu. First, the arrival of the euro is the first serious challenge to the global hegemony of the dollar since the 1930s. The euro will be to the dollar what Airbus is to Boeing. If the euro were to challenge the dollar, that would not be something the US could afford to take lightly. The US gains much from printing the world's reserve currency. Seignorage – the revenue that accrues to the federal government from the ubiquity of hundreds of billions of dollars in banknotes – is one benefit. More important, the primacy of the dollar means the U S has no trouble financing its huge external needs – a $160 billion current account deficit – in its own currency, inoculating debt service costs against currency volatility.

Second, Emu optimists believe, the U S is nervous about the efficiencies they expect monetary union to bring the European economy. These, they think, will turn the euro zone into a forceful global competitor. It is true there is some concern in Washington about the implications of Emu for U S dominance of the global financial system. But it is hard to find many U S policymakers who regard the threat as anything other than very distant. Mr Summers has repeatedly pointed out that it took many years of U S economic strength before the dollar achieved its supremacy. A global reserve currency, he has argued, is not simply legislated into existence. He reckons it will take years before the euro builds enough credibility to become a serious threat.

Few in the U S administration worry that any long-term economic gains Europe makes will damage the U S. A vibrant and integrated European market poses more opportunities than dangers for U S companies. On this, at any rate, it seems reasonable to take U S officials at their word. It is not the success of Emu that worries us, but the possibility that it will be somewhat less than successful, says one.

What are the dangers, then, for the U S and the rest of the world of an unsuccessful Emu? The main one is economic. The concern (widespread among economists) is that monetary union will be subject to immense strains if the necessary structural changes are not made. Though U S officials are anxious to stress they believe the Emu countries will reform, there is concern they may not. Specifically, the U S believes urgent action is needed to make labour markets more flexible to compensate for the lack of exchange-rate flexibility by individual countries. It is also widely felt that the absence of a common fiscal policy could make regional disparities much worse.

Reforms are needed in Europe, says Janet Yellen, chair of Mr Clinton's Council of Economic Advisers. Rigidities in labour markets will be a problem in a world where you have a common currency and countries have given up any flexibility in monetary policy. Some observers attribute this line of criticism, with some justification, to the vogue for U S economic triumphalism. The remarkably good performance of the U S economy in the past few years – solid growth with no inflation – is hailed by even cautious U S policymakers as a vindication of the distinctive American model: flexible labour markets, small government, a weak welfare net, dynamic capital markets and deregulated markets. Europe, by contrast, mostly stagnant for the past five years, is viewed by Americans as a model of economic failure and antediluvian rigidities.

According to this view, Emu not only fails to answer Europe's problems, but acts as a dangerous distraction. 'It's like seeing a good friend who has a heart condition insist on going to see a dentist to get his problems fixed,' says one official. 'In the mean time the heart condition gets ever more life-threatening.' This line is reinforced by the spectacle of the UK standing aside from the Emu project. There is a consensus in Washington that Britain has enjoyed twenty years of economic transformation at least in part because it has endorsed the US entrepreneurial model and turned its back on the continental European social market approach.

Some of these views smack of hubris. But many Americans genuinely worry that an Emu built on unreformed economies would produce persistent unemployment and sluggish growth. That in turn would mean the euro would be a weak currency against the dollar, undermining the competitiveness of US companies in world markets. In short, the risk is that Europe under Emu could become another Japan, exporting its way to growth, while ignoring its underlying structural problems. But in Japan, these structural faults have built up to such a point that they could pose serious problems for Asia and the rest of the world. European governments reject this parallel. They insist their currency will remain strong, underpinned by sound monetary policies. Just as important, Emu will promote structural reforms.

For the time being, the world accepts European promises in good faith. But the arguments between France and the rest about who should be president of the European Central Bank have tested this assumption: if Europe breaks its promises and the ECB falls under the spell of politicians, there will be trouble.

So much for Emu's possible economic effects. There is a separate debate taking shape in the US about its likely political consequences. As more Americans have woken up to the project, many have come to the conclusion that Emu will be bad news for the US. Part of this concern is a familiar hostility among some US conservatives to the EU, which they have always regarded as an unreliable partner. But the imminent arrival of the euro has broadened the base of those expressing doubts. The most forthright contribution so far was that of Martin Feldstein, one of the country's most respected economists and chairman of former President Ronald Reagan's Council of Economic Advisers. Mr Feldstein argued in November 1997, in an article in *Foreign Affairs*, that Emu represented a step too far for European integration that the economic strains it would produce in Europe would lead to serious political unrest – even war. If Emu does come into existence, it will change the political character of Europe in ways that could lead to conflicts in Europe and confrontations with the United States, he wrote.

Though these views are not widely shared, there is a growing belief that Emu represents a watershed for transatlantic relations. As with the economists, the foreign-policymakers generally believe that, if Emu works well, the gains from closer integration will suit the rest of the world too. But the unspoken fear is that, if it does not succeed, the stakes will have been raised considerably higher.

First appeared 5 May 1998

Midsummer madness: *the euro should be delayed until Europe comes to its senses on economic policy*

STEVEN RATTNER

For months, American devotees of economic policy have watched as the meanderings of Europe have grown more and more curious. Now, if France's post-election manoeuvrings are anything to go by, continental Europe appears to have gone economically bonkers.

Most bizarre is the embrace by France of statist ideas that lost all credibility in the US more than a decade ago. Not even the most fringe element in America today would argue that more public sector jobs, larger budget deficits and an interventionist state would constitute a proper tonic for slow growth and lagging competitiveness.

Almost as surreal were the efforts at the Amsterdam summit in June 1997 and elsewhere to continue to push the euro through in the face of weakened commitment to the Maastricht criteria and uncertain obeisance to the terms of the French left. The euro would probably not have worked under pre-election circumstances, and Europe is now far from those seemingly halcyon days.

It is time to put the euro out of its misery. The project should at least be postponed until Europe comes to recognize the fantasy of believing that a unified currency and a set of arbitrary fiscal benchmarks could turn a variety of inert economies into a match for the vibrant American colossus.

For all the countless trees that have been felled to publish thoughtful words about the euro, most Europeans remain oblivious to what has made the US experience successful and why the euro cannot succeed. True, as the euro obsession implies, the US success is partly about disciplined fiscal and monetary policies that have driven our budget deficit to below 1 per cent of gross domestic product.

But equally important, US success has been based on a flexible economy that prizes innovation, that taxes and regulates less, that permits labour market terms and conditions to adjust freely, that allows regional disparities to be diminished by the free movement of labour and capital, and that affords its immigrant and minority workers the chance to make their best contribution. Furthermore, the system funds its growth through highly liquid financial markets that attract capital by promising investors the opportunity to profit – or lose – without the risk of government changing the rules.

By itself, the euro would distract Europe while addressing few – if any – of these challenges. A single currency would bring certain efficiencies by eliminating foreign exchange mechanics in Europe. It could challenge the dollar's role as the world's reserve currency, though the value of that is not wholly apparent. It would lead perhaps to a one-off demand for euros that might temporarily improve the euro/dollar exchange rate, but this would soon return to fundamentals.

The French have not been alone in their confusion. Countries throughout Europe have dodged the real issues in their rush to meet the Maastricht criteria, rather like Cinderella's stepsisters trying to jam their oversized feet into the glass slipper. Only the UK seems to have retained a modicum of sense, maintaining a careful distance from the euro panic, improving its management of monetary policy and exchanging a tired government for some new blood.

Most worrying, the French elections provide a preview of the social and political consequences of adopting the euro in a vacuum. Monetary integration alone cannot possibly force the 'convergence' of participating economies. National governments retain control of a huge array of policies, including over tax and spending. Having a euro would not prevent the French from going down the road on which they are now embarking. Even as 1999 approaches, European states continue to demonstrate their readiness to fiddle the numbers, as the recent attempt to refinance gold reserves by the normally sensible Germans shows. If countries are willing to go to such lengths just to join, imagine what liberties might be taken later.

Even with genuinely integrated policies, the experience of the US suggests that competitiveness might not always converge. Take our experience with productivity, which increased rapidly in the 1950s and 1960s, slowly in the next two decades, and may have risen somewhat faster in the 1990s. But we know neither why productivity slowed nor even how fast it is growing at the moment – much less how government policies influence it.

Without convergence of competitiveness, different growth rates will inevitably develop. Without monetary and exchange-rate policy to redress these imbalances, the consequences of adjustment will be magnified:

rising unemployment, enormous downward pressure on wages, loss of investment to more competitive countries and the like.

France provides an important lesson of why the euro cannot work on its own. Once historic currencies have been abolished and only the euro remains, what will happen when the populace of a country like France decides not to bear the pain any longer? The answer is a move to expansionary policies such as those now being adopted by Paris. This would be destructive.

Proponents of the euro have argued that a single currency will help bring about greater political integration. In that sense, the French elections also provide an important lesson by showing, if nothing else, that when the going gets tough, political convergence becomes less, not more, likely. In reality, the euro has a chance of succeeding only once true political integration exists.

Supporters of the euro continue to argue that the US has had one currency and yet has worked through differences in regional growth rates without huge dislocations. That comparison should be recognized as weak. For two centuries, the US has had a strong central government with a dominant role in formulating fiscal and regulatory policy, easy migration of labour, few language or regional cultural differences and a variety of federal programmes to ease the pain when a region goes into recession.

The US experience holds other lessons for Europe as well. We have learned over the past two decades, for example, that in such a fast-changing world, categories of money supply hold so little meaning that the Federal Reserve has embraced a more impressionistic approach to guiding our economy, concentrating on price stability and full employment. How would such decisions be made in a Europe of varying unemployment and inflation rates?

A perception permeates the European press that the US is somehow frightened of an integrated Europe. That is simply not true. Weak European economies intensify our own balance of payments challenges. Weak European economies distract from the integration and rebuilding of eastern bloc countries. And weak European economies mean a lack of strong political leadership to help maintain global tranquillity.

A truly integrated Europe would hold great promise, not only for itself but for the rest of the world. Unfortunately, the present course of events offers little reason for optimism.

First appeared 18 June 1997

Pragmatic Europe: *Americans sceptical about whether economic and monetary union will work underestimate Europe's ability to adapt*

LIONEL BARBER

Lionel Jospin, France's Socialist prime minister, visited Washington in June 1998 and promptly announced that he had changed his views about the US. It was time to pay tribute to America's success in employment policy, he said. Contrary to what his countrymen often asserted – and maybe even believed – most new jobs in the US were not of the hamburger-flipping variety but rather jobs of the future in services and technology.

Mr Jospin's admission that red-blooded Anglo-Saxon capitalism may have some merits has been heralded as the most impressive conversion since Saul trod the road to Damascus. But there is more to his American experience than meets the eye.

The Socialist government has recently secured passage of the 35-hour working week and French business says the new law will damage competitiveness. Mr Jospin – steadily encroaching on the foreign policy domain of a weakened President Jacques Chirac – is keen to counter the impression that France wants to turn the rest of Europe into an industrial museum.

France is changing. It is the world's third-largest importer and exporter of capital and the fourth-largest trading nation. Mr Jospin and his able lieutenant, Dominique Strauss-Kahn, the finance minister, have understood that they must live with the markets as well as their election campaign promises. Since they came to power, the Socialists have shown themselves to be more pragmatic and open-minded than their critics predicted. Hence Mr Jospin's call in Washington that it was time for France and the US to ditch the stereotypes that bedevil bilateral relations.

How unfortunate that many US policymakers and opinion-formers are unwilling to respond in kind. Their views about France and Europe, especially the prospects for a successful economic and monetary union, are often out of touch or out of date. At least this is my impression from three conferences on Emu, which I have spent in the company of distinguished American academics.

The most recent took place in June 1998 in Talloires, France, organized by the Weatherhead Centre for International Affairs at Harvard University. No one went as far as Martin Feldstein, the former Reagan administration economist and Harvard academic, who has predicted that the single currency could provoke conflict in western Europe. But scepticism about the merits and viability of the single currency was pervasive.

One speaker declared that the European Central Bank was a monetary dictatorship, that Britain would not join the euro zone before 2010 and that the euro would not be a serious rival to the dollar for fifteen to twenty years. A Harvard Business School colleague at a conference in Stockholm was gloomier still: France was congenitally incapable of pushing through labour market reforms needed to make monetary union work. Western Europe was doomed unless it mended its ways.

American snootiness towards Emu is understandable. The US economy is booming, the stock market defies gravity. The US took more than 120 years to create a central bank with a common currency, the Europeans are pushing ahead after forty years without the safety net of political union. All the same, there are at least four reasons why prevailing US pessimism is overdone.

First, American commentators are treating the architecture of Emu, notably the draconian stability pact on fiscal discipline, as hard and fast economic rules. They are, in fact, political agreements. Their ambiguity need not be a disadvantage. Provided that each contracting party has a reasonable hope that its interpretation will prevail, an equilibrium, however uneasy, can exist.

Second, Americans underestimate the Europeans' capacity for improvisation. Five years ago, the European exchange-rate mechanism virtually collapsed under a wave of speculation, but the politicians and central bankers widened the margins of fluctuations for currencies in the ERM and Emu lived to fight another day. Expect similar institutional innovation if Emu gets into trouble.

Third, although the independent European Central Bank's commitment to price stability is enshrined in the Maastricht treaty, Wim Duisenberg and his new executive board in Frankfurt know they cannot operate in a political vacuum. Mr Duisenberg has already agreed to give testimony to the European Parliament four times a year. His dictatorship will be more benign than some imagine.

Finally, American academics are committing the cardinal sin of not watching the markets. Those who assume that the euro will not be a credible challenge to the dollar anytime soon underestimate the dramatic effect of the single currency in accelerating the creation of a truly liquid pan-European debt market.

Of course, the EU cannot hope to replicate overnight the highly efficient, round-the-clock market in US Treasury bills. But the consolidation of the European banking industry and the sharpening competition between Paris and Frankfurt to establish a benchmark in long-term euro-denominated debt is a harbinger of the coming revolution in Europe's capital markets.

A prominent European central banker in Talloires offered another pointer to change, which occurred in late 1995 but whose significance escaped many observers. At the time, the German government and the Bundesbank were opposed to converting German public debt from D-Marks into euros on Emu's launch. After a tense negotiation, the Germans agreed to issue new debt in euros, but balked at denominating existing debt in the new currency on the grounds that it would upset a jittery German public. The central bankers explained that the position was illogical and untenable. Eventually, the Germans bowed to the market.

Americans should observe what Europeans do rather than what they say. Mr Jospin is an obvious example.

First appeared 24 June 1998

Appendix
The Emu project – an outline

Source: Emu Net

1957

March

Treaty of Rome signed. Members encouraged to regard their exchange-rate policies as a 'matter of common concern'.

1958

January

European Economic Community (EEC) established.

1969

December

Hague summit requests report on Emu, stipulating 1980 as target date.

1971

February

Werner Report published proposing a three-stage process for achieving Emu, including permanent fixing of exchange rates, a single monetary authority and monetary policy and an EEC fiscal policy.

August

US dollar floated, affecting exchange rate stability in Europe.

1972

March

Creation of the 'Snake in the Tunnel' by the six EEC countries; soon joined by sterling, the punt and Danish and Norwegian kroner.

October

Heads of government meeting in Paris endorsed Werner Report.

1979

March

Start of the European Monetary System (EMS); Exchange Rate Mechanism (ERM) set up with eight member currencies within 2.25

per cent fluctuation margins, although peseta, lira, escudo and sterling to be allowed a 'broad band' of 6 per cent. Introduction of the Ecu as weighted average of all European currencies.

September

ERM parities first changed: revaluation of D-mark, devaluation of Danish krona.

1985

July

Mass devaluation within ERM of Belgian and French francs, Danish krona, Irish punt, Dutch gilder, Italian lira, German mark.

1986

February

Single European Act (SEA) signed, formalizing Single Market programme.

April

French franc devalued. Belgian franc, krona, guilder and D-mark revalued.

August

Irish punt revalued.

1988

June

European Council in Hanover requests Delors Report outlining 'concrete stages' leading to Emu.

1989

April

Delors Report published.

June

Spanish peseta joins ERM with 6 per cent fluctuation bands.
Madrid European Council decides to liberalize capital movements in Europe – Stage 1 of Emu.

1990

July

Stage 1 of Emu begins. Removal of exchange controls across Europe.

October

UK joins ERM with 6 per cent bands at 2.95 marks per pound sterling.

1991

December

Heads of government agree Treaty on European Union at Maastricht.

1992

February

Maastricht Treaty signed.

April

Portuguese escudo joins ERM with 6 per cent bands.

June

'No' in Maastricht referendum in Denmark.

July

Irish vote for Maastricht Treaty.

September

Black Wednesday: UK leaves ERM. Lira suspended. Peseta devalued. 'Yes' in referendum in France, with 51.05 per cent in favour. Exchange controls temporarily imposed in Ireland, Spain, Portugal.

November

Peseta, escudo devalued. French franc, Danish krona and Irish punt under siege from markets.

1993

January

Single Market '1992' programme starts. Irish punt devalued by 10 per cent.

May

Peseta and escudo devalued. Danes vote for Maastricht in second referendum.

July

Bundesbank buys French francs on markets.

August

French franc dips below ERM floor. Widening of ERM bands to 15 per cent. D-mark and guilder stay at 2.25 per cent.

November

Maastricht Treaty enters into force. Composition of Ecu basket frozen. German Constitutional Court (Karlsruhe) rules in favour of Maastricht Treaty.

1994

January

Stage 2 of Emu begins: European Monetary Institute (EMI) established. Member States strive to fulfil convergence criteria. Final deadline of 1 January 1999 agreed for beginning Stage 3 of Emu, regardless of the number of Member States qualifying and of general economic climate.

1995

January

Austria, Sweden and Finland join EU.

European Commission publishes Green Paper on 'Practical Arrangements for the Introduction of the Single Currency'.

November

EMI 'Report on the transition to the Euro' published.

December

European Council meeting in Madrid. The name 'Euro' agreed for the Single Currency. Ministers endorse EMI plan envisaging conversion to the Euro over four-year timetable.

1996

October

Finnish markka joins ERM with 15 per cent fluctuation bands.

November

Lira re-enters ERM at 990 per D-mark.

December

European Council meeting in Dublin. The legal framework and exchange-rate relations between the 'ins' and 'outs' discussed. Agreement reached on Stability and Growth Pact, enhancing the coordination of economic policies.

1997

January

EMI specifies regulatory and organizational framework for the European Central Bank and the European System of Central Banks (the national central banks of the euro countries that will implement the ECB's monetary policy).

May

Socialist government held by Lionel Jospin gains power in France. New uncertainty over Emu, focusing on Stability and Growth Pact.

June

Draft Amsterdam Treaty agreed. France and Germany agree to retain terms of Stability and Growth Pact. Unemployment figures large as an issue.

September

Finance Ministers agree to fix bilateral conversion rates between participating countries in advance, at the time when qualifying countries chosen in May 1998.

October

British Chancellor, Gordon Brown, announces that UK unlikely to enter Emu before next UK general election (i.e. no entry before 2002/3), and that UK membership will depend upon the economy meeting five economic tests.

Basis for 'Euro-11' or 'X' committee established: a new council for Emu participants' Finance ministers to meet informally before EcoFin meetings and deliberate on tax and spending, labour markets, exchange rates.

December

European leaders agree on the broad terms for the 'Euro-11' committee in which euro-zone countries will discuss economic issues.

1998

March

European Commission and European Monetary Institute publish 'convergence reports', recommending that all applicant countries qualify for monetary union. A report by the Bundesbank criticizes overblown deficits of Belgium and Italy.

May

Emu begins. Heads of State decide which countries qualify for Emu, fix bilateral conversion rates and agree to maintain their economies in line with the Maastricht convergence criteria.

June

European Central Bank officially inaugurated and comes into operation.

September

Frankfurt – ECB Governing Council to meet.

ECB General Council (all fifteen EU central bank heads) meets.

October and November

Frankfurt – ECB Governing Council (Executive Board plus Euro-11 national bank governors) to meet.

December

Frankfurt – ECB Governing Council (Executive Board plus Euro-11 national bank governors) to meet.

ECB General Council (all fifteen EU central bank heads) meets.

Vienna – European Council meeting of heads of state and government.

Euro conversion rates decided, using spot market rates on the day.

'Conversion weekend' starts: financial market players make systems fully euro-compatible.

1999

January

Stage 3 of Emu begins: the Euro comes into formal existence.
European Central Bank becomes fully operative.
EcoFin council meeting to confirm Euro exchange rate rates.
Exchange rates to be 'irrevocably fixed' amongst those countries qualifying for Emu.
European Central Bank takes over operation of Emu area monetary policy.
ESCB to use only the Euro in its money market and foreign exchange operations.
TARGET system comes into operation for cross-border settlements.

Further reading

Understanding the Euro edited by Andrew Duff; published by the Federal Trust

Will the Euro work? The ins and outs of Emu by David Currie; published by the Economist Intelligence Unit

The Euro edited by Paul Temperton; published by Wiley

Euro futures by David Smith; published by Capstone

The Ostrich and the Emu: policy choices facing the UK an independent panel of experts chaired by Rupert Pennant-Lea; published by the Centre for Economic Policy Research

The single European currency a practical guide by the Hundred Group of Finance Directors

Britain and Emu published by the Centre for European Reform; contact (44) 171 233 1199

Getting the end game right by David Begg, Francesco Giavazzi, Jurgen von Hagen and Charles Wyplosz, published by the Centre for Economic Policy Studies

The pros and cons of Emu by David Currie; published by the Economist Intelligence Unit

The politics and economics of single currency by Martin Wolf, Hans-Ekhart Scharrer and Christopher Johnson; RIIA Discussion Paper 69

Britain and the European Union: dialogue of the deaf by Lord Beloff; published by Macmillan

User guide to the Euro edited by Graham Bishop, Jose Peres and Sammy van Tuyll; published by the Federal Trust

In with the Euro, out with the pound by Christopher Johnson; published by Penguin

Maastricht and beyond: building the European Union edited by Andrew Duff, John Pinder and Roy Price; published by Routledge for the Federal Trust

EMU 2000? Prospects for monetary union by Christopher Taylor; published by Pinter and Cassell for the Royal Institute for Economic Affairs

Sources of information on the Internet

Exchanges

London Stock Exchange
http://www.stockex.co.uk
LIFFE
http://www.liffe.com
London Metal Exchange
http://www.lme.co.uk/cgi-bin/php/mainl.htm

Government

UK Euro web site
http://www.euro.gov.uk
10 Downing Street
http://www.number-10.gov.uk
Foreign Office (FCO)
http://www.fco.gov.uk
UK Permanent Representation, Brussels
http://ukrep.fco.gov.uk
HM Treasury
http://www.hm-treasury.gov.uk
Department of Trade and Industry (DTI)
http://www.dti.gov.uk
Bank of England
http://www.bankofengland.co.uk/publica.htm#europe
Central Office of Information – government press releases
http://www.coi.gov.uk/coi/depts/deptlist.html
Her Majesty's Stationery Office (HMSO)
http://www.hmso.gov.uk
Office for National Statistics
http://www.ons.gov.uk
European Central Bank
http://www.ecb.int

EU
  http://www.europa.eu.int
EU Euro page
  http://www.euro.eu.int
European Commission
  http://www.europa.eu.int/en/comm.html
European Parliament euro website
  http://www.europarl.eu.int/dg3/euro/en/default.htm
Eurostat
  http://www.europa.eu.int/en/comm/eurostat/servern/home.htm

Special interest groups

British Chambers of Commerce
  http://www.britishchambers.org.uk
Confederation of British Industry (CBI)
  http://www.cbi.org.uk
Institute of Directors
  http://www.iod.co.uk
Federation of Small Businesses
  http://www.fsb.org.uk
Consumers' Association
  http://www.which.net
Trades Union Congress (TUC)
  http://www.tuc.org.uk

Think tanks, research, lobbying

Adam Smith Institute
  http://www.cyberpoint.co.uk/asi/index.htm
Association for the Monetary Union of Europe
  http://amue.lf.net
British Council
  http://www.britcoun.org
Centre for Economic Performance, LSE
  http://cep.lse.ac.uk
Centre for European Reform
  http://www.cer.org.uk
Centre for Policy Studies
  http://www.cps.org.uk
Centre for Economic Forecasting, LBS
  http://www.lbs.ac.uk/cef
Centre for the Study of Financial Innovation
  http://www.csfi.demon.co.uk

Charter 88
http://www.gn.apc.org/charter88/home.html
Conservative Way Forward
http://www.conwayfor.org
Critical European Group
http://www.keele.ac.uk/socs/ks40/ceghome.html
Demos
http://www.demos.co.uk
Economic and Social Research Council
http://www.esrc.ac.uk
Emunet
http://www.euro-emu.co.uk
European Movement
http://www.euromove.org.uk
Federal Trust
http://www.compulink.co.uk/fedtrust
Institute of Economic Affairs
http://www.iea.org.uk
Institute for Fiscal Studies
http://www.ifs.org.uk
Institute of Public Policy Research
http://www.ippr.org.uk
Labour Research Department
http://www.lrd.org.uk/labres.html
National Institute of Economic and Social Research
http://www.niesr.ac.uk
Political Studies Association
http://www.lgu.ac.uk/psa/psa.html
Political Economy Research Centre
http://www.shef.ac.uk/uni/academic/N-Q/perc
Royal Economic Society
http://www.res.org.uk
Royal Institute for International Affairs
http://www.riia.org

Business help

Business Link
http://www.businesslink.co.uk
Enterprise Zone
http://www.enterprisezone.org.uk
European Information Centres (EICs)
http://www.euro-info.org.uk

Training and Enterprise Centres (TECs)
http://www.tec.co.uk/tecnc/index/html
DTI Overseas Technologies Service
http://www.dti.gov.uk/ots
Trade UK
http://www.tradeuk.com
DataOp Alliance
http://www.dataop.com
Expert Access System
http://www.xas.co.uk
Europe Online
http://www.europeonline.com/biznet

Business directories on the web

The Business Information Zone
http://www.thebiz.co.uk
The Business Bureau (UK)
http://www.u-net.com/bureau
Yahoo! Small business info
http://www.yahoo.com/business/Small_Business_Information

READ MORE IN PENGUIN

In every corner of the world, on every subject under the sun, Penguin represents quality and variety – the very best in publishing today.

For complete information about books available from Penguin – including Puffins, Penguin Classics and Arkana – and how to order them, write to us at the appropriate address below. Please note that for copyright reasons the selection of books varies from country to country.

In the United Kingdom: Please write to *Dept. EP, Penguin Books Ltd, Bath Road, Harmondsworth, West Drayton, Middlesex UB7 ODA*

In the United States: Please write to *Consumer Sales, Penguin Putnam Inc., P.O. Box 999, Dept. 17109, Bergenfield, New Jersey 07621-0120.* VISA and MasterCard holders call 1-800-253-6476 to order Penguin titles

In Canada: Please write to *Penguin Books Canada Ltd, 10 Alcorn Avenue, Suite 300, Toronto, Ontario M4V 3B2*

In Australia: Please write to *Penguin Books Australia Ltd, P.O. Box 257, Ringwood, Victoria 3134*

In New Zealand: Please write to *Penguin Books (NZ) Ltd, Private Bag 102902, North Shore Mail Centre, Auckland 10*

In India: Please write to *Penguin Books India Pvt Ltd, 210 Chiranjiv Tower, 43 Nehru Place, New Delhi 110 019*

In the Netherlands: Please write to *Penguin Books Netherlands bv, Postbus 3507, NL-1001 AH Amsterdam*

In Germany: Please write to *Penguin Books Deutschland GmbH, Metzlerstrasse 26, 60594 Frankfurt am Main*

In Spain: Please write to *Penguin Books S. A., Bravo Murillo 19, 1° B, 28015 Madrid*

In Italy: Please write to *Penguin Italia s.r.l., Via Benedetto Croce 2, 20094 Corsico, Milano*

In France: Please write to *Penguin France, Le Carré Wilson, 62 rue Benjamin Baillaud, 31500 Toulouse*

In Japan: Please write to *Penguin Books Japan Ltd, Kaneko Building, 2-3-25 Koraku, Bunkyo-Ku, Tokyo 112*

In South Africa: Please write to *Penguin Books South Africa (Pty) Ltd, Private Bag X14, Parkview, 2122 Johannesburg*

READ MORE IN PENGUIN